THE HISTORY OF TROY
IN MIDDLE ENGLISH LITERATURE

THE HISTORY OF TROY IN MIDDLE ENGLISH LITERATURE

Guido delle Colonne's *Historia Destructionis Troiae* in Medieval England

C. David Benson

D. S. BREWER · ROWMAN & LITTLEFIELD

© C. David Benson 1980
Published by D. S. Brewer, an imprint of
Boydell & Brewer Ltd, PO Box 9, Woodbridge, Suffolk IP12 3DF

First published 1980

British Library Cataloguing in Publication Data

Benson, C David
    The history of Troy in Middle English literature.
    1. Trojans in literature
    2. English literature—Middle English, 1100–1500
    —History and criticism
    I. Title
820'.9'376   PR275.T/

ISBN 0-85991-059-8

US ISBN 0 8476 6289 6

Photoset by Rowland Phototypesetting Ltd, Bury St Edmunds, Suffolk
Printed by St Edmundsbury Press, Haverhill, Suffolk

CONTENTS

To the Memory of
LEE
and Bob and June

ACKNOWLEDGEMENTS

I am pleased to offer thanks to several institutions and individuals for their help with this book:

To the Committee on University Scholarly Publications (CUSP) of the University of Colorado for their generous award of a subvention that supported the publication of this book. Particular thanks to James Kincaid and Paul Levitt.

To the Indiana University Press for permission to use portions of the translation of Guido delle Colonne by Mary Elizabeth Meek, *Historia Destructionis Troiae* (Bloomington, 1974).

To the *American Benedictine Review* for permission to reprint, in altered form, material from two articles first published there: 'The Ancient World in John Lydgate's *Troy Book*,' 24 (1973), 299–312 and 'Prudence, Othea, and Lydgate's Death of Hector,' 26 (1975), 115–23; also to the *Chaucer Review* for permission to reprint material from two articles first published there: 'Troilus and Cresseid in Henryson's *Testament*,' 13 (1979), 263–71 and ' "O Nyce World": What Chaucer Really Found in Guido delle Colonne's History of Troy,' 13 (1980), 308–15.

To three readers of early drafts of this book for their generous help: Emerson Brown, Deborah Signer, and Charles Muscatine; and to two more recent readers who have tried to instruct me in logical argument: Larry Sklute, always the most helpful and demanding of teachers, and Linda Georgianna, a fine critic and a friend indeed.

To Alain Renoir, my director when this work began as a dissertation many years ago, and to Robert Hanning and Donald Baker, my colleagues at Columbia and Colorado. My gratitude to them goes well beyond their substantial help with this book, for their benefactions to me have been continuous. In their learning and goodness, all three have been my models of what a teacher, scholar, and man ought to be.

Finally, my deepest thanks and love go to my wife, Pamela. Her scholarship and good judgment have improved each of these pages, as she herself has my life.

PART ONE

THE MEDIEVAL HISTORY OF TROY

I

The Medieval History of Troy: Guido delle Colonne

Introduction

From Homer to Joyce, the Trojan War has been the most persistent non-religious subject in Western literature, but one aspect of the complex tradition has been neglected by modern scholarship: the medieval history of Troy. In the Middle Ages, the story of Troy was not only a legend or poetic fancy; it was also available in eye-witness journals believed to have been kept during the war itself by Dares, on the Trojan side, and Dictys, on the Greek. These works, whose truth was accepted by all, were first combined in the *Roman de Troie* of Benoît de Saint-Maure, and the material was then put into authoritative form by Guido delle Colonne in his *Historia Destructionis Troiae*. The *Historia* was itself translated into Middle English verse on three separate occasions. The modern reader who knows only classical versions of the Trojan War is at some disadvantage when he meets the story in medieval literature. His conception of Troy and its fate will usually be very different from that of the author he is reading because medieval Troy is not the classical city. The Greek dramatists were unknown to the European Middle Ages, and Homer was available only in a crude Latin redaction. Even those classical works that were read, like Ovid or Vergil, contain only part of the medieval knowledge of Troy.

My subject is the other, neglected version of the Troy story in the Middle Ages: the historical tradition, in the form produced by Guido delle Colonne. In order better to understand the history's difference from classical accounts, we must begin with some knowledge of its descent from the mysterious reporters Dares and Dictys. The former's *De Excidio Troiae Historia* and the latter's *Ephemeris de Historia Belli Troiani* are fully extant only in Latin versions. A papyrus fragment of the original Dictys in Greek has been found, and it is assumed that there was once a Greek Dares.[1] Dictys's work was written during the first century of the

Christian era and the original Dares probably at about the same time, although the Latin translation we now have of the latter is dated to the early sixth century A.D. We do not know the circumstances surrounding the creation of either. They are odd works, brief and crude, the unlikely progenitors of so numerous a race of medieval literary descendants.[2] Although Dictys is a moralist and a patriot (he is bitterly scornful of the Trojan barbarians), both writers are of interest to us primarily because of their apparent factuality. R. M. Frazer notes that 'they use none of the divine machinery typical of epic poetry, and they tend to describe super-natural occurrences in rationalistic terms.'[3] Both banish the gods from the fighting and instead provide character portraits, precise battle accounts, and other realistic details that convinced the Middle Ages that each was indeed a true history.

About 1160 Benoît de Saint-Maure used the Dares and Dictys material, and his imagination even more, to create one of the first French romances, the lavish *Roman de Troie,* whose 30,300 lines are full of desperate love stories and exotic, marvellous people, places, and things.[4] In one way it is unfortunate that our concern is with Guido delle Colonne's *Historia Destructionis Troiae* and not with the *Roman de Troie* because the latter is far superior in style and inventiveness. We shall not meet its equal as poetry until the discussion of Chaucer and Henryson in the last chapter. The *Roman de Troie,* whose influence on French romance was immense, is an exciting poem and genuinely original. Like Chaucer, but unlike the Middle English historians of Troy, Benoît sees the Troy story as something to be exploited for artistic effect, not merely conserved for its historical truth.

More than a century after Benoît, in 1287, Guido delle Colonne, a Sicilian judge and perhaps the poet mentioned by Dante in the *De Vulgari Eloquentia,* translated Benoît's poem into a Latin prose work now called the *Historia Destructionis Troiae,* which de-emphasizes the love stories and drops, reduces, or doubts Benoît's marvels.[5] Guido never names his real source, but insists he is keeping alive the full account of the two original reporters. Indeed, for a long time the *Historia* was thought to have preceded the romance. Guido was not necessarily guilty of conscious fraud, however; he may sincerely have believed that Benoît's poem was a corrupted version of the true history, solid and respectable once its garish decoration had been removed. If he knew Dares and Dictys in the form we know them, as he probably did, he might well have regarded their accounts as no more than the working notes or outline of the complete history. Guido's real opinion of his own work and his motive for writing it may never be known, but, whatever he thought he was doing, the educated world soon accepted his *Historia* for the genuine history of Troy. Benoît's poem, when considered at all, was regarded as only a romanticized version of the full history.[6] Although the Renaissance began to raise questions about the tradition, Sir Philip Sidney was still able to contrast the 'feigned Aeneas in Virgil' to 'the right Aeneas in Dares Phrygius.'[7] Full enlightenment came late. Not until the eighteenth century did Jacob Perizonius demonstrate beyond question the forgery of Dares and Dictys,[8] and only in the nineteenth century was it shown that Guido had used Benoît and that the story had moved from poetry to prose, as well as from romance to history.

Since the Middle Ages accepted Guido's history of Troy as absolutely genuine, it is misleading and an improper use of modern hindsight to label the *Historia* and its English translations as *romance* or *legend*.[9] In fact, the Trojan War is the only major classical tale that was available during the Middle Ages in the form of history. Because of Dares and Dictys, the events at Troy appeared in a fully rationalized and believable form almost totally devoid of gods and myths. The case is different with the other matters of antiquity. Thebes was also a great city, also besieged and destroyed. In the late Middle Ages a reader could find a classical epic on each of the cities (the *Aeneid* and *Thebaid*) and also a French romance on each (the *Roman de Troie* and *Roman de Thebes*),[10] but only Troy had a *Historia Destructionis*. Poems about Alexander are everywhere in the Middle Ages, and of course they trace their ultimate origin to true events, yet it is not hard to see why the Trojan poems had greater historical warrant. The Alexander stories do not exist in a single tradition, and they are full of marvels that even a medieval audience might doubt: griffin rides to heaven, bizarre Indian creatures, and prophetic trees.[11] Fascinating and exciting no doubt, but just the kind of fabulous material Guido systematically excised from Benoît as historically suspect. The seemingly analogous work of Geoffrey of Monmouth and his 'Arthurian' descendants is also unlike the medieval history of Troy. The truth of Arthur was suspect from the beginning, and it quickly gave way to romance and individual invention. Renouncing any serious claim to history, the Arthurian material could metamorphosize into great literature. Respect for the truth of the Trojan history, however, caused writers to try to preserve it without corruption and guard it from mutation.

Guido's Trojan history, in addition to being considered factually true, forms a special variety of medieval history that has so far gone unrecognized. Guido and his English followers wrote histories that are neither Providential nor nationalistic, but which may be defined as classical chronicles. They report the ancient past with the same eyewitness detail found in late-medieval chronicles of contemporary events, like those written by Froissart. Although the medieval history of Troy no longer has the ability to appeal to a wide audience, it deserves to be taken seriously and judged on its own principles.

At this point it should be made clear that the subject of the present study is a limited one: the fate of Guido's medieval history of Troy in Middle English literature. When I use the term *medieval history of Troy*, I am referring generally to the historical tradition of Troy that descends from

Dares and Dictys, and specifically to Guido's *Historia*. Although the exact relationship of Guido to Benoît needs more detailed study than it has yet received, that cannot be attempted here. My discussion largely depends on passages that are original with Guido, but even when he is doing little more than translating Benoît's French verse into Latin prose, I shall approach his work as though it were actually the original compilation of Dares and Dictys the Middle Ages believed it to be. The popularity of the *Historia* throughout Europe was immense (translations were produced in several languages, at least eight printed editions appeared between 1473–94, and as many as one hundred and fifty manuscripts may still be extant), but my study is confined to its career in Middle English. Medieval England knew many different stories of Troy—versions of the founding of Britain by Trojan Brute, the pseudo-classical *Excidium Troiae* and its Middle English translations, and the classical accounts of Vergil and Ovid, to name only the most prominent—but my concern is only with the historical tradition that derives from the *Historia*. After a discussion of Guido's *Historia* itself, I will analyze in detail the three full-length translations of it into Middle English verse: the alliterative *Destruction of Troy*, the *Laud Troy Book*, and Lydgate's *Troy Book*. My purpose is to define the medieval history of Troy, show its place in the general English historical tradition, and describe the success and failure of the three writers who independently labored to put the history into Middle English. Unlike Dares and Dictys, or Guido himself, the English translators of the *Historia* are poets as well as historians, and they constantly struggle to remain true to both offices. The attempt to serve two such disparate masters almost inevitably produces strains and failure, but this does not diminish the ambition of their effort nor the skill and ability each demonstrates in the struggle. Their effort to tell history in verse is a neglected but revealing chapter in the story of both English history and poetry. My second concern is with two greater English poets, Chaucer and Henryson, who make significant, though limited, use of the medieval history of Troy. Unlike the three historians, they are not burdened by the obligation to preserve the entire record of the Trojan War; nevertheless, its material is more important to both than has usually been believed.

History and Chronicle

Anything like a complete discussion of historical writing in the Middle Ages is obviously impossible here—the subject is vast and never simple. All that can be attempted is a sketch of some of the most important characteristics of the discipline, especially as practiced in England, so that its relation to the *Historia* and its English translations will be clear.[12]

Guido's own conception of his place in the medieval historical tradition is not the concern of this study; our subject instead is the fate of his history in late-medieval England. Thus the *Historia* will not be considered simply for its own sake, but primarily as it might have been understood by readers at the later time of the *Destruction of Troy*, the *Laud Troy Book*, and Lydgate's *Troy Book*.

Gervase of Canterbury (ca. 1200) begins his chronicle with a distinction between formal history and chronicle that V. H. Galbraith argues 'was the common assumption of historical writers for a thousand years, and lies at the root of all medieval thinking about history.' Gervase says that history and chronicle both use the same material and aim for truth, but that they differ in method:

> The historian is the master-man; to him is appropriate grandeur of style, 'bombast and swelling words' (*ampullas et sesquipedalia verba*); he proceeds diffusely and elegantly, lulling his hearers—or readers—by the charm of his narrative, and his cunning selection of facts. The task of the humbler chronicler is to get his dates right, and year by year record briefly the acts of kings and princes, and such other events, portents and miracles as occur from time to time.[13]

Gervase's primary concern is with style and form (*modus* and *forma*), but the differences he notes reflect a real distinction in Christian histori- ography—between chronicles, which give only a factual record of public events, and histories, which probe the hidden significance of that record and reveal God's Providential plan. These two kinds of history exist in the *Bible*, especially in the Old Testament, where purely factual records like genealogies exist along with more ambitious attempts to discover the ultimate meaning of these facts. A similar mixture of these two kinds of truth is found in medieval Biblical exegesis. Old Testament events may be shown to prefigure the New Dispensation of Christ, but the spiritual level, however sublime, in no way obliterates or diminishes the historical.[14]

Modern scholarship has not always recognized the two strains in medieval historiography. R. G. Collingwood, for example, finds only Providential history in the Middle Ages: 'The great task of medieval historiography was the task of discovering and expounding this objective or divine plan.'[15] D. W. Robertson, Jr., a leading 'historical' critic of literature, also insists that the Middle Ages knew only one kind of history, which is history proper in Gervase's terms:

> With reference to 'history', no one in the Middle Ages had any notion of a detached record of events produced for its own sake. Events in the past belonged to the order of Providence, so that both these events and the persons who participated in them

had an exemplary character, immediately relevant to life in the present. To find the 'truth' of history was then not simply to discover the facts, but to find the exemplary force of the events adduced, or, in other words, their Providential implications.[16]

Although Robertson adequately defines Providential history, he ignores the aim and achievement of the chroniclers. Viewed less tendentiously, it is clear that any attempt to illuminate the Providential meaning of history must be based on an accurate and detached record of events. The higher truth is a function of the lower, and thus the chronicler's task is humble but essential: he assembles the basic materials that historians proper will use to construct their lofty edifices.[17]

Some writers can be quickly assigned to the camp of either history or chronicle. In the *City of God*, St. Augustine searches beyond the deceptive motions of the earthly creation to find the sublime Creator and his love: Augustine is a historian in Gervase's terms. The 'St. Albans School,' which included Roger of Wendover, Matthew Paris, Thomas Walsingham (and perhaps others), offers excellent examples of chroniclers. Concerning Paris, Richard Vaughan writes that 'evidently his primary object was the recording of contemporary events,' and Galbraith sees Walsingham's merits as 'those of the conscientious compiler. He made no attempt to subdue his facts to any theory: his point of view reflects the most orthodox opinion of his day.'[18] Other writers have claim to both titles. Eusebius's *Ecclesiastical History* is a seminal example of Providential history; however, he had previously composed a two-part work on chronology, which, in Jerome's translation, became authoritative. In the *History* he calls the chronology a summary of his present work; in other words, the facts without the meaning: a chronicle from which to construct a history.[19] Bede composed a treatise on chronology, *De Temporum Ratione*, as well as his grander *Historia Ecclesiastica Gentis Anglorum*. Otto of Freising imitates Augustine's title and approach in the *Chronica sive Historia de Duabus Civitatibus;* he also wrote a chronicle, albeit a magnificent one, in the *Gesta Friderici I Imperatoris*.

One of the two kinds of medieval history can now be dismissed. Guido's *Historia* and its English translations are forms of the chronicle and have nothing in common with the more exalted variety of medieval history. The limited scope of the history of Troy is perhaps explained by its unique descent. Dares and Dictys each produced works whose brevity and self-conscious emphasis on the factual almost necessarily exclude any genuine 'philosophy of history.' Dares is anti-Greek and Dictys anti-Trojan. Nationalism, virtually racism in Dictys, plus the determination to tell the real story of Troy as opposed to Homer's poetic fancies, exhaust their theoretical aims. Neither work has any tendency toward Providential history—no attempt is made to discover the divine will at work and, indeed, no proof exists that 'Dares' and 'Dictys,' whoever they really were, had any part in the Judeo-Christian tradition. When Benoît refashioned their two journals into his *Roman de Troie*, he did nothing to shape the material into either history or chronicle. His additions were love stories, speeches, elaborate rhetorical descriptions, palaces with magical columns, and even an elaborate plumbing system that is capable of forever preserving Hector's corpse. Typical of the writers in the first, lush period of romance, Benoît stressed the marvelous, the foreign, even the bizarre: his intention was to dazzle and fascinate the reader, not to instruct him in the ways of Providence. When Guido redid the *Roman* his main effort was to omit or tone down Benoît's more exotic fancies to produce what seemed to others, and probably even to himself, a factual record of the Trojan War. Once he had removed Benoît's major additions, and with them most of Benoît's characteristically twelfth-century themes, he was left with a mass of specific data unattached to any ideological scheme.

Clerical Chronicles and the Historia

To a late-medieval English audience, Guido's approach to history would not have been unfamiliar. In the prologue to his *Historia*, the Sicilian judge defines history writing in terms similar to those used by the authors of English clerical chronicles. First, he states that the task of the historian is to preserve the past from oblivion:

> Although every day past events are obliterated by more recent ones, still certain past events happened a long time ago which are so worthy of memory on account of their enduring greatness that age does not succeed in destroying them by imperceptible corrosion, nor do the previous cycles of time gone by end in dull silence. In their case, uninterrupted records flourish on account of the greatness of the events, as long as the tale of what is past is handed down to posterity. Writings of the ancients, faithful preservers of tradition, depict the past as if it were the present, and, by the attentive readings of books, endow valiant heroes with the courageous spirit they are imagined to have had, just as if they were alive—heroes whom the extensive age of the world long ago swallowed up by death. It is fitting, therefore, that the fall of the city of Troy should not be blotted out by a long duration of time. To keep it alive in the minds of succeeding generations, by means of continuous records, the pen of many writers described it in a trustworthy account.[20]

Following from this, Guido insists that his version is indeed the true one and not a fanciful poetic invention. Unlike the fictions of Homer, Vergil, and Ovid, the *Historia* has faithfully transcribed the material of 'Dictys the Greek and Dares the Phrygian, who were at the time of the Trojan War continually present in their armies and were the most trustworthy reporters of those things which they saw' (Pro. 41–43; p. 4).

Guido's two claims for Dares and Dictys would have been recognized by the English translators of the *Historia,* and by their readers, as the same ones made again and again by clerical chroniclers: (1) the purpose of history is to preserve contemporary events for posterity, and (2) eye-witness testimony is the surest guarantee of truth. In the prologue to his *Ecclesiastical History,* Bede insists that 'in accordance with the principles of true history (*quod uera lex historiae est*), I have simply sought to commit to writing what I have collected from common report, for the instruction of posterity.' Bede seems most confident of his Northumbrian material because 'apart from those matters of which I had personal knowledge, I have learned not from any one source (*auctore*) but from the faithful testimony of innumerable witnesses, who either knew or remembered these things.'[21] The English historians who came after Bede not only continue his chronology, they also obey the same historical laws. Eadmer's preface is perhaps the closest to Guido's. He praises those who 'with an eye to the good of future generations have committed to writing a record of events of their own times.' His own generation lacks the comfort and strength that comes from a knowledge of one's predecessors 'because of the scarcity of written documents which has resulted in the events being all too quickly buried in oblivion.' Therefore he intends (like Dares and Dictys) to keep alive the memory of his own time and will 'set down in writing the things which I have seen with my own eyes and myself heard.'[22] Others in the twelfth century, the golden age of medieval English historiography, also make the same two points. Ordericus Vitalis, whose preface cites Dares and Trogus Pompeius as Gentile historians, defines his aim in words that remind us of Guido's claim for his sources: 'as the history of the past has been handed down to us by preceding writers, so also a relation of what is going on around us should be transmitted to future generations by the pen of contemporaries.' The events he will record are 'both such as have passed under my own observation, and those which, occurring in neighbouring countries, have come to my knowledge.'[23]

Similar statements are made by the estimable Henry of Huntingdon and William of Malmesbury.[24] The author of the *Itinerarium Peregrinorum et Gesta Regis Ricardi* claims that historical writing was begun to save the fame of exceptional deeds from being erased by the course of time, and he cites Dares to show that the best history is written by eyewitnesses like himself.[25] These views continued to be held in the period of the *Historia*'s English translators. In the fourteenth century the delightfully named Adam Murimuth announces that he intends to keep the past alive through writing and that he will rely on personal observation for the record of his own times.[26]

To an English reader of history in the fourteenth century, Dares and Dictys would have appeared to be eyewitness reporters who preserved the truth of their own time just as contemporary clerical chroniclers were preserving the present. The same reader would have no reason to doubt that Dares and Dictys had, in fact, accomplished what Guido claims for them. Wherever he looked the authority of their history was supported. They had no rivals; no other complete version of the Troy story existed, except for various poetic fictions which were easily dismissed, and thus with the matter of Troy there was no need to combine or choose among sources. The descent is straight and unencumbered. We have noted that Ordericus Vitalis and the author of the *Itinerarium Peregrinorum* cite Dares as precedent. They had warrant to do so. Isidore of Seville states that Moses was the first historian in the Judeo-Christian tradition and that among the Gentiles the first was Dares Phrygius.[27] This information had wide circulation and is included in Hugh of St. Victor's *Didascalicon*.[28] The *Polychronicon* of Ranulf Higden begins its account of the Trojan War with some preliminary material from Trogus Pompeius (after Justin's *Epitome*), but the main story, as Higden himself states, is that of Dares.

The history begun by Dares and Dictys is not like the clerical chronicle in all ways, however. One purpose of the clerical chronicle, perhaps its most important one, is conspicuously not claimed by Guido: moral instruction. Bede is clear on the moral as opposed to the merely intellectual effect that history should have: 'should history tell of good men and their good estate, the thoughtful listener is spurred on to imitate the good; should it record the evil ends of wicked men, no less effectively the devout and earnest listener or reader is kindled to eschew what is harmful and perverse, and himself with greater care pursue those things which he has learned to be good and pleasing in the sight of God.'[29] Interestingly enough, the historian becomes a teacher only when he shows his audience the factual truth of the past, because only then he is informing them of things previously unknown. The moral purpose of history is more the job of the reader himself; he must 'imitate the good,' which is not something new, but already known: 'those things he has learned (*cognouerit*) to be good and pleasing in the sight of God.' The chronicle's recording purpose is an act of instruction, its moral purpose one of inspiration. Ordericus Vitalis, Jocelin of Brakelond, Roger of Wendover, and Matthew Paris all insist that the reader should use the examples of good and evil included in their histories as example and warning.[30] Henry of Huntingdon on the utility of history anticipates Sidney on poetry. He argues that history is much better than philosophy in presenting vice and virtue because it is a more entertaining form, and he sees a wonderful effect in it: 'So, also, in the annals of all people, which indeed display the providence of God, clemency, munificence, honesty, circumspection, and the like, with their opposites, not only provoke believers to what is good, and deter them from evil, but even attract worldly men to goodness, and arm them against wickedness.'[31] In the fourteenth century, the *Polychronicon* is still repeating the same ideas.[32]

But Guido is different. Neither in his prologue, nor elsewhere in the *Historia* does he profess to inspire the reader to good or warn him from bad. Guido's purpose is never seriously theological or moral. The apparently moralistic passages Guido adds to Benoît are too rhetorical and contradictory to qualify as serious instruction. The superficiality of these proverbial lessons will be discussed below. Guido shares the clerical chroniclers' desire to produce an accurate record, and yet his work finally differs essentially from Christian history, be it Providential or chronicle, because of his refusal to interpret the events he narrates. He does not, like the Providential historian, see each event as a strand in God's divine web; nor like the clerical chronicler, does he believe that an individual act can be abstracted into a generally applicable lesson. Guido satisfies those who want to know exactly what happened at Troy; he makes no attempt to locate the city's role in God's plan or to draw consistent examples of morally good or bad conduct. Yet these different final goals should not obscure the *Historia*'s basic similarity to the clerical chronicle—each claims to be a record of factual, eyewitness history.

The Aristocratic Chronicle

A second kind of medieval chronicle, one that was especially popular at the time of Guido's Middle English translators, contains other characteristics of the *Historia*. In this group, which has been called the aristocratic chronicle in a recent study by William J. Brandt, are the *Chronicles* of Jordan Fantosme and Pierre de Langtoft, Thomas Gray's *Scalacronica*, the *Life of the Black Prince* by the herald of Sir John Chandos, and, most importantly, the *Chronicles* of Jean Froissart.[33] Brandt's rigid division of chronicles into two groups (aristocratic and clerical) is too artificial and extreme, as Robert Stepsis has shown,[34] but his discussion of specific characteristics in the aristocratic chronicles can help us better understand why the *Historia* was accepted as genuine history by the later Middle Ages. Although the two groups overlap in practice, it can be generally said that the *Historia* is most like the clerical chronicle in its commitment to preserve the truth of the past and most like the aristocratic chronicle in its narrative style and structure. Again I must note that it is not relevant to my argument whether Guido himself was actually influenced by either the aristocratic or clerical chronicle (indeed, most of those discussed here were written after his time), my only claim is that to its English translators and their audiences, the *Historia* would have seemed much like both varieties.

Brandt argues that aristocratic chronicles are more limited than clerical ones in scope and subject: 'They are concerned only with the knightly class, and they are concerned with that class as heroes of council and field.'[35] While clerical chronicles tend to be simply 'collections of incidents or events' with no continuity of action, aristocratic chronicles are essentially narratives and are thus 'primarily concerned with relating this continuous action . . . of things happening in time.'[36] Two other distinguishing marks of the aristocratic chronicle noted by Brandt are its aim 'to celebrate, not to explain' action, and the 'alternating reportage, first of one side and then of the other.'[37] Brandt's conclusions indicate how much the *Historia* would have seemed like a contemporary aristocratic chronicle to its Middle English translators. Guido's main interest is the same: knighthood seen in and between battles. His method of narration is also like the aristocratic chronicle. The clerical chronicle, especially in England where the annalistic tradition remained strong, makes simple chronology its chief principle of organization. Each year is a separate container and every thing that happened during it is tossed in together. The *Historia*'s material is also basically chronological, but the aim is narration—story—and not simply a record of single and often disparate events. Guido's subject is the whole story of Troy and its final destruction, no more and no less. Finally, the *Historia* is like the aristocratic chronicle in alternating its narration between the Greek and Trojan sides during both truce and battle.

Both the aristocratic chronicle and Guido's *Historia* focus on the deeds and pageantry of knighthood—military campaigns, their preparation, and their aftermath. Other matters of state and other events in the realm, prominent in the clerical chronicle, are generally absent in these works. Since gentle folk, not monks, supplied both audience and subject for aristocratic chronicles, the Latin of the clerical chronicle gives way to the vernacular. The decision of three individual authors to translate the *Historia* into English suggests that they anticipated its appeal to the same lay readers.

The late-medieval aristocratic chronicle invariably deals with a limited amount of time and space, usually that which had been personally experienced by the author. Clerical chroniclers, on the other hand, even if they write only about their own period, often add their work to existing universal histories (so both Eadmer and Henry of Huntingdon announce that they are followers of Bede). Whatever the root cause of the aristocratic chronicle's narrow focus,[38] the *Historia* observes similar limits. Although Guido goes beyond the Trojan War to trace its origins in the quest of the Argonauts and to show its aftermath in the return of the Greeks, the entire period covered is less than a man's lifetime and the work narrates a story complete in itself.

In its most essential interests and form, therefore, the *Historia* must have seemed to do for the age of Priam what writers like Froissart were doing for the present. The *Historia* can be considered an aristocratic chronicle on a classical theme. Today we can see the many differences between Guido and the medieval aristocratic chronicle, but our English translators must have been drawn to and delighted by the degree of similarity. The events at Troy happened far away, the city and all its glory had been buried for ages, and yet because of the work of Dares and Dictys, and the later writers who preserved them, fourteenth-century Englishmen believed that they were able to confront the ancient 'past as if it were the present' (Pro. 9; p. 3).

The Historia as Classical Chronicle

A reader who knows the story of Troy only as it appears in classical literature will be unsettled by Guido's *Historia* much in the way Odysseus was by his return to Ithaca. Much will be generally recognizable, but everything is somewhat altered, and the total effect is strange indeed. The *Historia* is pro-Trojan; and so while Hector still dies by the hand of Achilles, he is far and away the superior warrior who only falls because of a sneak attack. Love stories abound in the medieval version. Achilles sulks in his tent, not from wounded pride, but because he is love-sick for Polyxena, the daughter of Priam. The passion of Troilus and Cressida (here named Briseida) first appears in the medieval story, and even Paris and Helen are made more romantic. But the most important change, though one that has gone largely unrecognized, is that the medieval Troy story is given the form of chronicle. The *Historia* claims to tell all— 'everything that took place according to the complete history, both in general and in particular' (Pro. 52–53; p. 4)—and seems to contain the kind of convincing documentation that truth requires.

Early in the work we are given a list of the principal heroes fighting for Troy and a similar list of Greeks—each portrait full of specific details apparently drawn from life. There is also a complete list of Greek ships and Trojan allies. Truth must surely be contained in such a profusion of names, both personal and geographical, and specific numbers. When a battle occurs, and battle is the essential stuff of the *Historia*, we know who leads which battalion of how many men, who engages whom in single combat, and who dies by whose hand. We are told exactly when a battle ends, given a complete casualty report (wounds and fatalities), and informed when a truce has been agreed upon and how long it will last. The documentation and detail, the names and numbers, are constant, and their cumulative effect is convincing. If Guido's verisimilitude is suspect at some points, it is usually because he is trying to cope with confusions in his source. Dares and Dictys each tell a different story about Ajax, son of Telamon, and since Benoît gives them both so does Guido.

Guido is careful never to strain the credibility of his history with fantastic decoration. He is ever diligent to expose mere poetic fancy and isolate it from the true history. The Golden Fleece, he tells us, is nothing more than a mass of treasure in sheep's clothing (1.88–93; p. 7). The poets may have invented fictions about the divine birth (4.7–15; p. 33) and stellar fate (8.114–27; p. 83) of Castor and Pollux, but Guido is not fooled, and he takes pains that the reader should not be either. While marvels occur throughout the *Historia*, they are generally reduced and rationalized from Benoît and are of the sort that a medieval audience could believe possible. Guido shows us the magic by which Medea is able to defeat the beasts that guard the Golden Fleece, but he is careful also to establish the limits of her powers. Skilled as she may have been in astrology and witchcraft, Medea did not, as the pagans believed and Ovid wrote, mock the injunctions of God (2.190–234; pp. 16–17). When Guido comes to the Chamber of Beauty, one of Benoît's most elaborate rhetorical and architectural set-pieces, he can no longer remain silent and in his desire for truth even questions the veracity of Dares. As a faithful transmitter of the historical record, he briefly records the main features of the Chamber, but balks at describing four gold images constructed by magic. Even though 'Dares' vouches for their truth, Guido's honesty compels him to pronounce them 'empty dreams rather than factual truths' (21.12; p. 171).

The Eyewitness Style of Guido's Historia

Guido's repeated claim that he is offering only unadorned truth has not, of course, been accepted by modern scholars, but it has caused them to ignore the *Historia*'s literary form. Nevertheless, Guido's presentation of the story of Troy is more complex than it at first seems, and three of his work's qualities are especially interesting: (1) the *Historia*'s objective, eyewitness narration, (2) its focus on individual heroes and presentation of all human action as battle, and (3) its deep pessimism concerning man's ability to control or even understand his fate.

Like the medieval chroniclers discussed above, Guido believes that truth lies in public information available to an eyewitness observer. Paul Archambault has defined a late-medieval school of such chroniclers (Froissart is its most famous member) whom he calls 'phenomenalists' or 'mirror' historians. The aim of such chroniclers is the surface representation of things using 'neither shadow nor high relief'; accurate in detail they have 'no moral or political thesis to prove'; their only general ideas are of 'a devastating banality,' and their perspective is that of a 'naive spectator.'[39] Guido boasts of his veracity and sneers at poetic fables because he has the reports of Dares and Dictys who, like these later chroniclers, 'were at the time of the Trojan War continually present in their armies and were the most trustworthy reporters of those things which they saw' (Pro. 41–43; p. 4). Nevertheless, the price Guido must pay for such authority is heavy: he is prevented from going beyond the surface of things to explore those truths not contained in observable fact. As a result, his accounts of even public events are curiously incomplete, and more subjective scenes, those dealing with human character and emotion, quickly become ludicrous.

The limits of the eyewitness style are apparent even with material that is relatively concrete. Battle is the essential stuff of the *Historia*, but Guido is not a particularly good war reporter. Rarely does he describe military action so that it involves or excites us; instead he remains at a great distance from his material. His profusion of names and numbers, his items of eyewitness fact, cannot substitute for other, deeper kinds of truth. As a consequence the *Historia* often reads like the box-score of a baseball game. The statistical information is all there—the hits, runs, errors—but missing is any of the real drama.

Guido is unable or unwilling to analyze large-scale fighting. When he tries to provide an overview of battle, he describes a melée. We never really discover the men at all—only the noise of their lances and swords, the sight of their bodies and gore. Nor does Guido ever examine the deeper patterns of war. All is a chaotic and bloody blur until he focuses on individual fights. Battle action in the *Historia* frequently has the intricacy of a TV soap opera, but it is presented without ideology or any sense of strategy and is always reducible to units of simple conflict—usually knight against knight. Here as elsewhere Guido presents objective fact— the public face of an event available to an eyewitness. He tells us what the warriors do, while avoiding any serious examination of why or how they do it.

The extremely paratactic style of Guido's battle description precludes any serious analysis of larger or more subtle forces behind the events themselves, as in this example from the fourth battle:

> Meanwhile there was a very great struggle in fighting between King Arastrus and Ulysses. Ulysses hurled him from his horse, and when he had seized the horse, he ordered it taken to his tent. Polimedes attacked old Ampon and wounded him fatally so that he breathed his last and died from the wound. Neoptolemus approached King Archilogus and both fell from their horses. Polydamas rushed upon Palamedes whom he hurled wounded from his horse, and jeered at his weakness with vile words. King Stelenus and King Caras met to fight with each other. King Stelenus hurled King Caras, wounded, from his horse. Philimenis rushed upon the duke of Athens,

whom he cast from his horse, took the horse from him and handed it over to his own men. Philitoas rushed upon King Remus and both fell from their horses. King Theseus and King Euryalus both met fighting, wounded each other, and courageously cast each other from their horses. (17.74–87; p. 153)

To realize Guido's extraordinary shallowness as a war reporter, we need only compare him with Froissart. Although he also treats only the surface of things, and is hardly a serious analyst of war in the modern sense, Froissart describes real fighting and demonstrates an appreciation of strategy and tactics almost totally absent in the *Historia*. Froissart tells us that, before the battle of Crécy, the English king ordered his commanders to survey the terrain and determine the most advantageous position to place their troops. The careful preparation and perfect discipline of the English army pay off as the weary and disorganized French, forced to attack with the sun in their eyes, are mowed down almost effortlessly.[40] The military tactics described by Froissart are rather elementary, but they are worthy of a Napoleon or Caesar when compared to the lone example of strategy in the *Historia*: the plan to conquer Laomedon's Troy. Hercules suggests the Greek army be divided into two parts. One will hide in the woods near the city while the other remains by the ships to invite the attack of the Trojans in the morning, and thus Laomedon's army will be surrounded and cut off from Troy (4.120–48; pp. 36–37). Hercules's plan in wonderfully childish, though we are told it actually works, and yet in the major Trojan War there is not even this level of tactical sophistication.

Guido depends on this same eyewitness style to portray human character; in the *Historia* men as well as arms remain one-dimensional. Brandt finds traits in clerical chronicles that are similar to Guido's approach, and this suggests again how familiar the *Historia* would have seemed to a history-reading audience in the fourteenth or fifteenth century. Character portraits in clerical chronicles, according to Brandt, lack any organizing principle and assume 'that the truth about an individual could be summarized by a series of adjectives.' Missing is a hierarchy of motives and values, a sense of an individual's mainspring of action because, for the clerical chronicle, 'human nature remained a collection of manifestations. The characteristics noted by the chroniclers are free floating; they do not spring from any sort of unifying ground.'[41] An identical method of characterization is used by Guido for his portraits of important Greeks and Trojans in Book Eight. When Chaucer suddenly offers similar descriptions of Troilus, Diomedes, and Criseyde late in his *Troilus and Criseyde* (probably from Dares by way of Joseph of Exeter), we are shocked because of the crude contrast to the complex investigation of mind and emotions undertaken in the rest of the poem. It is as if a surgeon suddenly picked up a jack-knife in the middle of a delicate heart operation. Guido, unlike Chaucer, at no time has the slightest interest in the human psyche; his approach to character is not a poet's, but that of an alert yet distant observer.

Guido pauses to explain Dares's method (which is also his own) before presenting the portraits themselves: 'For very often during truces made between the armies he went to the Greek tents, and he observed the nature of each of the chief people, gazing at them so that he would know how to describe their characteristics in his work' (8.132–35; p. 83). Guido insists that the portraits are eyewitness reports to insure that the reader will accept their factual truth; in so doing, however, he must also concede that their information does not go beyond that apparent to an outside observer. The claim to exterior truth eliminates any to interior truth, and so each description in Book Eight takes the form identified by Brandt—a list of individual qualities: 'Antenor was tall and slim, full of talk but intelligent. He was a man of greatest enterprise, very cautious, the beloved favorite of King Priam, and when the occasion presented itself, he mocked his companions with great wit. Nevertheless he was absolutely mature in all seriousness' (8.247–51; p. 86). By any measure this is a fascinating collection of attributes, but its potential remains unexploited. Each quality is stillborn and is never used to explain the hero's curious and important role in the history of Troy. Antenor is a puzzle: he moves from trusted ambassador to conniving traitor and finally betrays even his co-conspirator Aeneas, but in the *Historia*, while the pieces are there, they remain unassembled.

Throughout the *Historia*, in a variety of situations, Guido provides a list where we would expect analysis—a factual if narrow way of present-ing history. In this method, quality is most characteristically represented by quantity: the value of a forest is measured by the number of its trees. Perhaps the most surprising of these lists occurs during the first meeting of Paris and Helen, who share the one love story expanded from Benoît. We are told that as soon as Paris saw Helen, 'he coveted her, and . . . he seethed with intense desire' (7.169–71; p. 71); then, from his perspective, we are given a full accounting of the queen's attributes, down to such details as eyelashes, teeth, shoulder blades, and fingernails (7.173–230; pp. 71–73). The catalogue is a rhetorical convention to be sure (although this one is original with Guido), but rarely is it intended to explain a lover's emotions. However, that which makes the list so ludicrous to us—the distant numbering and cold detail of the items—is precisely the measure of the intensity of Paris's ardor in the eyewitness style. To imagine the love of Paris and Helen from within would make Guido a poet, an inventor of fictions. Instead he aims only for history and, in his conception of that office, must remain in the world of tangible and observable fact, however false that may sometimes seem to the situation at hand.

Because its notion of truth is so superficial, the eyewitness style tends to view each event as isolated and without context. Time and again in the *Historia* a character's action in one situation will seem to contradict his action in another, but Guido never apologizes or explains. In this he is like Froissart whose characters, according to Archambault, 'do not seem to profit from their mistakes. The reader is never allowed to get inside their skin or grasp them intuitively, even when they suffer. He must subjectify them, read into their character through their outside delin- eations. Froissart allows for no other response.'[42] We have seen this with Paris's infatuation for Helen; an even more important silence concerns Hector's attitude toward the war itself.

After the failure of Antenor's peace mission, Priam turns to Hector, his eldest son, for support in waging a war of revenge on Greece and appoints him 'sole leader and chief in this undertaking' (6.96; p. 59). Hector, while admitting the justice of revenge, argues that war with Greece would be extremely risky, accomplish little good, and subject the peace and prosperity of Troy to the malign influence of Fortune (6.108–66; pp. 59–60). Hector's advice is not, however, accepted, and the Trojans decide to send Paris against Greece. Curiously, Hector's anti-war position is never again discussed in the *Historia*. The grim satisfaction he might be expected to take in the fulfillment of his prophecy goes unmentioned, and any conflict between his initial opposition and later participation in the war is unexplored. A modern historian might wonder if Hector's commitment to the war was ever whole-hearted or was in any way undermined by bitterness because his views had been ignored. Guido's eyewitness style is incapable of raising, let alone answering, these or similar questions. Remaining so resolutely on the surface of things, it cannot even provide evidence from which the reader might speculate. Guido's eyewitness style challenges the English historians of Troy to preserve its facts, and, at the same time, it provides them with opportunities to fill its many pyschological voids.

The Importance of Heroes and Battles in the Historia

Because it sees life as a series of discrete and unconnected events, the *Historia* has difficulty interpreting its story at any depth. Brandt's descrip- tion of military action in the aristocratic chronicle is also true for the *Historia*: 'The aristocratic chronicler did not see a conflict as having a structure of its own. Each party to a conflict pursued his line of action, which he initiated by an act of will. The opposing forces in a conflict hence remain distinct from one another because their actions were seen as manifestations of individual wills and not as a part of an enveloping structure.'[43] Individual acts of will are important in the *Historia* also, and even potentially complex events are presented superficially.

   The most common motive for action in the *Historia* is revenge, but a
revenge that almost always remains mechanical because Guido never
probes beneath the surface of things. Jason returns to claim the throne of
Thessaly having won both the Golden Fleece and Medea, but he is
incapable of enjoying either until he has exacted 'revenge and reprisal'
against Laomedon for the insult of refusing to let him land at Troy (3.406;
p. 32). Priam rebuilds Troy into a rich and flourishing city, yet he remains
unsatisfied: 'he turned his restless thoughts back to the serious injuries
which had been offered him a while ago by the Greeks' (5.252–53; p. 50).
In the Trojan debate over whether to go to war over Hesione, even Hector,
who argues against it because of the risks involved, confesses that the
'great nobility' of the Trojans makes 'the slightest injury . . . very shameful' (6.111–12; p. 59). Thus it is easy for Troilus's passionate insistence
that 'it is not to be borne that the Greeks offered us such a great dishonor
without retaliation and vengeance' (6.310–11; p. 64) to carry the day
against Hector's good sense. The basic narrative structure of the *Historia*
is a simple pattern of action and reaction. Time and again in battle a knight
will see a comrade wounded or killed and, especially if the fallen warrior is
a kinsman, feel compelled to seek revenge against the winner. Should he
succeed, a knight on the other side will come forward to revenge this new
injury, and a chain of violence as unbreakable as a Sicilian feud is thus
created.
   In the *Historia* the will of individual heroes is crucial; yet their extraordinary abilities are never explained or analyzed, only celebrated. The
ordinary knight's revenge produces, at most, the death of his enemy;
when a hero seeks revenge, however, the whole tide of battle turns. In the
first war at Troy, each side is holding its own until Laomedon sees his
nephew Pollux fall dead before him:

> Then King Laomedon burst into floods of tears, miserably
> bewailing the fall of his nephew. In pain and deep anguish, he
> called together his whole army, which he urged by doleful
> tears to make a powerful attack in reprisal for the death of his
> nephew. Then, when he had sounded a blast on his horn,
> about seven thousand knights advanced to the king at the
> sound of the horn. When they had made the attack against the
> Greeks, they valiantly assaulted them, killed, wounded, and
> slew them cruelly at the point of the sword so that they turned
> disgracefully in flight. (4.273–81; p. 40)

To us the scene is ludicrous. How does one call together an entire army in
the midst of battle? Exactly what tearful words did Laomedon use, and just
how were the seven thousand troops arranged to such devastating effect?
Does the horn have any special meaning? These questions and similar
ones are totally inappropriate in the *Historia*. They might explain things

for us, but not for Guido. For him, the hero is absolute, and heroic desire is irresistible by definition.

In the *Historia*, Hector is the champion most able singlehandedly to stem a rout of his own men or create one in the enemy. His prowess is first seen during the Greek landing. Under the assault of a series of individual Greek champions, the Trojans have been 'forced to turn their backs and save themselves by flight' (14.238–39; p. 125). Enter *fortissimus* Hector whose deeds cause the enemy to flee 'before his face, unable to stand his deadly blows, and thus while he persisted the Greeks failed' (14.259–61; p. 125). When Hector then wearies and retires, the Greeks are able to regain the initiative under their hero, Achilles. Guido does not trouble to explain Hector's sudden weariness, anymore than he does the capacity of the Trojan champion to sweep all before him. Guido makes his heroes the determining factor in any battle because like extraordinary forces of nature (a hurricane or a tornado), their great effect needs no explanation, only statement. His concern is not to analyze his heroes, but to celebrate them—whether Greek or Trojan. When Hector dies, the Trojans feel doomed, as do the Greeks at the death of Achilles; Troy shuts its gates and refuses any longer to fight when its last champion, Penthesilea, has been defeated. The Trojan War in the *Historia* is not between armies or divisions, nor even between the strategies of rival commanders, it is between individual heroes. Froissart seems to expect that his audience will recognize that the Trojan War is so described. In the account of James Douglas's attempt to stem a retreat all by himself during the battle of Chevy Chase, Froissart says the Scotsman advanced 'furiously forward, as though he was a Trojan Hector expecting to win the battle single-handed.'[44]

The direct conflict of battle is Guido's model for action off the field as well as on. In the frequent councils held by both Greeks and Trojans, issues are never seriously explored or analyzed; instead, two clearly opposed sides each fights for its own position until the most powerful side gains total victory over the other, just as one knight will use his greater strength to wound or kill a lesser warrior. A clear example of this repeated pattern occurs in response to the death of Achilles. The Greeks are deeply shaken by the loss of their champion, and 'agreed among themselves that with Achilles taken away from them, there remained no hope of seizing the city' (27.58–59; p. 208). A council is therefore held, and Agamemnon sets the question in the form of a debate: does the army wish to continue the war or return to Greece? Inevitably the result is a direct clash: 'The opinions of the hearers were divided according to their different wishes; some approved of the war, others said the return was pleasing' (27.71–73; p. 208). Although Guido gives no persuasive speeches, in the next sentence a winner emerges: 'At last they all agreed upon and heartily approved of one opinion—to continue the war, saying that even if they lacked Achilles, they did not lack the promises of the gods . . .' (27.73–76;

p. 208). The victorious position is not only unanimous, it is the direct opposite of the Greeks' initial attitude: now they trust in the promises of the gods. We are never told why this argument becomes decisive or how its proponents manage so completely to win over the other side, any more than we know why one knight is able to conquer another. One party is simply stronger than the other. This may do to explain battle, but is inadequate for more subtle conflicts.

Guido's inability to see human relationships in any terms other than those of pitched battle reveals itself in unexpected places. A particularly puzzling example is Hector's final parting from his wife and family. One night Andromache dreams that Hector will be killed in the next day's battle. Terrified, she wakes her husband, but his harsh reaction transforms her concern into conflict: 'She implored him with devoted prayers to pay attention to the meaning of the vision and not to dare to go to battle that day. Hector then, exceedingly angry at his wife's words, rebuked her and reproached her with very bitter words, claiming it was not wise to believe the deceptions of dreams which always delude dreamers' (21.48–53; p. 172). Having lost this first skirmish, Andromache next warns Priam and Hecuba and begs them to stop Hector. Priam agrees and while sending the Trojan battalions into battle, 'he ordered Hector expressly not to mingle in the fray' (21.64–65; p. 172). This enrages Hector at both wife and father. He insults Andromache and, 'disregarding his father's orders,' arms himself (21.69; p. 172). With her cause almost lost, Andromache throws herself at Hector's feet while clutching their child. Hecuba, Cassandra, Polyxena, and Helen join the lament, but Hector's response is resolute: 'he was not moved by their tears and prayers' (21.82; p. 173). Instead he finishes arming and mounts his horse. Andromache in grief rallies Priam with weeping and self-mutilation, urging him to bring back Hector. Priam quickly overtakes Hector and 'with angry heart' (21.95; p. 173) seizes his son's reins and both orders and begs him to go no farther: 'Finally, with great objection to his father's orders, Hector obeyed. He returned unwillingly and went up into his palace, but did not, however, trouble to remove the armor with which he was clad' (21.97–100; p. 173). Unhappily, Hector soon gets his way. When told that Achilles has slain his natural brother Margariton, he becomes furious and without Priam's knowledge enters the battle to receive the death Andromache had foreseen.

What are we to make of this account of Guido's principal hero? During these last moments with his family, Hector shows nothing but an inexcusable anger and cruelty. He appears to care nothing for his wife and child and acts like the callowest of adolescents toward his father. As mad for war as Hotspur, he has Edmund's feeling for family. And yet we know this does not truly represent Guido's view of Hector. From the first the hero's fierceness in battle is matched by prudence, generosity, and a nature beloved by all. He is as wise as he is powerful; a chivalrous knight as well as a conquering warrior. His affection and care for Priam are stressed throughout, and in his formal portrait Guido says that 'No offensive or improper word ever left his mouth' (8.218; p. 85). The explanation, I believe, lies in Guido's view of all human action as battle. When he comes to this final, potentially complex scene, he can only understand it as a series of simple and absolute conflicts. Guido has no way of exploring a person's inner thoughts or feelings directly; he must objectify them as exterior action and then define them through direct opposition. Any chance for subtlety is lost in the process with the result that Hector becomes monstrous. No shadows or twilight exist in the minds or relationships of Guido's characters, just as there are no friends across a battlefield—everyone is on one side or the other. Given Guido's method, Hector cannot disagree with his wife and father without becoming their bitter enemy. Guido was wise to choose a subject that contains little more than war and the preparations for war—battle is the model by which he understands all human behavior.

The Pessimism of the Historia

Although it is generally faithful to Benoît's poem, the *Historia* contains a class of additions that lead us to its most remarkable quality: Guido's deep pessimism concerning man's ability to shape or even comprehend his own destiny. In a series of emotional laments, uttered in a distinct, almost personal voice far different from the formal one used to narrate historical events, Guido looks back across the centuries and agonizes over the trivial faults and unknowing mistakes that bring about the ruin of Troy. Guido's anguish comes from the conflict between his characters' ignorance and his own historical perspective. He knows, as they cannot, how things will turn out. Even long after the fact, Guido never offers the assurance that God is behind the events at Troy. The *Historia* does not show us the just punishment of sin, only the futility of human plans and effort. The villain of the Trojan War is simply the ignorance and weakness of the human condition. No one man is responsible, nor one country. All men are fallible, nursing old injuries and unable to foresee the consequences of their actions. Violence escalates with each side's turn to respond, growing from the trivial fault of Laomedon to almost total destruction for both Greece and Troy. Guido does not avoid the pain of his history by turning it into allegory; he chronicles the suffering brought on by real events. He does not assess blame or discover an underlying Providential design; instead he weeps at the human ignorance and impotence revealed by his history and can offer only truisms as advice. This pessimism is the *Historia*'s most fascinating quality, yet it has gone largely unrecognized.

In the most ambitious study yet written on Guido, Walter B. Wigginton argues that the *Historia* is 'a traditional, quasi-allegorical moral history' which follows the school of Providential history as taught by such as Augustine and Otto of Freising.[45] The war at Troy is horrible, but ultimately under the hand of God: it is 'the working out, through men, of some divine purpose.'[46] We are not to feel pity, according to Wigginton, at the wretched ends that befall Laomedon and Priam, only a sense of justice. Both are symbols of worldly ambition and pride; Priam especially is guilty and centrally responsible for the war: it is clear from the start 'that Priam brought it on himself.'[47] I believe that this view of the *Historia* is fundamentally mistaken. The story of Troy is, of course, ripe for allegorical treatment (Wigginton notes many medieval examples), but this is not Guido's aim in the *Historia*. He is a chronicler of real events, not a maker of allegories, and always respects the literal truth of his history.

A closer look at the *Historia* will show that the two chief sinners identified by Wigginton—Laomedon and Priam—are caught by fate rather than models of conscious evil. Laomedon's first encounter with the forces that will destroy him and his city is not the result of his own action, and his response is not blameworthy. The Argonauts land outside Troy for rest and water while on route to the Golden Fleece. The reader knows the Greek force is not hostile because Guido tells us so; unfortunately for him, Laomedon gets a more ambiguous report:

> While Jason and Hercules and their followers were resting in the port of Simois, the report about them reached Laomedon, king of the Trojans, that a certain people unknown to the Trojans, that is, the Greeks, had entered the Phrygian territories in a strange ship, perhaps to spy out secrets in the little Trojan kingdom, or, more probably, to lay waste the country of Troy. (2.56–62; p. 12)

Given this information, Laomedon quite naturally orders Jason and his men to leave the country, in response to which 'accursed plan' Guido comments parenthetically '(if only he never had!)' (2.64–65; p. 12). This is an expression of regret, not of blame,[48] and is possible only because of Guido's long perspective: he, unlike Laomedon, knows the Greeks' intent was innocent and what disasters this decision will occasion. Laomedon does not know this, cannot know it, and thus is not culpable. His decision, though based on faulty reports, is both moderate and logical. He is not especially aggressive and, though insisting that the Argonauts must leave, he does not attack them. As a practical matter, the chance that Laomedon would ever suffer from this expulsion had to be extremely small. For the narrator, however, Laomedon's dreadful end is already a long-established historical fact, and he can do nothing but lament as he retells the first, avoidable steps of this tragedy.

There is no need to find a hidden allegorical lesson in the story of Laomedon; Guido clearly tells us who is responsible. He does not blame

Laomedon but fate. As he describes the Argonauts' arrival at Troy for rest and water, Guido explicitly denies any element of human responsibility: 'The envious course of the fates, however, which always troubles the repose of mortal men, *for no cause* drew causes for enmity and offense out from unexpected hiding places' (2.7–9; p. 11—my emphasis). Nor do subsequent events during this first destruction reveal examples of good rewarded and evil punished, because finally no one wins: Troy is razed and its people killed or enslaved; and even though Greece conquers, 'still for a long time the damage done by the death of its people and the slaughter of its best men destroyed the reward of victory' (2.16–18; p. 11). The *Historia* finds no Providential design behind these events, only ignorance and folly. Long after the fact, these events still have not formed a clear pattern. Concerning the destruction of Laomedon's city, Guido acknowledges how unsettling it is to men's minds 'that a punishment of such severity had to be inflicted for such a trivial fault' (2.20–21; p. 11). He briefly wonders if the founding of Rome and other European settlements might be a justification for 'the amount of evil which took place' (2.22; p. 11), before concluding helplessly that 'the human mind is uncertain whether the cause of such a great betrayal was finally the cause of subsequent good' (2.54–55; p. 12).

After the actual fall of the city, Guido reveals his pessimism at its starkest:

> For the envious course of the fates, the enemy of happiness, always prevents the highest things from remaining on the heights for very long, and in order to bring the condition of men more easily to ruin, it attacks the mighty, through unperceived and obscure snares, and leads them to misfortune, taking its cause from trivial and unthought-of matters, so that by using foresight and with the aid of caution they are not able to protect themselves. (5.14–21; p. 43)

The mighty are totally exposed, but no one is safe. The fates, not here connected in any way to God's Providence as in Boethius or Dante, continually set hidden snares that are beyond men's ability to unravel: 'they are not able to protect themselves' no matter how hard they try. Laomedon is not guilty, or at least not unusually so, only especially unlucky. Guido sees the lot of man, especially of those in high estate, as that of a sand castle before the incoming tide. The *Historia* is not a record of Providential design; the wicked are not punished nor the good saved— all are destroyed.

It is equally wrong to see Priam as the principal negative exemplum in the *Historia*: the chief sinner directly responsible for the war.[49] Guido's pessimism is all-embracing and does not stop at individuals. The Trojan king makes mistakes, misjudges reality, and gives way to passion and error; but he is not exceptionally or irredeemably evil. Before trying force to recover Hesione, he sends Antenor to try to win her through diplomacy. Guido regrets Priam's subsequent ire when this fails, but actual blame is avoided: 'But, say, King Priam, what unhappy quirk of fate incited your peaceful heart to such unfortunate boldness, so that you were not able in the least to restrain the impulses of your heart by mature counsels (although, granted, these impulses are not in the control of man)' (6.8–12; p. 56). This is not a criticism of Priam so much as a defense. Priam is finally not responsible because he was incited by a quirk of fate, and because it is impossible for man to harness the impulses of his heart. After the war council decides to send Paris on a vengeance raid, Guido laments that those in favor of peace were not listened to: 'Oh, would that they had agreed with them, for perhaps those outrages which followed afterward would never have taken place! But because the inevitable fates establish future calamities, it pleased everyone that Paris should go to Greece with the navy' (6.380–84; p. 66). If only Priam and the Trojans had known, Guido cries; but that is precisely the point: how could they have known? Only in retrospect is Hector's advice against war more correct than Troilus's argument for it. The thrust of Guido's lament is not toward fixing blame, rather the opposite. The 'invincible fates' so dominate the affairs of men that only 'perhaps' would those future outrages have been avoided had the peace party prevailed. Neither culpability nor responsibility is possible, for Priam or anyone else, in such a world. Certainly Priam is not alone in folly. Cassandra utters true prophecies of disasters that will befall the returning Greeks as she had prophecied disaster for Troy (31.189–99; p. 242). She is heeded neither time. The passion among the Greeks to return home is reminiscent of Priam's desire to attack: 'then ill-advised heedlessness moved the hearts of the Greeks with the blind passion of eagerness' (31.224–26; p. 243).

In the midst of such chaos, the only lessons Guido's narrator dares to offer are not Christian allegories but simple proverbs—truisms that ignore the questions raised and which, like his laments, are possible only because he knows the end of the story. Here is his remedy for Laomedon's fall:

> Farseeing men should therefore earnestly consider that such are the unforeseen results of actions in this world. For this reason it is necessary that men refrain from trivial and even slight offenses. For slight injuries quite frequently tend to be like fire, whose little spark, nourished with hidden sustenance, suddenly bursts out from under the ashes into very great, searing flames. (5.6–11; p. 43)

The advice is sound but meaningless. It cannot be applied to any new situation because it both begs the question (the offense to the Argonauts is unnecessary) and knows the future (a great war will spring from this trivial act). The difficulty with proverbial advice is that it is so often contradictory (which is the appropriate maxim—'look before you leap' or 'he who hesitates is lost'?) and can only accurately be applied after the event. Guido's narrator gives opposing lessons following two different Trojan councils. In Book 19, Hector properly objects to the granting of a truce, and this leads Guido to advise the wise man to say his piece, even if it is unpopular (19.27–35; p. 160). Ten books later, after Amphimachus speaks against the final, fraudulent truce and thereby earns the traitors' implacable enmity, Guido offers the opposite lesson: if your views are unpopular, better keep them to yourself (29.313–17; p. 226). Guido's conclusions are correct in each case, but only because of his historical perspective. In an almost God-like way, he knows the conclusion of each event.

The only general lesson to be learned from Guido's contradictory advice is that this world is a dangerous and uncertain place, and one would do well always to walk carefully, taking care to disturb as little as possible. Such advice is totally indifferent to Christian morality; it is worldly wisdom, practical and expedient. However much Guido may have sincerely believed in the truths of the Church (and there is no reason to doubt his frequent professions), those truths do not operate in the world of the *Historia*. Guido remains an objective chronicler who sticks to his sources and allows the action to play out in its own terms.[50] The pagan gods, often invoked but never directly seen (except by Paris in a dream), are the deities who have power in Greece and Troy. At Delphos they inform both Calchas and the Greeks how long the war will last and who will triumph; their predictions are absolute truth. Many of the most crucial events in the story are engineered by the gods. They guard the Golden Fleece with 'irresistible power' (2.364; p. 20) according to Medea, who herself is capable of the supernatural; and Paris regards his dream as a sign from them (6.185; p. 61). The gods actually appear in his dream and their promises are true if somewhat misleading.

Of even more importance than the gods to events at Troy, however, are the vaguer, and thus less obviously nonChristian, forces of fate and fortune. Fortune is frequently presented in the Middle Ages as an ultimately benevolent force; however haphazardly the goddess may appear to grant her favors, she is in truth the direct agent of Providence, and as such her every action is directed by God. So we find her in Augustine, Boethius, and Dante. Less sophisticated writers draw a cruder figure who openly works to reward the good and overthrow the wicked, as we shall see in Lydgate's *Troy Book*. In either case Fortune is ultimately good and part of the divine plan for mankind. The *Historia*, however, is no part of this tradition; instead it resorts to an older and more super-stitious school, found also in other medieval works like the alliterative *Morte Arthure*, that does not recognize Providence, only malignant chance.[51] This view was held long before Christ, and one of its appeals to

Guido may have been its harmony with the pagan perspective of Dares and Dictys. No beneficial or divine order sends forth the fortune of the *Historia,* it proceeds rather from chaos and flux. This fortune is not the vivacious, if skittish, goddess Boethius personified in such detail, but a distant abstraction, never capitalized or personalized and interchangeable with the equally vague *fata* (which often means no more than chance or luck). Fortune and the fates are the most powerful forces in the *Historia* and generate unending disaster, yet their operation is no part of any clear controlling order, not even a wicked one. They do not even seem to be consciously hostile to mankind, but are instead distantly and randomly malignant.

While these forces resist clear definition, there is never any doubt that their power is absolute and their effect on men devastating, as we have seen with Laomedon and Priam. Laomedon unwittingly subjected himself to fortune when he rejected the Argonauts, unable to imagine that this single spark would ignite such a holocaust (5.7–21; p. 42). Priam seems even more surely the victim of fate, for we recall that Guido seems to doubt whether he ever had a real choice: 'because the inevitable fates establish future calamities, it pleased everyone that Paris should go to Greece with the navy' (6.382–84; p. 66). Human freedom is denied even more flatly in a later consideration of Priam's act: 'But after the inexorable Fates decree that misfortunes and evils shall happen, they represent the opposite and contrary in the minds of men and recommend them as favorable' (6.409–11; p. 67).

Like Vergil, Guido understands that the Fall of Troy is the story of men eagerly and happily arranging their own destruction. Once when the Trojans are on the verge of total victory, Hector encounters his cousin Ajax, son of Hesione and Telamon, and invites him back to the city to meet his relatives. Ajax refuses but does persuade Hector to call off the Trojan advance. Judged on its own merits, the act illustrates the highest virtues of chivalry. In practical effect, however, Hector's *beau geste* is as fatal to Troy as Laomedon's expulsion of the Argonauts or Priam's pursuit of revenge. It robs Troy of its one opportunity for absolute victory: 'This was the trivial cause for which the Trojans on that day ceased from obtaining their victory which they never afterward were able to reach, because the fates opposed' (15.694–96; p. 147). While pride and rashness make one especially vulnerable to bad fortune, prudence and virtue are no sure protection against it. Man's ignorance of the consequences of his actions is so great that one cannot anticipate when a generous act like Hector's will pull the heavens down upon him: 'But the fates, who arrange for future adversities to happen, destroy everything by hidden snares, by which they complete those adversities which they have arranged for the future' (15.647–49; p. 146).[52]

The *Historia* may well be one of the most despairing books ever written. Fortune and the fates, however impersonal and unknowable, seem to offer some real explanation for the war at Troy, until the reader at last realizes that they are only literary metaphors for the wretched condition of mankind. The *Historia* does not recognize any order or purpose in the world—no deities or even historical forces—only the bleak certainty that things will always get worse. As the war continues, the level of violence rises and with it comes an increase in treachery and sheer bad luck. Clerical distrust of the world, as in Innocent's *De Contemptu Mundi*, may be an influence here, but Guido offers no compensating hope of heaven to redeem the tears. His concern is only with this world and its inhabitants, and what he reveals is a self-perpetuating cycle of mistake, revenge, and destruction that is beyond man's control. The history of Troy does not celebrate glory or heroism, but records with horror the destruction and futility of war.

Nobody wins in the *Historia Destructionis Troiae*. Achilles kills Hector treacherously, then abuses the dead body of Troilus, and is likewise slain himself through the deceptions of Paris and Hecuba, after having argued the futility of the whole enterprise. The Greeks claim victory: their prize is a gutted Troy, on the return from which most will die. Menelaus finally gets back his Helen and is condemned to live with her for the rest of his life.

Despair increases in the *Historia* as events unroll. The war of Laomedon's Troy is a relatively straightforward military engagement and so is the beginning of the great Trojan War, but soon viciousness and deceit begin to dominate. Hector's death, the beginning of the end for Troy, marks the transition from conventional fighting to horror. Before it there is heroism and even chivalry: Hector is warned away from danger by Theseus, a Greek, and he later returns the favor. After it, however, death becomes ignoble and wholesale. Hector is murdered in the first dishonorable combat in the *Historia* when Achilles sees him unprotected and kills him by a sneak attack (21.165–73; p. 175). This is soon followed by the awful death of Troilus, who is surrounded and made helpless by the whole troop of Myrmidons before Achilles dares to behead him. Achilles signals his glorious victory by shamefully dragging Troilus's body through the Greek army (26.262–64; p. 204). Guido explicitly recognizes this unpardonable violation of chivalric conduct with a passage addressed to Homer in which he criticizes the Greek poet for praising such an ignoble coward as Achilles (26.265–93; pp. 204–05). Achilles is not the only offender against honor and fair play. In response to the deaths of Hector and Troilus, Hecuba and Paris conspire to lure Achilles to the temple of Apollo on the pretext that he will be given Polyxena. Once there, he is surprised by a large force and 'wickedly killed' by Paris. Only the prayers of Helen keep his body from being thrown to the dogs (27. 1–49; pp. 206–08). The ugliness spreads and increases. In the very next battle, Paris kills Ajax with a poisoned arrow. The remaining heroes increasingly abandon any pretense to honorable conduct. When

Penthesilea is conquered by Pyrrhus, he 'in satisfaction of his vengeance, hacked her whole body to pieces' (28.201–02; p. 217). Treason and treachery are now standard behavior, and not only for Antenor and Aeneas. At the last, it is everyone for himself.

Learning that peace negotiations are underway, Helen, for whom the war had been fought, 'went secretly to Antenor under the shadows of night and begged him earnestly to negotiate her peace and reconciliation with Menelaus' (29.282–84; p. 225). The Palladium, Troy's guarantee of divine protection, is betrayed when its guardian, a priest, allows himself to be bribed. Guido is provoked to cry out against this extreme treachery: 'what place can be safe or secure if holiness which should be incorruptible is corrupted?' (30.41–42; p. 229).

The Trojan Horse is the appropriate symbol for the entire story. Called an offering for divine favor, it causes total ruin after it is joyfully drawn into position by the victims themselves—a token of ignorance and self-destruction. But terror and tragedy do not end with the fall of the city. The Greek victory is instantly stained with avarice and cruelty. Pyrrhus, who has already shown himself to be his father's son by the mutilation of a female warrior (Penthesilea) and the murder of an old, defenseless man (Priam), now cuts to pieces the innocent Polyxena on Achilles's tomb— an act whose viciousness sickens even his comrades. Violence then turns inward. Ajax Telamon is found hacked and pierced in his bed after a quarrel with Ulysses, which causes the wily one to depart from Troy in the dead of night (31.57–90; p. 239). Meanwhile back in what is left of Troy, Aeneas and Antenor arrange to have each other banished in an appropriately shabby end to the whole business.

Nor do the Greeks leave disaster behind when they depart Troy; instead events become even more irrational and beyond human control. An insidious story comes to the ears of King Nauplius that his son Palamedes did not die in battle (which the reader knows to be the truth), but at the hands of Ulysses and Diomedes with the secret approval of the whole Greek command. To revenge Palamedes, the King and Oectus, his other son, lure the returning Greek fleet onto the rocks of their coast: 'more than two hundred Greek ships with their sailors were sunk in this shipwreck on these cliffs and crags' (32.91–92; p. 248). Then they start spreading false rumors of their own that result in Diomedes being turned away by his wife into temporary exile. A similar story unleashes the most repulsive violence yet seen: Agamemnon's death by Clytemnestra and her own death by Orestes. Although Menelaus is horrified when he hears what his nephew has done, the quarrel is patched up so that Orestes can inherit his father's kingdom and marry Hermione, the daughter of Menelaus and Helen.

The story of Pyrrhus and Andromache follows and completely mocks both the reasons for which the war was fought and its outcome. After Pyrrhus returns from Troy with Andromache and Laomedon, her son by

Hector, he falls in love with Hermione and steals her away from her husband, Orestes. In a scene of extreme irony, Pyrrhus is at Delphos giving thanks 'for the great victory accomplished by the dead Achilles, his father, against the cruelly slain Paris' (34.205–07; p. 268), when he, who had imitated Paris in taking Hermione, is himself slain by Orestes. Orestes then takes Andromache back to his own kingdom where she gives birth to a son fathered by Pyrrhus who is named Achilleides. The end of the conflict between the royal families of Thessaly and Troy, which is one way of viewing the plot of the *Historia*,[53] is as neat as it is unexpected:

> This Achilleides grew up and crowned his brother Laomedon king of Thessaly, since he himself had renounced it, although the kingdom rightly belonged to him, and he also desired and commanded, on account of his love for his brother, that all the Trojans who were captives in Greece should enjoy complete freedom. (34.234–38; pp. 268–69)

Consider all the battles that have been fought, all the death and ruin, all the treachery and deceit—and for what end? For nothing except those evils themselves. Greece and Troy are finally represented by brothers, and Laomedon's great-grandson and namesake occupies the throne of Jason. Looked at in this way, the *Historia* becomes the blackest of comedies, a story of total absurdity.

Guido's motive in presenting such an unremittingly horrible tale, more despairing even than the noble tragedy he found in Benoît, is obscure and finally irrelevant to this study. Perhaps his knowledge of Sicilian history—the wars and betrayals he had seen or heard about and mass destruction like that during the Sicilian Vespers—persuaded Guido that mankind has an insatiable appetite for self-destruction. Faced with the misery of Trojan history, a cycle of increasing violence and treachery which grows ever more irrational and beyond human control, Guido is reduced to two almost contradictory responses: he struggles to achieve objective, factual truth in his history, and in his laments he expresses helpless sorrow for characters who are oblivious to the disasters he can see so clearly.

The *Historia* is not legend or romance, it is an unrecognized variety of medieval history, but Guido's dedication to eyewitness historical fact is practiced at the expense of other, deeper kinds of truth. Three different Middle English authors attempt to bring the raw material of the *Historia* to poetic life. In doing so, they ignore Guido's only serious interpretation of his material: the deep pessimism that runs through his story, which increases as the war unfolds. However, this despair is not completely without effect. It becomes an important element in the two best poems about Troy in Middle English, poems that otherwise use the medieval history of Troy very selectively—Chaucer's *Troilus and Criseyde* and Henryson's *Testament of Cresseid*.

PART TWO

THE MIDDLE ENGLISH HISTORY OF TROY

II

History into Verse: The Prologues to the Middle English History of Troy

Guido delle Colonne's *Historia Destructionis Troiae* was translated three times into Middle English verse between about 1400 and 1426. The alliterative *Destruction of Troy* is the most faithful version of Guido and contains the best poetry; the *Laud Troy Book* tries to appeal to the widest audience by using the form of a romance; and Lydgate's *Troy Book* is the most ambitious work both intellectually and rhetorically. Each poem presents the *Historia* in a different literary form (almost a separate *genre*), yet all three authors respect and conserve the historical truth of Guido's work. The struggle of Guido's English translators to turn history into verse, to be both historian and poet, is the subject of my next four chapters. No one author's solution is exactly like another's, yet all three are caught in the same contradiction of serving two disciplines. The Middle English historians of Troy are not failed romance writers or simply mechanical translators of Guido; instead they are skilled and intelligent craftsmen whose conscientious efforts to bring ancient history to an unlearned audience have been inadequately understood and insufficiently valued. Time has mocked their work (by showing the history to be false), but it nevertheless remains a revealing episode in the story of both medieval history and poetry.

The Middle English historians of Troy affirm their common dedication to both history and poetry in their individual prologues. The expressed goal of all three is identical: the true historical record must be preserved completely, while presented in a form that will appeal to a contemporary audience. The value of such an exacting effort is insisted on by Guido because he, like other medieval writers, is haunted by the transitoriness of human life and the constant care required to preserve the past from the oblivion of time. I quote from the *Destruction*'s rendering of his view:

> Sothe stories ben stoken vp, & straught out of mynde,
> And swolowet into swym by swiftenes of yeres,
> Ffor new þat ben now, next at our hond.[1]

Happily for us, Guido continues, the events at Troy have been kept alive by a continuous historical tradition derived from the eyewitness obser- vations of Dares and Dictys, who were 'continually present in their armies and were the most trustworthy reporters of those things which they saw' (Pro. 42–43; p. 4). In their work the reader will find not only the true story, but, equally important, the whole story: 'everything that took place according to the complete history, both in general and in particular' (Pro. 52–53; p. 4).

Each of the Middle English translators of the *Historia* offers a unique prologue to his work (because each is defining his own special approach to the subject), but all are careful to echo Guido's essential claims. The prologue to the alliterative *Destruction,* here as elsewhere the most faith- ful English version of the *Historia,* insists in two places on the eyewitness origin of the material (23 and 55–60) and at length on its completeness (77–95). The *Laud*'s prologue barely follows Guido's at all, but it does bring forth Dares and Dictys as the work's authority:

> For thei were euery day in the feld
> And alle here dedis thay be-held,—
> And as thei were thei wreten hem bothe.[2]

The *Laud*-poet assures the reader that his work contains the whole, true story, 'the werre sothe alle plenere' (65–86), because it derives from two men who wrote 'the sothe to say with-oute les' (93). Among the English historians of Troy, Lydgate provides the most rhetorically ambitious prologue. After a long series of invocations and dedications, he also insists on the absolute veracity of his material: 'Wher was remembrid, of auctours vs be-forn, / Of the dede the verreie trewe corn.'[3] In a nice rhetorical touch, Lydgate repeats the word *trewe,* or a close synonym, no less than twenty-six times within the next 160 or so lines. He, too, finds ultimate warrent in Dares and Dictys: 'They were present and seyen euerydel, / And as it fel they write trewe and wel' (Pro. 313–14). Guido is praised because, though he adds art and eloquence to the material, he does not once blemish its historical truth ('in effecte the substaunce is the same' [Pro. 356–59]). Lydgate vows not to tamper with this tradition himself and honors Guido, 'Whom I schal folwe as nyʒe as euer I may' (Pro. 375).

Although they repeat Guido's claims of historical truth, and seek to preserve his 'classical chronicle' as we shall see, the Middle English historians of Troy alter one significant part of the prologue to the

Historia: its attack on the classical poets of Troy. They must maintain, against Guido, that one can be both true historian and good poet. For Guido the division is absolute. Whatever their other merits, Homer, Ovid, and Vergil are guilty of undermining 'the truth of this very history, dealing with it lightly as poets do, in fanciful inventions by means of certain fictions, so that what they wrote seemed to their audiences to have recorded not the true things, but the fictitious ones instead' (Pro. 17–21; pp. 3–4). Only in the *Historia*, Guido maintains, can the West at last 'separate the true from the false' (Pro. 38–39; p. 4).

The English translators deliberately and necessarily modify Guido's judgment on poetry. They intend to use verse not to compromise but to preserve and extend the truth of the history: to make it appeal to a large audience incapable of reading Guido. In his one significant departure from the *Historia*'s prologue, the author of the *Destruction* will grant only that *some* (note the repetition of this word) poets have not told the truth about Troy:

> But sum poyetis full prist þat put hom þerto,
> With fablis and falshed fayned þere spechr.
> And made more of þat mater þan hom maister were:
> Sum lokyt ouer litle and lympit of the sothe. (33–36)

Although the *Destruction* follows the *Historia* in finding Homer unworthy of belief, since he is the author of 'trifuls' and 'feynit fare' (37–46), it then goes on to claim that other poets have corrected his errors:

> That [his errors] poyetis of prise have preuyt vntrew:
> Ouyde and othir þat onest were ay,
> Virgille þe virtuus, verrit for nobill,
> Thes dampnet his dedys & for dull holdyn. (47–50)

Guido had distinguished false poets from true historians; the alliterative poet distinguishes true from false poets.

Poetry and history may be judged antipathetic by both Guido and ourselves, but their union would have seemed perfectly legitimate in medieval England. The special passion for history among both the Anglo-Saxons and Normans is well-known. After 1066 vernacular historical literature continued in the victorious language, often in the form of poetry. There was already Anglo-Saxon precedent for this in works like the *Battle of Brunanburh* and the *Battle of Maldon*. In her important study of Anglo-Norman literature, Dominica Legge discusses those poems which are also genuine history. Gaimer, 'the oldest chronicler in the French language,'[4] set the pattern for popular history in England; and later historian-poets, like Jordan Fantosme and Pierre de Langtoft, are authoritative historians still worthy of belief today.[5] Two Anglo-Norman biographies in octosyllabic couplets demonstrate that genuine poetry and sound history can inhabit the same work: the thirteenth-century *Histoire de Guillaume le Maréchal* and the late fourteenth-century life of the Black Prince by the herald of Sir John Chandos, part of which was used by Froissart.[6]

The highly respected *Polychronicon* insists on the importance of 'scripta poetarum' in preserving the past,[7] and with the resurrection of English as a literary language came more vernacular histories in poetry: Langtoft was soon turned into English verse by Robert Manning of Brunne, and the *Short English Metrical Chronicle* derives from French historical poems.[8] Not content with translations only, Englishmen also produced original histories in verse. John Page's *Sege of Rouen* is an impressive example. According to C. L. Kingsford, it is 'the most authentic account which we possess' of the engagement.[9] Similarly, the Scottish *Bruce* (1375) is a work of real historical value.[10] Kingsford discusses the special historical importance of poetry in the fifteenth century: for then 'ballads are the most natural form for popular historical narrative, and verse is the commonest vehicle not only for political satire, but for political controversy as well.'[11] A late-medieval English audience, then, would be very familiar with the idea that true history could be contained in poetry. For the translators of Guido it was a natural medium to use, especially if they wished to interest a popular audience.

The Middle English historians of Troy do not, with the one exception in the *Destruction* already noted, directly confront Guido's bias against poetry. Instead, they justify their medium as a response to another section of the *Historia*'s prologue. The true historical tradition, Guido says, is able to 'depict the past as if it were the present,' so that ancient heroes are endowed with 'the courageous spirit they are imagined to have had, just as if they were alive' (Pro. 9–11; p. 3). The purpose of the *Historia* is to salvage the story of Troy: 'To keep it alive in the minds of succeeding generations' (Pro. 14–15; p. 3). The Middle English historians of Troy understand Guido to mean that the historian should not embalm the past, rather he must vivify it. If history is to live for new audiences and seem 'as if it were the present,' it must, to some degree and without compromise to its truth, adapt itself to each generation of readers. It must change in order to remain the same; and thus a superficial alteration of form will guarantee the essential continuity. The English historians of Troy faced the problem of any translator: how a new language and form can be used to retain as much as possible of the original. All of our authors choose poetry as a way of keeping the record both fresh and true, and their ultimate aim is even more ambitious. Not content with merely keeping the story up to date, each wants to make ancient, scholarly history appeal to a popular audience.

The alliterative poet opens with an attempt to win readers away from contemporary romance by insisting on the pleasures to be had from true records of the distant past:

But olde stories of stithe þat astate helde,
May be solas to sum þat it segh neuer,
Be writyng of wees þat wist it in dede,
With sight for to serche, of hom þat suet after,
To ken all the crafte how þe case felle,
By lokyng of letturs þat lefte were of olde. (21–26)

In the narrative itself, the poet several times uses a formula to demonstrate that truth is stranger than fiction. He insists that the characteristics
of Hector, the Trojan army, and the battle at the landing are so extraordinary that such marvels were 'neuer red in no Romanse' (3896, 5544,
and 5714). We have no way of knowing how successful the poet's efforts to
appeal to a wide, unlearned audience were, but they are in accord with the
spirit of the time. The authoritative *Polychronicon* was translated into
English by Trevisa in the 1380s and again by an anonymous author in the
next century; and Robert Manning wrote his *Story of England* in simple
vernacular verse in order, he says, to be understood by a wide audience of
lewed readers.[12]

None of the Middle English histories of Troy reaches out to a general
audience more directly than the *Laud Troy Book*. Ignoring most of
Guido's prologue, the poet, after a short prayer, opens with a catalogue of
standard romances (11–26); he then goes on to insist that the greatest hero
of all has been ignored:

But of the worthiest wyght in wede
That euere by-strod any stede,
Spekes no man, ne in romaunce redes
Off his batayle ne of his dedis.
Off that batayle spekes no man,
There alle prowes of knyghtes be-gan;
That was for-sothe of the batayle
That at Troye was saunfayle. (27–34)

The poet argues at length that the Trojan War was history's superlative
battle fought by the best knights ever (35–64). Like the author of the
Destruction, the *Laud*-poet reminds his audience throughout the
narrative that they are reading an exceptional story, fully as exciting as any
romance fiction. During one battle, he insists that, since men first bore
weapons or rode horses, 'Herde neuere man telle In boke ne rede / So
manye at ones lye dede' (6691–92). At another battle, he stops to note that
in 'gestes of douȝti men' we may be told of a battle that lasts for ten days, or
in the standard romances 'of Ywayn and Wade' the fighting may go on for
as long as two weeks, 'and that was kampiouns right' (9375–84); but here
Greek and Trojans fight not for three days, nor for fourteen, but 'With-
outen rest thei fauȝt al-weyes / Til thei hadden fouȝten.xxx.ti dayes'
(9391–21)! These examples could be multiplied and testify to the poet's

unremitting efforts to promote the history and make it attractive to a general audience.

The fullest discussion of the value of poetry in presenting history, as we might expect, is in the prologue to Lydgate's *Troy Book*. He tells us that King Henry commissioned the work expressly so that the story of Troy might be widely known:

> By-cause he wolde that to hyʒe and lowe
> The noble story openly wer knowe
> In oure tonge . . . (Pro. 111–13)

Yet popularity itself is not the final goal, truth is: 'That of the story þe trouthe we nat mys / No more than doth eche other nacioun' (Pro. 116–17). The achievement of the true historical writer is that he can make the past live in the present and thus preserve ancient deeds:

> For vn-to vs her bokes represent
> With-oute feynynge þe weie þat þei went
> In her daies, whan thei wer alyue. (Pro. 177–79)

Rhetorical and literary skill, far from being suspect, are seen as essential in the effort to hold off the ravages of time. We are reminded that ancient poets (or clerks as Lydgate calls them here) frequently used their art in the service of truth:

> Of hiʒe prowes, whiche clerkis in memorie
> Han trewly set thoruʒ diligent labour,
> And enlumyned with many corious flour
> Of rethorik, to make vs comprehende
> The trouthe of al, as it was in kende. (Pro. 216–20)

Lydgate accepts Guido's argument that some poets have lied (once again the examples cited are Homer, Ovid, and Vergil), but he precedes that with a long passage on the historical authority of another classical poet. If the reader wishes to learn about the ruin of ancient Thebes, 'Crop and rote, riʒt as it was in dede,' then he must 'On Stace loketh, and þer ʒe may it rede' (Pro. 229–30).

The *Historia* itself offers the ultimate proof for Lydgate that art need not undermine truth but is instead its surest defender. Guido is first commended for the accuracy of his historical record:

> That besied hym the tracys for to swe
> Of Dite and Dares, & cast hym nat transmwe
> In al the story a worde as in sentence.
> But folweth hem by swyche convenience,
> That in effecte the substaunce is the same. (Pro. 355–59)

What makes Guido's work unequaled and such a delight to the modern reader, however, is his artistry:

For he enlvmyneth by crafte & cadence
This noble story with many fresche colour
Of rethorik, and many riche flour
Of eloquence to make it sownde bet
He in the story hath ymped in and set,
That in good feythe I trowe he hath no pere,
To rekne alle þat write of this matere,
As in his boke ʒe may beholde and se. (Pro. 362–69)

This is the goal of each of the Middle English poet/historians of Troy: to tell the story of Troy faithfully and fully, with such literary skill that it would remain compelling to a wide audience of medieval readers. The achievement of each individual author in this effort is now our subject.

III

The Destruction of Troy: *History as Poetry*

Of the three medieval English translators of Guido's *Historia*, the anonymous author of the alliterative *Destruction of Troy* is at once the most faithful to his source and the best poet.[1] Like Guido, he undertook the telling of the whole history of Troy: every speech, every battle, every fact; unfortunately, the sheer bulk of this material and its intractability defeat even his considerable poetic skill. The history he so laboriously preserves is regarded today as no more than a tedious fiction, and all that can be honestly admired by most readers are a number of excellent passages scattered through the poem like raisins in a bland pudding. In the nineteenth century a slim volume might have been produced entitled *Beauties from the Destruction of Troy*. But the modern opinion of the *Destruction* is not the whole story. For its own time, the work accomplishes the double feat of involving its readers in an important ancient story and remaining faithful to the full historical record of Guido. The author of the *Destruction* is able to make the *Historia* a poem without turning it into fable. Although he is not especially learned and does not approach the history intellectually, the poet retells his story with extraordinary care and demonstrates a shrewd intelligence. Without going beyond the *Historia* itself, he makes its narrative clearer and more consistent. Most important of all, he uses his poetic skill to make the story come alive for a contemporary audience; the massed facts of Guido's eyewitness style, so frequently dull in the *Historia* itself, become the stuff of a concrete poetry that at times rivals the best work of the fourteenth-century Alliterative Revival.

The Destruction's Fidelity to the Historia

The poet of the *Destruction* considers his first duty to be the preservation of the true historical record of Troy. Everything else, including poetic excellence, is secondary. Most who have studied the *Destruction* recognize the care and accuracy with which it follows the *Historia*, but that opinion has not been unanimous. G. A. Panton, one of the original editors, concluded that the poem was 'a translation, though not a close and continuous one, of Guido's *Historia Trojana*.'[2] More recently, a similar opinion was offered by Robert Lumiansky: 'the poet handles Guido's material with great freedom and with an eye for literary effectiveness. He adds, omits, and condenses in an effort to present a balanced, acceptable, and vigorous account.'[3] Often the poet does transmute Guido's leaden prose into literary gold, but the phrase 'great freedom' is badly misleading and ignores the *Destruction*'s earnest claim to historical fidelity. Other students of the *Destruction*, especially E. Bagby Atwood and Gordon Wood in their unpublished dissertations, have demonstrated at length how close and continuous the translation is.[4]

Nathaniel Griffin's superb edition of the *Historia* may make the unwary reader believe the *Destruction* is freer with its source than it actually is. Wood has demonstrated that the poet's manuscript of Guido could not have been identical to any of those used by Griffin, though it must have been related in some way to the common ancestor of the two labeled A and H. Other readings in the *Destruction*, which appear to follow forms in Guido's own manuscript, are preserved in P^2.[5] Griffin's text is therefore often misleading, since many of the poet's apparent deviations from his source can be found in the variants. Moreover, since the manuscript from which the *Destruction* was translated is only related and not identical to A, H, and P^2, we may confidently assume that some other differences from Griffin's *Historia* are also accurate readings.

Before investigating the poet's method of translation in detail, it may be helpful to illustrate just how closely the *Destruction* often follows the *Historia*. The following passage, which I have chosen more or less at random, opens Book 20 in the *Historia* and describes the seventh battle of the war. For the sake of precise comparison and because the *Destruction* provides a sufficient gloss, I give Guido's original Latin.

Post igitur trium mensium	After the monethis were meuyt
emersas inducias, adueniente	of þe mene true,/Þen waknet vp
die sequenti, Troyani	were and myche wale sorow!/The
accinguntur ad bellum et,	secund day suyng, says me þe lyne,/
ordinatis per Hectorem	There bownet vnto batell from
Troianorum acciebus, ipse	the burgh euyn,/Mony triet men
Hector cum aciebus ipsis	of Troy, and tokyn þe fild,/
ad bellum primum exiuit,	Euyn ordant by Ector, after his
ducens secum xv milia	deuise./The prinse with his pouer
militum, quos sue deputauit	past on first,/With xv .M. fully,
tantummodo aciei. Quem	all of fyn knightes,/In his batell
cum aliis x milibus	full bold boun to þe feld:/And

militum est Troilus
illico insequtus. Deinde
Paris ciuitatem egreditur,
existentibus secum uiris
pugnantibus in arcubus et
sagittis, illis de Persia,
trium milium numero in
equis fortibus et bene
munitis; deinde Deyfebus
ad bellum exiuit cum aliis
iii milibus pugnatorum;
deinde Heneas cum aliis
ceteris paratis ad pugnam.
Qui omnes fuerunt tunc ex
parte Troyanorum centum
milia militum strenuorum
in multa uirtute bellandi,
prout Dares in codice suo
scripsit. Ex parte uero
Grecorum accessit ad bellum
rex Menelaus cum vii
milibus armatorum. Deinde
proximo Dyomedes cum
totidem; deinde Achilles
cum totidem; deinde rex
Antipus in trium milium
militum comitiua; deinde
rex Agamenon cum magni-
tudine magna nimis. De
Grecis autem rex Filis
cum acie sua primus
Troyanos aggreditur. Cui
statim Hector uenit obuius
incunctanter, quem sic
potenter sue lancee
percussit in ictu quod
ipsum mortuum prostrauit
ab equo. De morte igitur
regis Filis clamor fit
maximus. Bellum letale
committitur, ex quo
sequitur magna strages.
Ex parte uero Grecorum
dum rex Xantipus accessisset,
regis Filis uolens sui

Troiell with x .M. turnit forth
aftur./Then Paris put furth,
the percians hym with,—/Abill
men of archery, auntrus in wer,—/
Three M. thro and thristy of
hond,/Vppon horses full hoge,
hardy men all./Then Deffibus
drogh furth, & to þe dede went,/
With thre M. thro men, þrepond
in armys./Eneas afturward with
angardly mony,/And oþer kynges
full kant, as þere course fell./
As Dares in his dyting duly me
tellus,/The sowme of the sow-
diouris, that fro þe Cité came,/
ffor to tell at this tyme of
triet men & noble,/A C.M. all
hoole, herty to stryke!/ ffro
the tenttes come tyte of the
triet grekes,/Menelay full
monly, with a manur pepull,/
Seuyn M. be sowme assignet for
hym./Then meuit with as mony,
mighty Dyomydes,/And Achilles
with choise men chosen of the
same./Than sought furth Xantippus
with sad men a hepe,/Thre
thowsaund thristy, þrong to the
fild./Than Agamynon the grete
gird on the last,/With a noyus
nowmbur, nait men of strenght./
The first, þat to fight past,
was Philoc the kyng,/Put hym
furth prudly, presit to þe Troiens!/
Ector met hym with mayn, macchit
hym so harde,/That he gird to
the ground & the gost past./Myche
clamur & crye for the kynges
sake,/And dynttes full dedly
delt hom betwene./Then girde o
the greke halfe with grym fare,/
Xantipus, a sure Kyng, with a
sad wepyn,/ffor to dere for þe
dethe of his dere vncle./He
suet furth sadly to þe sure

mortem auunculi uindicare, | prinse,/And stoke hym full
multos Troyanos interfecit. | stithly with a stiff sworde./
Hectorem insequitur, | Ector turnet with tene, toke
ipsum inuadit. Sed Hector | hym on þe hed,/Þat he slode
conuersus in iram in | doun sleghly, & sleppit euer after.
ipsum irruit, sic ipsum | (8182–8225)
grauiter uulnerauit quod
ad terram dilabitur
interfectus.
(pp. 166–67)

Of course the *Destruction* does not always reproduce the *Historia* with this precision, yet the passage is not exceptional. The poet's willingness to sacrifice all to preserve faithfully the history is clear. Although the requirements of alliterative verse demand some rearrangement (as in the expansion of the first six lines), often the poet is translating virtually word for word (note especially 8187–88, 8196–97, and 8217). The only factual differences between the two passages are the forms of two names: *Xantippus* and *Philoc*. Spelling is notoriously flexible in the Middle Ages, but the poet is justified in both cases. *Xantippus* (8209), for Guido's *Antipus*, follows the spelling in two manuscripts of the *Historia* known to be related to the poet's (A and P[2]),[6] and although Griffin does not give the variant *Philoc* (8213) for *Filiis* at this point, variants much like it are recorded when the same character appears earlier (6357 and 7487).[7]

Even when the fidelity of the *Destruction* to the *Historia* has been noticed, the alliterative poet is sometimes censured for so limiting himself. George Kane complains that 'he laboured under an excessive reverence for his material which made him unwilling to shorten his account.'[8] Such judgments expose modern assumptions about both the function of poetry and the legendary nature of the medieval Troy story. One might as well fault a medieval churchman for laboring under an excessive reverence for orthodox doctrine, without which he could develop a wonderfully original creed of his own. An accurate reproduction of Guido's material, which he believed to be the true history of Troy, is the poet's most basic aim. He wishes to make the history popular, but not at the expense of its factual integrity. The poet forgoes many opportunities to make his work better art in order to preserve its historical truth.

One example of the seriousness with which *Destruction*-poet approaches the historical record of the *Historia* is his precision as a translator. Only a sound knowledge of Latin could have permitted him to translate the *Historia* so accurately, for Guido's language is often obscure. Misunderstandings of the Latin by the poet are few and minor. One example is found when Jason returns to the court at Colchis bearing the Golden Fleece. In the *Historia*, Medea is overjoyed to see her lover, but does not show it openly: 'Although, if she could have, she would have given him the pleasant reward of many kisses in the sight of all these people, yet at the command of the king she sat next to Jason as if full of shyness' (3.360–62; p. 31). In the *Destruction* her wish becomes deed (though the word *curtesly* suggests a certain formality in the greeting):

> Medea the mayden with a mylde chere,
> Was Joyfull of Jason, Aioynit hym to,
> Kyst hym full curtesly, and of his come fayne. (973–75)

Another apparent mistranslation occurs during a Greek council at which Palamedes is critical of Agamemnon's command of the army. In reply, Agamemnon notes that Palamedes had joined the expedition only after a delay of two years, and he sarcastically concludes that past actions had somehow managed to work out satisfactorily: 'For you cannot say, Lord Palamedes, that our army cannot be led without your advice, since in your absence and without the precepts of your counsel many acts and deeds have been done in this army, which have turned out well enough for all in common' (22.148–52; p. 180). The alliterative version misses both Agamemnon's general sarcasm and his specific allusion to Palamedes's late arrival:

> Ne, þi self may not say, ne for sothe telle,
> Without assent of all somyn, sothely till now,
> Þat any dede has be don, or to dom past,
> But þou in person aprevit, & all oure prise kynges,
> And by agrement of the gret, & þe graunt hoole. (8911–15)

As error goes, the two examples just seen are pretty thin stuff, but they are the worst among the small number I was able to find in the *Destruction*.[9]

Additions and Omissions

Determined as he is to preserve the true record of Troy, the poet is more than just an English mirror of Guido; he is instead an intelligent adapter who alters his source with minor additions and omissions. Previous scholars have compiled lists of these changes, though none is complete nor could it be since change is hard to define exactly.[10] At first thought, these differences might seem to argue against the poet's commitment to preserve the whole history of Troy, but further consideration will prove the opposite. The poet is engaged in the complex and serious business of displaying the *Historia*'s truth in a form that will attract the contemporary reader. A piece of hackwork that simply turns Guido's Latin into English will not do; instead the *Historia* must be re-created, while keeping its accuracy intact, so that its story might live again in fourteenth-century England. If the author of the *Destruction* had produced no more than a mechanical translation of the *Historia*, he would not be worth our study; if he had felt free to change the source at will, he could hardly be called a historian. As it is, the small number of these changes and their relative unimportance to the narrative prove how deliberately he has chosen fidelity to the history over originality.

I have found examples of both omissions and additions unrecorded in previous studies, but another formal listing of changes in the *Destruction* is not as useful as recognition of the motive behind them. The poet's general practice is to separate historical fact from decoration. Guido's moral and rhetorical additions to the story are eliminated almost at will, but any nuggets of genuine historical information contained in them, however small, are preserved. Guido's frequent condemnations of women are examples of this detachable decoration. When King Aeëtes seats Medea next to Jason and unknowingly initiates their secret passion, Guido launches into a tirade on the lust and inconstancy of women (2.241–69; pp. 17–18). Included is a mock-scholastic comparison that equates women's desiring men to matter seeking form. These sentiments are shortened considerably in the *Destruction*, though the poet retains the central point that the king should not have trusted his daughter: 'Syn wemen are wilfull & þere wit chaunges,/And so likrus of loue in likyng of yowthe' (443–44). The actual consummation of the affair produces more rhetorical excess that begins with a lurid description of Medea's deflowering ('Jason opened the gates of virginity in Medea') and concludes in dismay over the insatiable appetite for pleasure one finds in lovers (3.112–26; p. 25). By contrast, the English version is as concise as it is tasteful:

> Þai solast hom samyn, as hom-seluon liket,
> With venus werkes, þat hom well pleasid:
> þat sorily dessauis, & men to sorow bringes. (752–54)

Similarly, Clytemnestra's liaison with Aegisthus prompts Guido to generalize on the taste in lascivious women for low-born men (32.126–38; pp. 248–49). The *Destruction* eliminates the questionable conclusion, but retains the historical fact that Aegisthus was not of noble rank (12741–44). Despite these reductions, and others like them, James Oakden, who had clearly not read the *Historia*, could claim that the poet is always biased against women.[11] His conclusion shows the dangers in judging any of the English histories of Troy unless precise comparison with its source has been made.

The poet's handling of Guido's thoughts on women teaches us two things. First, the English writer makes a clear distinction between history proper and moralizing: the latter may be in the narrative, but it is not of it. The poet does not regard such passages as the end toward which the entire work has been directed, but as detachable and rather obvious local conclusions. They are a common form of literary decoration and can be eliminated without compromising the truth of the history in order to make the factual narrative more exciting. Secondly, while he does not hesitate to rid his poem of rhetorical chaff, the poet is always alert to pluck out and save any bits of historical fruit contained therein. He is a careful historian.

A similar discrimination shapes the poet's handling of those passages in which Guido displays his learning. The Englishman tends to drop obviously classical references from his source, while retaining any important historical information. Thus he keeps Ulysses's statement that half of his ships were sucked into the depths (13299–304) but omits the *Historia*'s specific mention of Scylla and Charybdis (33.270; p. 260).[12] The same historical principle holds for other kinds of decorative knowledge. In his account of the Myrmidons, the poet drops Guido's mention of both their supposed Sicilian origin and their appearance in the apocryphal gospel of St. Matthew (1:5–27), and he makes only a passing reference to the Ovidian story, saying, 'More of thies Myrmydons mell I not now' (109). The omissions are deliberate. The Myrmidons are important characters in the Trojan War, and the *Destruction* includes a full account of their later actions, but false theories of their Sicilian origin, fables from Ovid, and allusions to them in apocryphal gospels are no part of the historical record and can safely be omitted to speed the narrative.

Throughout the *Destruction*, its hard-working poet uses his good judgment to eliminate information prompted by the narrative but not actually essential to it. Guido is forever wandering from the story of Troy itself down by-paths it suggests; the author of the *Destruction* often decides not to follow. Thus he omits two astronomical passages in the *Historia* (2.192–201; p. 16; and 11.81–87; p. 101), and many geographical speculations, especially those dealing with Sicily (e.g., Pro. 55–61; pp. 4–5; and 13.116–32; pp. 113–14). This last material was no doubt interesting to Guido's immediate audience, but has little to do with the fall of Troy. Of course, some omissions are undoubtedly the result of the manuscript the poet was using. The list of Priam's thirty bastard sons is certainly important historical information, and yet it is missing from the *Destruction*. The reason, almost surely, is neither carelessness nor prudery, but simply that the names were not in the poet's manuscript as they are not in related manuscripts A and H.[13]

The Learning and Good Sense of the Destruction-Poet

The author of the *Destruction* is a good Latinist and a careful translator of Guido, but he seems to be no scholar. His skill in arranging and presenting the factual material of the *Historia* sometimes deserts him when dealing with Guido's more learned additions. What evidence we have of the poet's classical learning is not impressive. In Book One, Guido refers to the rejuvenation of Aeson by Medea as described by Ovid in the *Metamorphoses* (1.36–40; p. 6). The *Destruction* changes this title to *Eroydos* (123 and errata), but Medea's letter to Jason in the *Heroides* (XII), which seems to be the intended reference, does not mention Aeson's return to youth, though a full account is found in *Metamorphoses* VII, 179–349. The alliterative poet gives no evidence of being better read in Vergil. He keeps Guido's claim that Achates was a stone Aeneas brought to Carthage (790–93), says that Anchises was Aeneas's mother (12900, though this may be a scribal error), and mistranslates Telamon's claim to have kill King Polymnester and Polydorus, one of Priam's sons under Polymnester's protection (31.17–22; p. 238). In the *Destruction*, 'Polidarius' is said to be the son of Polymnester himself and in the care of Priam (12183–87).[14] Alliterative poets have the habit of disguising their learning as opposed to Chaucer's flaunting of his (the *Gawain*-poet is clearly well-read but makes only occasional references to other works), but our author's ignorance seems genuine.[15]

The *Destruction* severely reduces Guido's longest learned addition: his digression on idolatry in Book 10. One reason for the truncation, as with the other omissions discussed above, is surely the poet's desire to make the story exciting for a contemporary audience, but another is that he finds himself out of his depth in this material. At two points the poet indicates that he recognizes the problem. Near the end of a description of Delos, the *Historia* says that, according to Isidore, the pagans claimed the sun and moon, Apollo and Diana, were born on the island and notes that it was also known as '*Ortigia*,' quail in Greek, because that bird was thought to have originated there (10.84–95; p. 93). The *Destruction* follows the first part of the passage, but trouble develops in the discussion of the sun and moon:

> Perfore gentils aiugget, & for iuste held,
> Þat in þat bare yle bothe borne were þai first.
> Þat lede in þere langage lyuely can call
> The pure sun in hir pride, appollus doughter;
> And Ediana, also, þai amyt hit to nome.
> The mone in his myldnes, þai menyt to hat
> Ortigia, ouer all honouret with grekes.
> Of þis mater nomore but meue to our tale. (4271–78)

The abrupt and rather gruff last line suggests that the poet may have recognized he had made a muddle of things and was determined to take the quickest way out. A similar note is heard at the end of the entire digression, the last part of which the poet has severely reduced:

> Of þis mater of mawmentry nomore at this tyme:
> Þis sufficis forsothe. Ses we now here,
> And turne to our tale & take þere we lefte. (4456–58)

Nevertheless, if the alliterative poet is not a scholar, he is certainly no fool. His intelligence and judgment, which we will see elsewhere in the *Destruction,* are also occasionally evident in his handling of Guido's learned digressions. Witness his version of Hercules's attempt to recuit Castor and Pollux for the first assault on Troy. For Guido the episode is an opportunity to display his knowledge of this famous pair and their sister, Helen. The result is not fortunate. He begins by naming Danaë as the mother of the three (two manuscripts read Leda), ends with mention of the supposed connection of Sicily with these stories, and includes what may well be the most remarkable, not to say awkward, metamorphosis in literature: Jupiter's seduction of Danaë while he is disguised as an egg:

> It is stated dogmatically by the poets that these brothers were the sons of Jupiter, borne to him by Danaë, loveliest of women, who, they allege, also bore Helen, who is thus the sister of these kings. In connection with the birth of this Helen, the poets fictitiously claim that Jupiter lay with the aforesaid Danaë in the likeness of an egg. For this reason someone stated 'Jupiter said, "I exult because Tyndaris came from an egg," ' calling the same Helen, Tyndaris, from a certain place which was called Tyndaris. Some say this place is in Sicily, on the northern coast, opposite the Aeolian Islands, not very far from the city of Messina. (4.7–17; p. 33)

The *Destruction*'s version of this nonsense is a brief, clear presentation of the essential information:

> As poyetis han put, plainly þo two
> Were getyn by a gode on a grete lady,
> Þe fairest of ffeturs þat euer on fote yode:
> And a suster to þe same, sothly, was Elyn,
> Getyn of þe same god in a goode tyme. (1016–20)

Whatever classical learning the English poet may lack, he is clever enough to avoid Guido's confusion.

The Destruction-Poet as Diligent Historian

The poet of the *Destruction* has never been given proper credit for the intelligence and care with which he translates the *Historia.* Because he believed the *Historia* contained the true and complete history of Troy, he did not supplement or conflate it with other material. Yet without ever leaving the closed system of the *Historia* itself, he finds an amazing number of Guido's errors, confusions, and inconsistencies, and he works hard to make the often stubborn text of his source as clear and consistent as possible.

In Book 19, a Greek request for a truce sets off a long debate in Troy; when it is over, Guido notes that the truce is granted but gives no further details (19.37–40; p. 160). The announcement is considerably expanded in the *Destruction*:

> Then takyn was the true, and with trauthe fest,
> Thre monethes & no more, þo mighty betwene,
> By assurans full sad vpon suche wise,
> Þat non offens shuld þere fall þo freikes betwene;
> But yche kyng & knight comyn with other,
> Bothe in tent & in towne, while the true last. (7874–79)

The terms of the truce, not directly given in the *Historia*, do not come from the poet's imagination. Rather he has deduced them from information in the *Historia* presented both before and after this passage. He assumes the truce is for three months because the Greeks requested that length before the Trojan debate (19.9; p. 160), and he reasons the agreement must have permitted visits between the two armies because Guido later describes Hector's appearance in the Greek camp during this period (19.56–126; pp. 161–62).

A more revealing change is to the brief description of one of the Greek battalion leaders: 'King Polidarius and King Machaon led the seventeenth' (15.185–86; p. 133). The *Destruction*'s version includes one additional detail: 'Polidarius, the porknell, and his pere Machaon,/Suet with the xvij, sad men & noble' (6368–69). At first glance *porknell*, or little pig, seems no more than a humorous detail chosen to complete the alliteration, but the poet is not taking undue liberties with his source even here. Almost 2500 lines earlier he had described Polidarius's corpulence while exactly translating Guido's catalogue of Greek heroes:

> Polidarius was pluccid as a porke fat,
> ffull grete in the grippe, all of grese hoge.
> So bolnet was his body, þat burthen hade ynoghe
> The fete of þat freke to ferke hym aboute,
> Or stond vppo streght for his strong charge. (3837–41)

In a work of over 14,000 lines these changes (details about a truce and the fatness of a Greek leader) may seem puny, but they tell us much about the poet's aims and abilities. He clearly knows the *Historia* so well that he can supply a detail from a later section or remember one for thousands of lines. He is no mechanical translator turning Latin into English by the pageful, but a writer of intelligence and judgment.

In his pioneering study of the poem, E. Bagby Atwood examined the *Destruction*'s attempt to deal with one set of inconsistencies in its source and concluded that the result was only confusion compounded. The problem is that Guido inherited two Ajax's from Benoît: Ajax Telamomius and Ajax Oileus. The former is first killed by Paris but soon reappears, apparently none the worse for the experience, only to be murdered in his bed by Ulysses:

> Ajax Oileus, who has set sail for home, is overtaken by a terrible tempest which wrecks his ships and casts him ashore half dead. This, says Guido, is because Minerva was wroth on account of Ajax's sacrilege in dragging Cassandra from her refuge in the Temple;—the worthy judge seems to have forgotten that it was the other Ajax who committed that outrage. The author of our poem was evidently conscious of these discrepancies; for after the first death of Ajax T. he refers to him only as Telamonius—and he evidently remembers the Cassandra episode aright, for he tells us that Ajax Oileus was shipwrecked because 'Telamon' had dragged that lady from her sanctuary![16]

Given this distortion of classical stories in both the *Historia* and *Destruction*, the modern reader may easily adopt Atwood's indulgent contempt. If we look at the problem from the poet's view, however, our attitude will be less patronizing. Obviously, as even Atwood suggests, the poet recognizes the confusion surrounding the two Ajax's in Guido and tries to correct it while remaining as close to his text as possible. We may laugh if we choose, but we should also admire the poet's conscientiousness. He demonstrates here both the ability to see as a whole the isolated episodes in which the two Greek heroes appear and a desire to make their stories consistent. The result may be, in one sense, foolish; the intention is historical truth.[17]

Examples can be found throughout the *Destruction* of its author's unflagging concern that his history be clear and complete. The *Historia* briefly describes the death of *Hupon*, king of Larissa, at the hand of Achilles (18.59–62; p. 156). The poet omits the warrior's name and calls him only 'the kyng of Larris' (7640) because he wishes to avoid confusion with an *Ampon* (17.76–78), whose death he had just described and whom he probably knew as *Hupon* (this is how the name appears in manuscripts A and H).[18] Likewise, the *Historia*'s *Margariton* (*Emargaron* in AH), a Trojan killed by the Myrmidons (26:90–91; p. 199), becomes *Swargadon* in the *Destruction* to avoid the appearance of resurrecting Priam's natural son *Margariton*, whose death shortly before had incited Hector to enter the battle in which he dies (21:123–25; p. 174).

The poet often makes a scene more complete by bringing in details from elsewhere in the *Historia*. When Ulysses and Diomedes come on their embassy to Troy, Guido says only that after entering the city, the Greeks 'went to the grand palace of King Priam' (12.104; p. 106). The poet remembers the name of the palace from the description of Troy in Book 5, and he writes that the envoys 'Entred into Elion [Ilion], þat honerable Palis' (4950). Before the first pitched battle of the siege, Guido has Hector send out a battalion 'in the name of the gods' (15.18–19; p. 127). In the *Destruction* Neptune has been added (6094) because he is elsewhere called the principal god of Troy.

Occasionally the poet makes original additions to his source. They have little effect on the historical narrative and usually seem motivated by a desire to make the story clearer and more complete by filling in any minor silences. Guido describes how Priam, after he has rebuilt Troy, begins to brood on the injuries he has suffered from the Greeks. The *Destruction* supplements this with two lines that remind the reader of exactly what those injuries were: 'His fader & his fryndis ferkit out of lyue,/And his suster into seruage þat hym sore noyet' (1700–01). Similarly, the poet sometimes supplies the logical extension to a scene in the *Historia*. Guido describes a battle in which Hector and Achilles unhorse one another (18.137–48; p. 159). Although Guido does not say so, the poet naturally assumes that Hector would have soon returned to the fray, and so he adds a brief account of the hero fighting (7790–95).

Other small additions occur elsewhere. Guido mentions the tombs of Achilles and Paris, but avoids any description on the grounds that it would be superfluous (27.63–64; p. 208; and 172–75; p. 211). In fact, he is probably reacting against the lavish accounts of these tombs in Benoît, which he judged inappropriate for a sober history. The alliterative poet, ignorant of Benoît and so free from such inhibitions, must have felt that Guido's silence undercut the completeness of the history, and so he cautiously adds a few details: Achilles's 'toure' was 'Meruelously made with masons deuyse,/With Jemmes, & iuwells, & other ioly stonys' (10584–85), and Paris was placed in a 'tabernacle' that was 'Made all of marbill, of mason deuyse,/With mony staryng stone stondyng aboute' (10782–83).

The *Destruction* also contains rhetorical additions. Although the poet usually shortens such passages in the *Historia*, especially those that moralize, he adds a few lines to the account of festivals at Venus's Cytherean temple that question the motives of the pilgrims there: 'More Janglyng of Japes þen any Juste werkes,/And for solas & sight þen sacrifice to do' (2873–74).[19] This brief flourish is a nice preparation for Helen's arrival and anticipates a long digression, reproduced from the *Historia* soon after, on the lascivious behavior at such rites. The examples just examined are a fair sample of additions made in the poem. They are few in number and only become apparent in a line-by-line comparison of the two texts. None is major, none changes the history in any significant way, and none is without warrant in the source. Considered together, they demonstrate once again the care with which the poet turned the *Historia* into English and his concern to make the history clear and complete.

Sense of History in the Destruction

The alliterative poet is clever, shrewd, and diligent, but his conception of history is not intellectual. He is concerned only with the factual record itself and is much less sophisticated than some of his contemporaries in depicting the ancient world of Troy. Morton Bloomfield has shown that Chaucer, especially in his later works, reveals 'an increasing preoccupation with both accurate chronology and cultural diversity and a strong feeling for the past, the present and the future.'[20] A similar 'sense of history' can be found in Robert Henryson's *Testament of Cresseid* and John Lydgate's *Troy Book*. With the limited historical material and vision available to them, all three writers work to create a Troy that contemporary audiences could believe historically accurate. The author of the *Destruction*, however, is not in their company. He has no feeling for the way in which pagan culture differs from his own and only a vague hostility toward its practices. Instead, he appeals to a contemporary audience by making the world of Troy seem familiar.

Although the alliterative poet often mentions religious sacrifices that are not in his source (e.g., 2869 and 2884), this does not indicate a genuine sense of the past, as do such additions in the *Knight's Tale*, for example. The poet's frequent citation of this ritual is no more than a habit of style: the overuse of an alliterative formula composed of the world *sacrifice* and some form of *solenite*. He employs the formula to describe funerals (5364, 7160, 9094, and 9615), other ceremonies like knighting (10948), oath-taking (11448), receiving the Trojan Horse (11871), and prayer (13709). He is so fond of the phrase that it appears after the slightest of hints: Helen's desire to go to the 'ceremonies of this festival' (7.107)—*festiuitatis sollempnia* (p. 70)—becomes her desire 'with Sacrafice solempne to seche vnto Venus' (2915); and the statement that a marriage is celebrated with 'solemnity' (33.124)—*sollempniter* (p. 256)—becomes 'With Solenité & Sacrifice' (13103).

Although the *Historia* is generally quite careful to avoid obvious and naive anachronisms, the *Destruction* makes no such effort. Some of its apparent chronological lapses are clearly due to the English language (*priest* for *sacerdotis*, for example), but others reveal the poet's own insensitivity to differences between Christianity and paganism. Within a few lines he has Priam refer to 'Our goddes' (2113) and also to 'God' (2115); the *Historia*'s one reference at this point is in the plural (6.47; p. 57). Later in the poem Priam prays to 'oure pure sanctys' (6279) and calls on 'our lord' (11543). When the priest who guards the Palladium is bribed to hand it over to the Greeks, Guido adds a lamentation on covetousness (30.39–47; p. 229). The *Destruction* transforms the passage into a contemporary sermon by the addition of specifically Christian terms and concepts like 'syns,' 'god one,' and 'the fend' (11775–81). The poet may not understand very much about pagan customs, but he knows what he doesn't like.

Guido, in his digression on idolatry, defines the gentiles as those '*sine lege*' (10.139–40; p. 94), meaning without the Mosaic Law. The English author adds real emotion and malice to his version: 'ffor no law in hor lede list hom to holde,/But folowit þere foule wille as fyndis hom taght' (4324–25).

Medieval terms and customs not associated with religion also undermine any genuine sense of historical distance. Jason is promised that he will become 'Duke' (242) of the kingdom of Thessaly; 'florence' (1367 and 1372) are among the treasure taken in the first destruction of Troy; Priam calls a 'perlament' to decide on war (2095); and Hector signals the end of his conflict with Ajax not 'when he had laid down his arms' (15.680; p. 146), but when he 'voidet his viser' (7092). These sorts of anachronisms are not especially flagrant, even Chaucer has a Duke of Athens in the *Knight's Tale* and a parliament in the *Troilus*; in the *Destruction*, however, they are never balanced by other passages that give a feeling for the past.

Although the alliterative poet has no real antiquarian sense, we must consider the possibility that his anachronisms are to some degree deliberate and meant to make the story real and understandable to his audience. Chaucer and Lydgate, with their more intellectual approach, insist on how much the past differs from the present, but the alliterative poet may be trying to win a popular audience to ancient history by showing similarities—making the story familiar to contemporary readers. The *Destruction* closely follows Guido in describing the glorious city of Troy built by Priam, until it comes to the list of Tradesmen; the occupations substituted in the English poem are almost all original and contemporary:

> Goldsmythes, Glouers, Girdillers noble;
> Sadlers, souters, Semsteris fyn;
> Tailours, Telers, Turners of vesselles;
> Wrightes, websters, walkers of clothe;
> Armurers, Arowsmythis with Axes of werre;
> Belmakers, bokebynders, brasiers fyn;
> Marchandes, Monymakers, Mongers of fyche;
> Parnters, painters, pynners also;
> Bochers, bladsmythis, baxters amonge;
> fferrers, flecchours, fele men of Crafte;
> Tauerners, tapsters, all the toune ouer;
> Sporiors, Spicers, Spynners of clothe;
> Cokes, condlers, coriours of ledur;
> Carpentours, cotelers, coucheours fyn;
> With barburs bigget in borders of the stretes. (1584–98)

The poet may not recognize the crafts originally listed by Guido, or he may feel his audience will not, and thus they need a contemporary catalogue if the passage is to be meaningful.[21]

The Destruction and Alliterative Poetry

Although the *Destruction of Troy* lacks deep learning and an intellectual sense of history, it is worth our interest because it contains such fine poetry. The need to turn Guido's huge bulk of factual information into verse sometimes overwhelms even this poet's great skill, prompting the charges of dullness and monotony that have often been leveled against him.[22] But these accusations are not the whole story. What makes the work so fascinating is the poet's genuine ability despite his ultimate failure. Although finally defeated by the material he is so careful to preserve, his artistry is equal to the best of the Alliterative Revival.[23] Unfortunately for him, he chose a subject, the Trojan War, and a goal, historical accuracy, that in ways he could not foresee doomed his efforts to almost total obscurity. Nevertheless it is our privilege as scholars to recognize genuine merit whatever its popular fate.

Many critics have recognized moments of poetic excellence in the *Destruction*, although little detailed analysis has been attempted.[24] Oakden even claimed to find a war council scene 'not unworthy of comparison with the one in *Paradise Lost*.'[25] This is surely going too far, but the poet does at times demonstrate remarkable control of alliterative verse. Most studies on the techniques of Middle English alliterative poetry have centered on *Gawain and the Green Knight,* and so we shall borrow their conclusions to analyze the *Destruction.* Larry Benson has observed that the critics of *Gawain,* who disagree about almost everything else, are remarkably unanimous about what makes *Gawain* an artistic success: the poet's command of concrete visual detail and his ability to organize it so that we can see each stage of an action.[26] Alain Renoir was the first to analyze the sequential presentation of images in *Gawain,* which he compares to the art of the film.[27] Renoir shows how a specific scene, the decapitation of the Green Knight, unfolds in a carefully designed series of pictures, or 'shots,' organized 'so as to emphasize the most strikingly suggestive details,'[28] Marie Borroff and Larry Benson have extended Renoir's perception by demonstrating that the narrative of *Gawain* is presented from limited and contrasting viewpoints. The result is that the observer of an action and the point of view from which it is seen are often more important than the action itself.[29]

These techniques are the common property of the best works in the Alliterative Revival. They are found in the *Morte Arthure,* for example, as Gawain and a company of British knights first catch sight of the enemy Roman camp:

Thise hende houez on a hille by the holte eynes,
Be-helde the howsynge fulle hye of hathene kynges—
They herde in theire herbergage hundrethez fulle many,
Hornez of olyfantez fulle helych blawene—
Palaisez proudliche pyghte, that palyd ware ryche,
Of palle and of purpure, wyth precyous stones;
Pensels and pomelle of ryche prynce armez,
Pighte in the playne mede, the pople to schewe.
And then the Romayns so ryche had arayede their tentez,
On rawe by the ryuere, vndyr the round hillez,
The emperour for honour ewyne in the myddes,
Wyth egles al ouer ennelled so faire:
And saw hyme and the sowdane, and senatours many,
Seke to-warde a sale with sextene kyngez,
Syland softely in, swettly by theme selfene,
To sowpe withe that soueraygne, ffulle selcouthe metez.[30]

The passage is a carefully designed sequence of distinct images, which moves from a general impression of the whole camp (1284–86), to some specific details (1287–90), to a description of how the tents are situated (1291–92), to a focusing in on the tent of the emperor himself (1293–94), and, finally, to individual people: the emperor and his chief men going to supper (1295–98). The last picture is particularly effective because it introduces motion into what had been a static description and so provides a transition back to the British knights who are about to ride down and interrupt the Romans at their meal. In addition, each of the images is seen from the specific, limited point of view of the Britains, a perspective clearly established at the beginning (1283). The narration is not omniscient, but a believable representation of how Gawain and his men would have first taken in the Roman camp: what they would have seen and in what order. Although it is a less successful work, the *Destruction* contains passages that are the equal of *Gawain* and *Morte Arthure*, as we shall now see.

The Poetry of Violent Action

Perhaps the greatest achievement of the *Destruction* is its ability to vivify the often dull facts of Guido's eyewitness style. By giving the ancient story of Troy a powerful sense of immediacy, the author of the *Destruction* is true to his double office and becomes both poet and historian. Nowhere is this clearer than in his concrete, visual descriptions of storm and battle. English poetry seems to fall naturally into alliteration at such moments; even Chaucer, who probably shared the Parson's low opinion of 'rum, ram, ruf,' is not immune, as the tournament in the *Knight's Tale* reveals

(A2605–13). The *Destruction* has been praised for such scenes since Oakden. Dorothy Everett, who has a generally low opinion of the poet's skill, is willing to concede that like 'other poets of the tradition, he is most impressive when describing violent action—battles and storms at sea in particular.'[31] Larry Benson, however, is almost alone in going beyond mere praise to describe and define the poet's technique. He has analyzed a 'marvellously detailed description' of a storm in the *Destruction* that signals the coming of winter (12467–74).[32] Two qualities that he finds particularly effective there are ones also characteristic of *Gawain*: (1) each detail is in its proper place, and (2) events are observed from a definite viewpoint.

An equally exciting example of the poet's technique can be found in the sea storm that occurs on Antenor's return from Greece; several critics have called attention to this passage, but no one has provided a close analysis.[33] The *Historia*'s version is unremarkable:

> As he was cutting the deep seas on his return, the hateful fury of a storm covered the sky with a dark fog, and the rains poured down with gusts of contrary winds in amazing peals of thunder and dreadful flashes of lightning. The waves, stirred up by the winds, rose in high mountains. Now the ship, diverted into the yawning troughs of the seas, sought the dangerous depths, now raised on the surges of the waves through the flood it sought the mountainous peaks of the tempest. The evident peril to their life weighed upon the sailors in the ship and they poured out various prayers to the gods for deliverance from the danger. Thus when this ship had been subjected to these obvious perils for three days, on the fourth day the distress of the storm ceased, and the rage of the wind was softened and ceased. The seas were calm, the waves were still, and the sailors, now snatched from a watery death, took comfort. (5. 438–52; pp. 55–56)

Without going beyond traditional formulas, the alliterative poet shows his intelligence and skill:

A TEMPAST ON ÞE SEE.

There a tempest hom toke on þe torres hegh:—
A rak and a royde wynde rose in hor saile,
A myst & a merkenes was meruell to se;
With a routond rayn ruthe to be holde,
Thonret full throly with a thicke haile;
With a leuenyng light as a low fyre,
Blaset all the brode see as it bren wold.
The flode with a felle course flowet on hepis,
Rose vppon rockes as any ranke hylles.

Wo wode were the waghes & þe wilde ythes,
All was like to be lost, þat no lond hade.
The ship ay shot furth o þe shire waghes,
As qwo clymbe at a clyffe, or a clent hille,—
Eft dump in the depe as all drowne wolde.
Was no stightlyng with stere, ne no stithe ropes,
Ne no sayle, þat might serue for vnsound wedur.
But all the buernes in the bote, as hom best liked,
Besoght vnto sainttes & to sere goddes;
With knelyng & crie to þere kynd halowes,
And with solempne sacrifice to seke þai awowet.
Pre dayes þroly þai þrappit with stormys,
Euer in point for to perysshe in the pale stremys;
With daunger and drede duret vnder hacche,
ffor wete of þe waghes þat wastis ouer hed.
The furthe day fell all þe fuerse wyndes,
And the wodenes of waghes wightly with droghe;
The se wex sober and þe sun clere,
Stormes were stille, Stremes abated,
All calme it be come, comferd þe pepull. (1983–2011)

It may take a second look to confirm, but these two passages contain essentially the same historical information. Although the poet does not alter his material, he does organize it more effectively. He exploits the paratactic tendency of alliterative verse by giving a single line to individual elements of the gathering storm—the wind, the dark mist, and the rain (1984–86). We see the tempest actually form before us, and then we feel it increase in danger with the rumble of thunder, the first sound mentioned, and the arrival of hail in line 1987. The eerie description of lightning on the ocean provides an appropriately fearsome climax (1988–89). The technique used here is that of *Gawain*: the narration of an event in 'a series of precisely differentiated stages.'[34] Guido's two comparisons of waves to mountains are fully developed in the *Destruction* (1990–91; 1994–96). The second is particularly good. Rhythm and alliteration first convey the sea's speed and violence (aided by the verb 'shot'), then picture the ship climbing slowly up the steep waves before its abrupt descent (the alliteration of 'dump' and 'depe' is especially effective).[35]

The poet's command of specific detail is sure. The force of the storm is measured by the utter uselessness of 'stere,' 'ropes,' and 'sayle' (1997–98). The desperate prayers of the sailors are made vivid when we see them kneel and cry (2001). Even a tired formula like 'pale stremys' (2004) takes on new life in the context of imminent death by water, the horror of which is underlined by the picture of lightning striking the water 'as it bren wold' (1989).[36] The poet's fidelity to his source prevents him from eliminating the information that the storm lasted a full three days, though

this does tend to dissipate the tension, but he does add a dramatic visual
image of the sailors crouched in the ship's hold as the threatening waves
roll over them. The episode ends with a series of quiet lines that re-
establish calm over the ocean and provide a contrast, in detail and rhythm,
to the storm's violent beginning (2009–11).[37]

The *Destruction* has also been generally praised for its battle scenes, a
real virtue in view of the unremitting warfare in the history.[38] While the
poet tends to depend on a small number of alliterative formulas—again
and again 'dyntees' are 'delt' or a wounded warrior is 'gird' to the
'ground,'—his description of battle is often precise and exciting, without
being unfaithful to Guido's historical facts. Others have given many
examples of good battle poetry in the *Destruction*, and there is no need to
repeat their work here. Nevertheless, the poet's skill at both war and
storm can be seen in one remarkable scene late in the siege. The *Historia*
begins its account with a general picture of the engagement after the two
armies clash:

> On account of this, a grim battle was waged between them,
> from which followed great carnage because of the dead. (25.
> 143–44; p. 194)

The alliterative translation uses conventional formulas but creates an
event that is more vivid and more serious:

> Brem was þe batell vpon both haluys!
> Mony gyrd to þe ground and to grym deth;
> Mony stoute þere was storuen vnder stel wedis;
> And mony britnet on bent, & blody by-ronnen! (9632–35)

In the next sentence, also short, Guido compares the rain to blood on
the ground:

> But though on that day the cloudy dark sky poured forth much
> rain, on the other hand, the blood of many dead was poured
> forth as the battle raged. (25.144–47; p. 194)

The comparison itself is trite, but the poet produces an impressive and
tangible description from it.

> That day was full derke, dymmyt with cloudes,
> With a Ropand Rayne rut fro the skewes;
> A myste & a merkenes in mountains aboute,
> All donkyt the dales with the dym showris.
> Yet the ledis on the land left not þerfore,
> But thrappit full throly, thryngyng thurgh sheldis,
> Till the bloberond blode blend with the rayn.
> And the ground, þat was gray, gret vnto red. (9636–43)

The passage proceeds logically from sky to ground, beginning with a wide, almost tranquil view of the natural scene and ending in a powerful close-up of the cluttered and bloody ground. The poet also uses color to create mood: the dark, cloudy sky, the misty hills, and the shrouded dales are suddenly contrasted to the red blood which transforms the grey ground.

The *Historia* next describes the entrance of Troilus into the battle and his quick rout of the Greeks who run back to their tents:

> As they fled through the torrents of rain, they turned toward their camp. The Trojans pursued them to their tents, but finally left them on account of the stormy weather and returned to their city and were received in it. (25.150–53; p. 194)

Once again the alliterative version makes improvements:

> Turnit to þere tenttes, tenyt full euyll,
> Thurgh the rug, & the rayn þat raiked aboue,
> All wery for wete, & for wan strokes;
> And ay the troiens with tene tyrnyn hom doun,
> ffely with fauchons folowet hom after,
> Dang hom to dethe in the dym water,
> Pursewit hom with pyne vnto þere pure tenttes,
> There leuit thay laike, and the laund past:
> ffor the wedur so wete, and the wan showres,
> Soght vnto the Citie soberly & faire,
> And entrid full easely, euyn as hom liked. (9651–61)

For Guido the rain is no more than an interesting meteorological fact; the English poet builds his whole passage around it. He makes us experience the full extent of the defeat by a series of pictures showing the Greek troops, exhausted and wet, struggling back to their tents through the 'rug & the rayn' as many fall dead into the 'dym water.' For the victorious Trojans, however, the weather is only an inconvenience—they call off their slaughter on account of rain ('ffor the wedur so wete').

The absolute military control enjoyed by the Trojans is also emphasized by the careful use of two words. We are told that the Trojans left their 'laike,' which often means no more than sport,[39] and passed from the 'launde.' *Laund* is a general word for field, though it often has pleasant connotations: the lush woods and garden around Colchis are called 'laundes' (334). The difference between winner and loser is also brought out by the description of each army's home. The Greeks are left among flooded and devastated tents that are strewn with the bodies of their comrades, while the Trojans return 'soberly & faire' to their families and enter the walls of the city 'full easely, euyn as hom liked.' Of course, there is an unexpressed irony here. However confident the Trojans are now and however disheartened the Greeks, the situation is soon to be reversed. Hector is already dead, and it is only a matter of time before the noble citadel itself will be more completely destroyed than the Greek tents.

In the first chapter we saw how vague and general Guido's eyewitness style could be in describing battle. His perspective is always distant and imprecise so that warfare usually appears as no more than a violent blur. He seems unable or unwilling to let the reader directly experience the events at Troy. Not so the alliterative poet. He makes the violent action mentioned in the *Historia* come alive for the reader by precise and skillful narration. While Guido is always careful to separate himself as historian from the poets, the English author strives to fulfill both offices. The poet's great talent is his ability to involve the reader in dry history; in so doing he no longer has to concern himself with the conflict between truth and art, for poet and historian are then one.

The Case for the Destruction-Poet

The *Destruction*-poet is especially skillful in presenting violent action, but this is not the limit of his abilities. In his poem he reveals the full range of alliterative narrative techniques without subverting Guido's history. One achievement of *Gawain*, we will remember, is its careful manipulation of point of view.[40] The power of several important scenes comes from the particular eyes through which we witness it. The Green Knight's entrance is the more horrible because we see it along with Arthur's courtiers, and the lady's first visit to Gawain's bedroom the more unsettling because we experience it with Gawain.[41] A particularly effective example of this same technique in the *Destruction* occurs during the first war at Troy. Laomedon routs what he thinks is the whole Greek army, and he is only just beginning to enjoy his triumph when a messenger races up to tell him that it was all a trick; he has only defeated a part of the invaders, and the main Greek force is now in control of the city. This is how Guido describes what Laomedon sees as he hurries back to Troy:

> King Laomedon had then not yet advanced far in the troop of his armed men when, looking from a distance, he saw a great part of his enemies had marched out of the city and were hastening toward him in armed phalanxes. Likewise he saw behind him that the Greeks, whom he had already more or less conquered on the shore, were hastening against him with renewed spirit and the greatest haste. He was bewildered and did not know what to do between these two forces, since he perceived he was in the midst of his enemies and hemmed in on all sides. Need I say more? (4. 291–300; p. 41)

The *Destruction* does say more and thereby develops the scene's full potential:

> The kyng is comyng kest vp his egh,
> Segh a batell full breme fro þe burghe come
> Prickand full prest vppon proude stedys.
> He blusshed ouer backeward to þe brode see,
> Se the Grekys come girdand with a grym noise,
> Þat fled were before & þe fild leuyt. (1313–18)

The point of view is more clearly Laomedon's in the *Destruction* (note 'kest vp his egh' and 'blusshed ouer backeward'). The king's terror when he realizes that he is caught in the vise of his enemies is heightened by describing the Greek armies in two sentences of equal length. The word *see*, which begins the second line of both sentences, reinforces the parallelism and also the perspective. We are given only brief descriptions of the two forces ('proude stedys' and 'with a grym noise'), but each clearly reflects the subjective reaction of the king who has seen his victory turn suddenly into complete defeat. The *Destruction* has not changed its source much, but enough to put the reader in the midst of the action.[42]

The poet of the *Destruction* also has gentler moods and shows his poetic skill in passages that have nothing to do with battle or storm. One such example is the coming of night to the Greek camp which opens Book 17 of the *Historia*:

> Accordingly when twilight came before the faces of men, and when everywhere in the space of the sky could be seen the stars that night, which impairs the eyes of those looking at the appearances of the rest of things, displays openly on account of the shadows of its darkness, all the kings, dukes, and princes of the Greeks assembled. (17.1–5; p. 151)

There is nothing remarkable here except the awkwardness in describing the visibility of the stars. Compare the alliterative version:

> When the day ouer drogh, & the derk entrid,
> The sternes full stithly starond o lofte;
> All merknet the mountens & mores aboute;
> The ffowles þere fethers, foldyn to gedur.
> Nightwacche for to wake, waites to blow;
> Tore fyres in the tenttes, tendlis olofte;
> All the gret of the grekes gedrit hom somyn. (7348–54)

Without being false to his source, the English poet has captured the tense quiet of twilight in the Greek camp. He creates the scene, and with it a mood, by a series of precise images whose order is carefully designed. First we see the vastness of the evening sky with its emerging stars, then the darkness over the mountains and moors. This wide view narrows even further to a close-up of birds preparing for the night. After these natural scenes, we are made ready for the council by a picture of the camp settling into its evening routine of military watchfulness. The image of light within darkness, so awkward in Guido, is nicely developed by the poet's counterpoint of natural starlight to man-made fire. This passage is both beautiful in itself and effective in creating the appropriate mood of nervous expectation—we soon learn that the Greeks, stung by Hector's military success, have assembled to plot his killing.

Frequently the poet makes us participate in the events at Troy by putting into dialogue what in the *Historia* is only description or indirect discourse. The poet can create effective scenes aurally as well as visually. At one point in the war, the Trojans are on the verge of complete rout, only Priam's sons are resisting the Greeks when Hector speaks to his forces:

> Hector spoke to them with affectionate words, reminding them of the injuries done them in the past by the Greeks, and recalled to their minds what the Greeks would do to them (let it not happen!) if they were by chance victorious. He advised them accordingly and urged them to grow more powerful in war and to strive wholeheartedly for victory from now on. (15. 539–44; p. 143)

The *Destruction* gives the speech in direct address:

> 'Now, bold men in batell, buske ye to fight,
> Haue mynd of þe malis, & the mykell harme,
> Þat vs wold happon to haue in a hond while,
> And the grekes may vs gripe, & to ground bryng!
> Therfore, feris, bes fell, fraistes your strenght,
> Let your hertes be hoole, hold you to-gedur!
> Bes frike on your fos, fell of your dynttes,
> Settes hom full sadly, sekir for to hit
> With all þe might & þe mayn of your mekill strenght!'
>
> (6943–51)

Just to hear Hector's voice at this exciting moment is a real improvement, and, in addition, his argument is so much more convincing than in the *Historia*. Guido has Hector remind his men of past injuries and future terrors without giving the specifics of either. His second sentence is particularly weak and, with minor changes, would be more appropriate for salesmen than for warriors. The speech in the *Destruction*, however, goes beyond mere chivalric convention; it seems addressed to a real army facing actual destruction. Hector ignores past grievances, and, in a exhortation that is forceful from the beginning, he confronts the immediate slaughter facing his men: 'the grekes may vs gripe, & to ground bryng.' The second part of the speech is a detailed, if formulaic, call to action which exploits the alliterative half-line to produce a compelling rhythm.[43]

Even speeches already in direct discourse are often more dramatic in the *Destruction*. Nestor is furious at Antenor's demand that Hesione be returned to Troy and threatens to punish the Trojan if he does not leave immediately:

> Assuredly, if my noble nature did not restrain me, I would order your tongue to be plucked out of your throat, because it is used in such speeches and for dishonor to your king. I should cause your limbs to be dismembered by having you dragged along the ground by horses. (5.429–33; p. 55)

This is hardly a gentle admonition, but it does not begin to equal the horrors detailed in the alliterative poem:

> But for noy of my nobilte & my nome gret,
> I shuld tere out þi tunge and þi tethe euyn,
> And chop þurghe þi chekes for chateryng so high:—
> Spede the to spille in spite of þi kynge,—
> To be hurlet with horses vpon hard stones,
> And drawen as a dog & to dethe broght:—
> Brittonet þi body into bare qwarters,
> And caste vnto curres as caren to ete. (1965–72)

There can be no doubt which speech would make Antenor depart with more speed.

The poet's ability to give a sense of immediacy to his source is usually found in brief, isolated passages, but occasionally he reveals the ability to manipulate somewhat larger units. When Antenor goes to regain Hesione, in the episode just discussed, he first visits Peleus, and the *Historia* notes briefly that the Trojan was 'honorably received by him' (5.321–22; p. 52). After Antenor presents Priam's demand for Hesione, however, the Greek king becomes incensed and orders Antenor to depart. Antenor quickly does so 'without seeking leave' (5.347–48; p. 53). The poet realizes the importance of this scene as a symbol not only of the failure of Antenor's mission but also of the inevitability of war. He therefore seizes on the hint in his source and makes Antenor's welcome nothing short of effusive:

> Antenor not tariet ne no tome hade,
> But went to the wale kyng on his way sone,
> Hailsit hym hendly, & he his honde toke,
> And welcomyt hym worthely as a wegh noble,
> And fraynit hym with frendship qwat the fre wold. (1790–94)

The result is to put into greater and more dramatic contrast Antenor's hasty departure, 'withoutyn lowtyng or lefe' (1823).

Just as events are described with precision and drama in the *Destruction*, so knighthood itself is no longer the dreamy ideal so often found in contemporary romance. The poet gives us real soldiers in serious combat.[44] Early in the war, the Trojans are routing the Greeks and on the verge of total victory when Hector encounters Ajax Telamon. Ajax declines his cousin's invitation to visit his relatives in Troy, but presumes on Hector's affection by asking him to call off the attack. Hector does so immediately. Guido mentions the army's return to Troy, but all he says of their feelings is that they are 'greatly disturbed and disappointed' (15.693; p. 147). They do not know it, but, as Guido notes, the city is doomed; never again will the Trojans have an opportunity for complete victory.

The *Destruction*'s account follows the *Historia* closely until the order to retreat. The poem then continues:

> But at the biddyng of þe bold, þat þe buernes led,
> Þai were assemblit full sone, & myche sorow hade,
> Wentton to þe wale toun wailyng in hert,
> Entrid with angur, and to þere Innes ʒode.
> Thus curstly þat knighthode for a cause light,
> Voidet þere victory for vanité of speche,
> Þat neuer auntrid hom aftur so ably to wyn. (7116–22)

These lines go beyond the aristocratic perspective of the *Historia* to provide a critique by ordinary men of chivalric pretensions. The poet understands the anger Hector's decision would cause in the ranks. They curse knighthood which 'for a cause light' destroyed 'þere' victory because of 'vanité of speche.' What scorn for their superiors is expressed in that last phrase. The result of the poet's addition is both a more dramatic scene and more convincing history.

The *Destruction*, like the other Middle English histories of Troy, is finally overwhelmed by the sheer weight of the material it must preserve, so that its full artistic potential is reached only occasionally. At its best, however, the *Destruction* is a very good poem indeed. The mere facts and often dull catalogues of Guido's *Historia* are brought to new life in the alliterative verse. Completely faithful to the historical record, the poet uses his art to enable the reader to experience directly the ancient events at Troy.

IV

The Laud Troy Book:
History as Romance

Like the other Middle English historians of Troy, the anonymous author
of the *Laud Troy Book* is both historian and poet.[1] He is faithful to the
essential facts of Guido and yet writes the freest translation of the *Historia*
in Middle English. As a poet, he is an exuberant story-teller whose racy
style and obvious pleasure in the violence of battle involve and excite the
reader. His special contribution to the medieval history is to retell it using
the forms and techniques of a popular *genre*, the Middle English romance;
but this is only part of his achievement. Beneath its romance trappings,
the *Laud* is a serious work of history whose dedication to the true record
of Troy is as deep as that of the other Middle English translations of
Guido. Although Hector, and a few other heroes, are given special
prominence in the *Laud*, they are not allowed to destroy the history in any
fundamental way. The poet is a surprisingly careful historian whose deep
knowledge of the *Historia* enables him to fill apparent gaps in his source.
No matter how original it may sometimes seem, the *Laud* never strays
very far from Guido's medieval history of Troy because its ultimate aim is
as much to conserve the historical truth of Troy as to make the story appeal
to a wide audience. The paradoxical nature of the *Laud Troy Book* has not
been examined seriously by previous scholars, nor has the poem ever
been viewed with much more respect than the airy condescension of R. K.
Root, who found the *Laud* 'quite untouched by any breath of true poesy.'[2]
The *Laud*-poet's attempt to produce a historical romance and his real
narrative skills deserve greater attention than they have received, and we
will begin with his energetic literary performance.

The Listening Audience

The *Laud* is the only Middle English version of the *Historia* to transform
Guido's distant narrative into a poem specifically intended for oral

recitation. The poet frequently addresses his audience directly, either urging them to hark and listen (e.g., 65, 103–04, 3243–45, and 3293–94) or calling their attention to an especially important incident (e.g., 7700, 10685–86, 12733–34, 15963–68, and 16125). The story is reduced in many places to make it more exciting and unified for those following by ear. The long opening section on the Argonauts is severely cut, and the Greek returns are eliminated entirely, along with most of Guido's learned and moral digressions and the catalogues of heroes and battalions. Instead, the poet adds many original summaries and foreshadowings, especially in the beginning, designed to help the audience keep the long and complicated story in mind (e.g., 1715–28, 3125–42, 3160–64, 3271–92, 4701–06, and 8583–94).[3] As in other Middle English romances, *Havelok* especially, the *Laud*'s narrator involves himself in the story and urges his listeners to do likewise. Except for his pessimistic laments, Guido's voice is always formal; even his most overheated rhetoric on the evils of women lacks any trace of a personal voice. How very different is the *Laud*-narrator, who extols his heroes and damns the villains. At one point he tries to infect us with his enthusiasm for Hector, his principal hero: 'Off suche a man haue ʒe non herd!' (4561); at another he interrupts the narrative to call on the enemy directly: 'Fals Gregeis, to ʒow I speke' (5393).

A more serious purpose of these outcries is to persuade his audience that ancient history can be as exciting as contemporary romance. The poet continually makes the most superlative claims for the siege of Troy:

> Off swyche a fyght as ther was one,
> In al this world was neuere none,
> Ne neuere schal be til domysday. (35–37)

This sort of promotion is a convention of the Middle English romance, but our poet often seems to undertake it with a special urgency. Guido's account of the Amazons is the sort of learned digression usually omitted in the *Laud*, but most of it is retained by the poet (15963–16036)—perhaps because he knows his audience will sit still for spicy details about these bizarre women and their irregular sexual arrangements. Nevertheless, the poet feels the need to introduce the material like a carnival pitchman:

> Bvt herkenes now of the quene,
> And of hir maydenes bolde & kene!
> I wol ʒow telle, if ʒe wol here,
> Off here lond the right manere;
> Where it is, and what lande,
> The manere schal ʒe vndirstande. (15963–68)

The *Laud*-poet is also skilled at creating dramatic speech for his characters, another conventional quality of the Middle English romance. Atwood has noted the poet's delight in battle insults and other forms of animated dialogue.[4] But beyond this, the poet aims to interest his audience by repeatedly transforming Guido's indirect discourse into strong, believable speeches and by giving dramatic life to formal monologues. A fateful moment for Troy occurs when Hector, leading a rout of the Greeks, meets his cousin Ajax and accedes to his request that the rampaging Trojan army be withdrawn. The speeches of each are summarized in the *Historia*:

> [Hector] promised to please [Ajax] in all things, and advised and asked him to come to Troy to see the large family of his kinsmen. He refused, however, and not neglecting the safety of his Greeks and his country, asked Hector, if he had such great affection for him, to manage it and bring it about that the Trojans would cease to fight further and would not pursue the fleeing Greeks further, but that they would go back to Troy, sending the Greeks away in peace on that day.
>
> (15.681–88; pp. 146–47)

The *Laud* gives the cousins' actual words:

> Ector seyde: 'my dere cosyn,
> Come to Troye and se thi kyn:
> Kyng Priamus, that is thin em,
> And his Baronage, and his barnetem.
> Gret worschepe—so god me saue!—
> Shaltow In Troye amonges hem haue.'
> There-with-al seyde Ayax: 'nay!
> But, dere Cosyn, I the pray,—
> As thow me louest and art curtais,—
> No more harme do thes Gregeis!
> But let hem be this day in pes,
> And bid thin men that thei wol ces!' (5973–84)

Despite the sing-song rhythm and exaggerated rhymes, these lines effectively focus Guido's repetitious vagueness into two short, sharp speeches whose exclamations ('so god me saue,' 'nay,' and 'I the pray') add to the effect of real speaking voices. Neither the *Destruction* nor Lydgate's *Troy Book* handles this scene so well. The alliterative poem offers only straightforward translation (7091–103); and though Lydgate puts Hector's words, but not Ajax's, into direct speech, he greatly expands the passage, as is his tendency, so that the dramatic point becomes even more confused (3. 2078–2121).[5]

The *Laud*-poet is versatile in his additions of direct speech. When appropriate, he can supply public, manipulative words, like those of Ulysses, whose speech to win Achilles back to battle begins with a conciliatory and shamelessly flattering preface not in the *Historia* (13047–60).[6] On a more sentimental occasion, Deiphobus's dying request to Paris for revenge is transformed from a formal demand ('I implore you earnestly to hasten speedily to my slayer, before this shaft is pulled from the wound in my chest, and that you will take great pains before I die that he who slew me will fall at your hands' [25.29–32; p. 190]) into an emotional statement of pain and brotherly affection:

> As I haue loued the, Paris, brother,
> In al my lyff be-fore alle other—
> Go aȝeyn & worche wisly,
> That he be ded rather than I! (12563–66; speech begins 12554)

Similes in the Laud

The poet's desire to make the history exciting for his listeners becomes even clearer when we examine his most flamboyant stylistic device: the large number of vivid similes, a few of which amount almost to conceits, that are worked into the narrative and especially into battle description.[7] Some of these use the traditional exotic beasts of chivalric romance and can be found in the *Historia* itself, though not in the same places;[8] but the most interesting and most numerous similes employ the familiar creatures and activities of English rural life. When Hector cuts Archilogus in half the poet says, 'He carf a-two bothe flesche and bon,/He culpunte him as he were an ele' (6254–55). Elsewhere the Greeks flee Hector 'as ffox to hole' (6117); Paris, knocked off his horse, rolls 'Ouer & ouer, as were a snayl' (6743); and Achilles destroys all he meets: 'Thei falle thikkere than heryng fletes,/In-myddes the se In here scole' (14204–05).[9] The poet's non-animal similes are also taken from common, rustic life. Hector, beating off some would-be captors, is said to 'cleue hem with his swordis egge,/As man doth the tre with wegge' (5025–26). Later he kills so many Greeks that they 'dyed thikkere then men dryues gece/To chepyng-toun for to selle' (7428–29), and still elsewhere he aids the Trojans who 'beten on hem [the Greeks], as don herdes/On weri bestis that drow In the plow' (9162–63).[10]

We should be wary in concluding from these similes that the *Laud* was intended for a low-born and unsophisticated audience. Although it was once widely assumed that most Middle English romances, including the *Laud*, were composed by wandering minstrels to be performed in mean taverns for crowds of beer-sodden peasants, recent studies, especially those by Albert C. Baugh, show how inadequate a picture this is.[11] In the case of the *Laud*, the fact of translation itself proves the poet's intent to make the history accessible to a wide and non-scholarly audience, but the audience need not be thought exclusively low and rustic on the evidence of his homely similes. No one in the fourteenth century was very far

removed from the farm in any case, and similar similes are used by
Chaucer, the cleverest and most well-read poet of the age, most notably in
the *Miller's Tale* but also throughout his work. The *Laud*-poet is no
Chaucer, but his similes also are deliberate and are employed to give
energy and wit to interminable battle scenes. The poet's comparisons to
homely and familiar things are a conscious, if conventional artistic device,
which allows him to display his cleverness while maintaining a popular
style. In the midst of monotonous bloodshed it is a delight to come upon
similes whose unexpected rhymes anticipate, however dimly, Alexander
Pope or Ogden Nash: 'And he ȝaff hem aȝeyn suche pattis,/That thei fel
doun as dede cattis' (8841–42); or 'He deled a-boute him euel knockis,/Her
armure ferde as it were frockis' (10599–1600).

The poet also uses similes to establish certain simple but effective
moods. Ajax's joy when he see fresh troops arrive to stem a route is
described thus:

> So mery was neuere Nightyngale
> Syngand In no hasel-crop,
> Ne no child playing with his top. (5548–50)[12]

A striking use of two rustic similes emphasizes the savagery of Hector's
revenge against Leochides, who had previously wounded the Trojan
hero:

> The duk hade of him suche a houselle,
> On bothe the sides his hors he felle;
> As he hadde ben a clouen hogge,
> The duke hanged as a frogge. (10749–52)

None of the above passages is especially subtle, that is a quality not often
found in the *Laud*, but all are memorable.

The Craft of the Laud-Poet

The poetry of the *Laud Troy Book* has a tendency to become flabby—often
it is clogged with meaningless tags and repetitious lines, which produce
the fatigue in the reader so brilliantly parodied by *Sir Thopas*. Yet when
the poet is excited by his subject, the result is dramatic and effectively
organized narration. Battle scenes, in particular, call forth his most
strenuous efforts; rarely is an opportunity missed to increase the violence
or call attention to the exploits of his favorite heroes, often with an
infectious enthusiasm and wit.

The *Laud*-poet's most consistent principle of translation is to add flesh
and blood to the many mere skeletons of battle description in the *Historia*.
He has many successes in so doing, as we shall see, but not all of his

changes are for the best. An example of his limitations, chosen at random, is the fight between Diomedes and Antiphus, recorded by Guido with extreme brevity: 'With great courage Diomedes slaughtered King Antiphus who was fighting against him' (18.63–64; p. 157). In the *Laud* this becomes:

> Diodemes and kyng Antipe,
> With-oute trompe or pipe
> Or any other Melodye,
> Thei redyn to-geder with gret envye;
> Here speres brast In splentes,
> But thei fel not with here dentes,
> With that Iustyng ne that Iornay.
> But thei ȝede not quyte a-way:
> Thei drow here swerdes of here scauberkis
> And smot on scheldes and hauberkes,
> The rynges barst, the nayles out,
> Thei were strawed al a-bout;
> Her woundes bledde, her flesch was tamet,
> The holest of hem ful sore was lamet.
> But at the laste be-tydde it so,
> That Diodemes smot In-two
> Thorow douȝtines duk Antipe gorge,
> With his swerd—was fair of forge,—
> That he fel ded on gresse and rote,
> Off that wounde he hadde no bote. (7393–412)

It is hard to find anything positive that has been gained by this expansion. The passage contains none of the precise visual images of physical action that are the glory of the alliterative *Destruction of Troy*. No real information, emotion, or drama has been added to Guido's short sentence, only some obvious padding and tired formulas (see especially 7403, 7405, 7407, 7412).

Even though disappointing passages similar to this one can be found throughout the *Laud*, they do not completely represent the poet or his achievement; he finds many ways to make numerous other battles interesting for his audience. Guido's growing despair before the limitless carnage at Troy is replaced in the *Laud* by a frank enjoyment of violence, the bloodier the better, which is often expressed through the crude verbal cleverness already seen in his similes. Before one battle the poet finds a powerful way to state that many Trojans will die:

> Many of hem come neuere to toun
> Hole aȝeyn, as thei ȝede out;
> Some lefft his hed, and som his snout. (7940–42)

This is the same sort of rough wit found in the poem's similes; any dismay we might feel at such obvious delight in violence would be to misinterpret the poet's tone and the degree of realism he intends. As with certain Icelandic epics or Western movies, the audience is meant to enjoy the bloody exaggeration and sheer exuberance for its own sake. The humor is certainly rough but not intentionally cruel. Perhaps the most outrageous example of the poet's gory wit is his account of the death of Archilogus. The *Historia* briefly gives the facts: 'Hector rushed upon him, and not being prevented by his armor, cut him in two with his sword, so that he gave up the ghost and died among the fighters' (16.118–20; p. 150). The *Laud* transmutes this into:

> He smote euen In-two his myddel
> Ryght euen at his gerdul,
> That half fel doun, and half sat stille,
> His armes myght not do ther-tille,
> Hit was a wondir sight to se,
> When þe hors be-gan to fle,
> A-mong the prese whan he ran,
> Op-on his bak with half a man. (6257–64)

Here, as so often in the *Laud*, narrative zest overcomes a certain crudeness of technique.

At other times the poet's craftmanship is much more impressive. Like the *Destruction*-poet, though to a lesser extent, he knows how to improve his source by narrating action from a limited or dramatic point of view and in a series of precise stages.[13] Description of battle in the *Historia* tends to be vague, omniscient, and distant: a summary rather than a blow-by-blow account, and a factual list rather than a dramatic narrative. Compare Guido's account of Hector's entrance into the battle at the landing with that in the *Laud*:

> Then that very valiant knight, the very brave Hector, as if aroused by the noise of the shouting, emerged from the city of Troy with a band of many men and entered the combat. He was flaming with kindled rage and gleaming in flashing arms and with a sharp lance; he carried a shield made of gleaming gold, adorned with the sign of three lions. He assaulted the Greeks powerfully, and as he cut the line right through the middle . . .
> (14.239–45; p. 125)

> The noyse was moche & gret clamour;
> Ector herde hem make sorow,
> For tene his herte began to bollen,
> And bothe his chekes gret swollen;
> He toke his armes and his atyre,
> That were as bryght as siluer wyre;

A better man was neuere on molde,
He bar a scheld of rede golde,
With thre lyons paynted her-In;
A delful note he thoght be-gyn.
Ector is armed, his stede be-strode,
He rod forth with-oute a-bode,
Toward his men gan he gange,
Him thoght he dwelled ther to longe.
He saw the Troyens faste fleand,
He rod to hem faste criand
And bad thei scholde a-ȝeyn turne,—
'Drede ȝow not ȝoure enemys sturne!'
Ihesu lord! what thei were glad,
When thei here noble leder had!
Was non so feble his voyce did here,
But it amendid herte and chere,
And turned a-ȝeyn with hardi herte
A-ȝeyn here enemys wonder smerte. (4531–54)

The difference between the two passages is not incident but approach. Guido remains aloof from the action and from the actors; he tells us what happened without showing us how or why. In contrast, the *Laud* forces us into the middle of events, which we experience as they would logically occur and from the characters' perspective. Guido tells us that Hector entered battle *as if* excited by the clamor ('quasi ad uoces clamancium excitatus'). In the *Laud*, the reader (or listener) is shown the incident itself: first Hector's perception of the noise of battle (4531–32) and then his intense reaction to it (4533–34). Guido's fact is transformed into human drama. Guido must interrupt the action to describe Hector's armor and weapons, while the English poem cleverly works in this information without loss of narrative tension. We learn about the equipment as we watch Hector don it (4535–40). Hector's actual entrance into battle is also much more effective in the *Laud* because we see it from two sharply defined points-of-view. First Hector's, as he desperately rides toward his men, sees them fleeing, and calls out encouragement (4541–48); then we are given the perspective of the Trojan troops as they hear their leader's words and immediately go on the offensive with renewed courage (4549–54). The poet's careful expansion of the *Historia* brings out the scene's full dramatic potential and allows his audience to participate in the action.

Narrative improvements in the *Laud* also include longer and more structurally elaborate passages. Penthesilea's first day of fighting is transformed from a random series of flatly described conflicts into a powerful drama of shame and conquest. The Queen of the Amazons arrives to aid Troy in its darkest hour. All of the city's heroes are now dead, and its inhabitants, hope almost completely gone, cower behind the famous walls, refusing to give the Greeks battle. Here is Guido's account of Penthesilea's entrance into the war as she leads out her troops and the remaining Trojans:

> The Greeks ran manfully up to them and received them powerfully with blows of their lances. A grim struggle was engaged in between them. Menelaus rushed upon Penthesilea, but Penthesilea thrust at Menelaus so powerfully that she cast him down from his horse. She took his horse from him and consigned it to her women. Diomedes, however, violently attacked Penthesilea in the swift charge of his horse and with a blow of his lance. Penthesilea met him courageously. Both thrust at each other with blows of their lances, but Penthesilea remained firmly on her horse. Diomedes was forced to sway at the blow of the attacker, likewise his horse. Penthesilea snatched Diomedes' shield from his neck and consigned it to one of her maidens. Telamon was not able to endure the things which were done in battle by Penthesilea and urged his horse in a charge against her. Penthesilea met him manfully and threw him from his horse to the ground, and rushing among the Greeks, fought with them fiercely. (28.43–57; pp. 212–13)

This passage represents Guido's usual description of battle. Events are given flatly and from a distance in the eyewitness style: no attempt is made to fit individual incidents into any larger pattern, nor are the motives and emotions of the characters at all explored. The *Laud* preserves Guido's essential facts, but expands the passage to 161 lines, adding emotion, suspense, and narrative structure. Penthesilea becomes an awesome figure whose victories are especially shameful to the Greeks because she is a woman.

The poet develops the scene in two sections: a greatly expanded initial mêlée followed by a series of Penthesilea's single encounters. One of his first additions describes the Greeks' astonishment as they see the embattled Trojans march from the city (16101–12); they wonder 'What it myght be that hem ayled/That thei come out so proude & gay' (16104–05). The Greeks anticipate an easy victory, and their smug self-confidence nicely sets up the surprise waiting on the battlefield. The *Laud* next provides a long account of Penthesilea's general military success (16125–54); for once the poet's reliance on tired battle formulas ('Scheldis ryue, & speres crake,/Eche man fightis with his make') does not weaken the narrative because the bloody confusion offers an effective contrast to the single combats that follow. These individual duels are the poet's most significant change: Guido's chance encounters become a series of deliberate efforts to beat Penthesilea by the principal Greek heroes.

The first attack on Penthesilea is by Menelaus; the *Laud* retains all of

Guido's facts (16155–68) but adds drama by showing us Menelaus as he plans his assault (16155–60). Diomedes is the next to try the queen, and he too is first introduced while watching from the sidelines: 'He saw the kyng [Menelaus] falle a-doun,/Vp the fete & doun the croun' (16171–72). The poet's tendency to describe war as slapstick comedy is here extremely effective given the Greeks' expectation of easy victory. Diomedes's actual encounter with Penthesilea is carefully organized: first he earnestly resolves to avenge Menelaus on the queen, then he attacks 'With al the myght that euere he hadde,' and finally he is unceremoniously and quickly dumped from his horse (16169–84). In the English work, Penthesilea not only gives Diomedes's shield to one of her maidens, as in Guido, but she also orders that it be borne every day in the war: 'In vilonye and In dispit/Off him that it auȝt, what so he hit' (16187–90). The result is further humiliation for the proud Greeks.

The third individual combat, Telamon against Penthesilea, is again prefaced by an original passage in which the next contestant observes his predecessor's defeat—a dramatic use of narrative point-of-view:

> Kyng Thelaman stode euere alone
> And saw the dedis that sche had done,
> He saw hir felle that douȝti kyng,
> And his scheld take with-oute lesyng
> Fro his nekke his vnthankes,
> And felde him doun at his hors schankes;
> And he was feld opon the grounde,
> And sche sat stille hol and sounde. (16191–98)

The presentation of these combats as jousts (made clear in 16170), with one knight after another picking up the challenge of Penthesilea, transforms Guido's random skirmishes into a carefully structured episode, showing the gradually more frustrating Greek effort to conquer the Amazon. Telamon's determination to avenge his comrades is the most passionate yet:

> Gret envy hadde he ther-ate,
> Opon hys hors ther he sate;
> He wex for tene blak as Cole,
> That schame myght be no lengur thole
> That sche hadde done the kynges two,
> He wolde assaye what he myght do:
> He toke a spere of stalworthe tre,—
> For he on hir wolde venged be,—
> And rode to hir with gret herte. (16201–09)

The suspense generated by these long preliminaries to battle is then sharply broken by the suddenness and brutality of the fight itself:

> And sche him kepis rapely & smerte,
> Sche smot him euen In-myddis the scheld
> That he fley out In-myddes the feld. (16210–12)

The *Laud*'s narrative is not always so skillful or careful, indeed the tension of this very scene is soon lost by the need to follow Guido's subsequent material, but the poet's skill as a sound literary craftsman needs to be acknowledged.

The Laud as Romance

Romance is one of those terms, like *liberty* or *love*, that everybody uses and no one can define. In Middle English it constantly overlaps other classifications like saints' lives or chronicle and includes works as diverse as *Sir Gawain and the Green Knight, Athelston,* and the *Siege of Jerusalem.* Nevertheless, however we define the Middle English romance, the *Laud* is more like one than any other English translation of Guido. On a few occasions the poet uses the very word to describe his work,[14] and, significantly, in his prologue he makes a special effort to associate the *Laud* with other, more famous romances:

> Many speken of men that romaunces rede
> That were sumtyme doughti in dede,
> The while that god hem lyff lente,
> That now ben dede and hennes wente:
> Off Bevis, Gy, and of Gauwayn,
> Off kyng Richard, & of Owayn,
> Off Tristram, and of Percyuale,
> Off Rouland Ris, and Aglauale,
> Off Archeroun, and of Octouian,
> Off Charles, & of Cassibaldan,
> Off Hauelok, Horne, & of Wade;—
> In Romaunces that of hem ben made
> That gestoures often dos of hem gestes
> At Mangeres and at grete ffestes.
> Here dedis ben in remembraunce
> In many fair Romaunce. (11–26)

In translating the medieval history of Troy, the *Laud*-poet claims to have produced a work not merely acceptable to a romance audience but one that is clearly the top of the line. His principal hero, Hector, is 'the worthiest wyght in wede' (27), and Troy is where the prowess of knight-hood first began (32)—where the greatest battle before Doomsday was fought (35–38) by the best warriors ever assembled (39–42). During one battle we are informed that from the beginning of warfare 'Herde neure

man telle In boke ne rede/So manye at ones lye dede' (6691–92); a later
encounter prompts similar superlatives:

> In erthe was neuere suche a semble;
> And that may alle men here & se
> That romaunce may vndirstonde & rede (13687–89)

The poet's self-promotion is not unique among medieval romance
writers, but here the special object is to prove that history, even ancient
history, can equal the usual romance in rousing action.

   Although associated with a wide range of works in its prologue, the
Laud is definitely in the English romance tradition and has little in
common with the continental model described by Auerbach: we find
nothing of the individual hero making a psychological journey or of a
world of marvels.[15] Dorothy Kempe and others have discussed at length
the elements added to the *Laud* that can also be found in contemporary
English romance.[16] Another full listing is unnecessary, but it would
include descriptions of armor (993–1000), dress (8039–64), tombs (12863–
66), feasting and sleep after battle (9313–19), councils (7075–86),
preparations for war (9313–19), and funeral ceremonies (11919–40). In
addition to battle itself, the *Laud*-poet is attracted to the trappings of
medieval warfare: the arming and marching out before combat and the
feasting after. Such passages of romance decoration are frequent in the
Laud, but they never threaten to choke the narrative itself with rhetorical
set-pieces, as in the *Roman de Troie*, and the poet declines many obvious
opportunities to add others. Almost without exception these passages
merely expand on some hint in the *Historia* and are not genuinely
original.

   The *Laud*-poet, like most authors of Middle English romance, is
careful not to appear too intellectual for his audience. George Kane insists
that 'the author's interests, if not always his gifts, are intellectual and
learned.'[17] He is certainly a good Latinist, is probably a cleric,[18] and
occasionally reveals tantalizing bits of learning: Statius is cited, though
possibly not directly, to explain why the Greeks waited on Tenedos for a
year (4139–42); and elsewhere the poet gives fairly detailed descriptions of
historical figures (including Alexander, Caesar, and Arthur) brought low
by Fortune (5919–54) and makes an original reference to Apollo (3360).
Yet if Lydgate often seems better-read than he really is, just the opposite
is probably true for the *Laud*-poet. However wide his actual learning, it is
rarely on display. His constant habit is to reduce Guido's classical stories,
and though he sometimes expands pagan rites for the color they provide,
his interest is not scholarly. Troilus's tomb and funeral get a bit more
space in the *Laud*, but the ceremony itself is performed by three bishops
and offerings are made by 'Erles, Dukes and of kynges' (15247–52).

   To a Middle English romance audience the world described in the *Laud* would seem quite familiar because so much of it is anachronistic. Although Guido is at some pains to avoid obvious medievalisms, and is generally followed by the faithful *Destruction* and by Lydgate, who displays a genuine antiquarian interest, the *Laud*-poet is extraordinarily permissive in allowing contemporary customs. He does this deliberately, I think, as part of a strategy to capture romance readers for the history of Troy. Armor and weapons are consistently those that would have been known to the audience (e.g., 7493–96 and 10213–14), and what fourteenth-century English reader would not feel at home at Troy with its parliaments (e.g., 3221, 3391, 3733, 11546, and 11590), sheriffs, and a mayor (18376)—especially when told that a captured warrior might be 'honge and drawe' (423), put in a 'depe dungoun' (6906), or held for ransom (5152), and that during truce time the heroes engage in the favorite sport of the medieval aristocracy: 'Thei go & hunte with her grehoundes,/With hauke, brache, & with kenetes' (13572–73)? Even more anachronistic are religious terms. Antenor swears by 'the rode' (1993), and elsewhere George and Christopher, among other saints, are evoked (16382 and 13603); Polyxena, facing death, prays 'so Crist me spede' (18558), and in the final destruction we are told that 'prest, ne clerk, ne sextayn/Leffte the Gregais non vn-sclayn' (18249–50). Many more such examples could be brought forth, all of which testify to the *Laud*'s popular, non-scholarly presentation of the history of Troy.

The *Laud* further establishes its place in the tradition of Middle English romance with its presentation of knighthood and chivalry. Guido, we will remember, takes a pessimistic view of the cycle of violence and treachery unleashed by the Trojan War. Not so the *Laud*-poet, whose delight in rousing battle action we have already discovered. He retains Guido's facts but banishes any despair in order that his audience may comfortably delight in the varied adventures of these extraordinary knights. Knighthood and all its works are of unquestioned value in the *Laud* and carefully emphasized.

The romance theme of honor and shame, the ultimate concern of every true knight but only a vain delusion that leads to death in the *Historia*, is taken seriously throughout the *Laud*. When Priam, because of his losses, locks the gates of Troy and refuses to fight anymore (28:4–5; p. 211), the *Laud* adds detail to Agamemnon's challenge (15910–22) that is designed to reflect on the Trojan king's honor. The end is especially stinging:

> For suche a kyng schulde euere dispice,
> For that was token of cowardise;
> And ligge not ther as an hog In sty,
> For that was to him a vilony. (15919–22)

No hero is more careful of his honor than Hector, the poet's favorite. The *Historia* at one point tells us briefly that King Epistrophus attacks Hector and insults him with 'many abusive words' (18:65–69; p. 157). In the *Laud* the incident is expanded (7445–78), and the Greek king, whom the poet labels 'that ape and owle' (7445), calls Hector 'fitz-a-putayn' and 'cherl velayn' (7447–48). Hector answers these challenges to his birth and class with pedantic seriousness in a long speech that meticulously offers a point-by-point defense of his rank, family, father, and mother:

> My moder is a gentil quene,
> A trewe lady, and euere hath bene;
> Sche did her lord neuere falshede,
> But euere was trewe In word and dede.
> It semes wel thanne, that I am fre,
> I may be skyl no cherl be! (7467–72)

He goes on in this way for twenty-five lines.

Benoît added romance in the modern sense to Dares and Dictys through the love stories of Achilles and Polyxena, Troilus and Briseida, Paris and Helen, and Jason and Medea. Guido's version of each story is awkwardly presented since his primary interest seems in the moralizations that can be drawn from them.[19] In the *Laud*, love is neither extravagantly narrated, as in Benoît, nor bitterly condemned, as in Guido, but, as in most Middle English romances, straightforwardly recorded. Amorous passion in the *Laud* at its worst can be a destroyer of noble knights like Achilles and Troilus, but at its best is a satisfying relaxation between doughty deeds.[20] In general the *Historia*'s love stories are simpler and less emotionally charged in the *Laud*, and they show an acceptance of immediate attraction and consummation found also in romances like *Richard Coeur de Lyon* and *Sir Launfal*. For Guido's tasteless and overblown description of Medea's deflowering and subsequent sexual insatiability (3.112–26; p. 25), the poet substitutes a matter-of-fact narration:

> When sche hadde take of him that oth,
> Thei caste of hem euery cloth
> And ȝede bothe in-to a bed,—
> With riche clothes hit was spred.
> Alle that nyȝt to-gedur thei lay,
> Til it was nere a-gayn the day. (881–86)

The most usual role for women in the *Laud* is as the inspiration for feats of derring-do. After Paris's raid, Menelaus in the *Historia* laments all the injuries that have been done him (the temple plundered, his people slaughtered, and captives including Helen taken), but in the *Laud* the Spartan king regrets, in courtly fashion, only the loss of 'faire Eleyn' (3067–80). The *Historia* notes that Paris feels shame because of Helen on one occasion when Menelaus unhorses him (17.72–73; p. 153), but the *Laud* elaborates the single sentence thus:

> Paris ther-of gret schame thoght,
> That he to grounde so sone was broght;
> He ros vp ful pale and wan
> For schame he hadde of fair Eleyn,
> He was ther-of wel sore aschamed,
> That he of Eleyne schulde be blamed,
> That sche saw so foule a falle,
> Ther sche was set In castel walle. (6745–52)

Similarly, an original romantic challenge is uttered by Hector in pursuit of King Teucer, who has just wounded him: 'A-byde, thow coward kyng Tentan,/For the love of thi lemman!' (5297–98).[21] But finally the *Laud*'s interest in love and women is minimal. Even Guido's misogyny is absent because the warriors' relations with women are just not important enough in the *Laud* to arouse resentment. As in the standard Middle English romance, the more idealistic or tender aspects of chivalry (love and honor), while present, remain clearly secondary to violent exploits on the field of battle.

The *Laud*'s fullest attention is devoted to the adventures of his sterling heroes and base villains: Guido's battles are consistently rewritten to highlight the deeds of individual leaders, as we saw with Penthesilea. For example, Guido's description of Menelaus's entrance into the seventh battle is factual and distant: 'At this point, however, Menelaus arrived to aid the Greeks in a company of three thousand armed knights, and they entered the battle. On account of this the Greeks, in the confidence of their strength, undertook with boldness to recover the field' (20.68–71; p. 168). The English poem, in contrast, emphasizes the leader, not his troops, and narrates the scene from his point of view:

> But Menelaus, when he beheld
> How thei of Grece had lorn the feld,
> Opon his stede the kyng him dresses,
> To Troiens euen he him gesses;
> He lased his helm, his spere he riȝtes,
> And rides thedir with alle his knyȝtes.
> He halp hem wel and wan hem erthe,
> He felde the thridde & sclow the ferthe;
> He and his bare Troiens ouer,
> And hem of Grece made hem couer
> And tok the feld the Troiens opon. (8997–9007)

So solicitous is the *Laud*-poet of his heroes that he will often explain away their smallest failings. When Troilus loses his horse to Diomedes, the poet adds the excuse that while the Greek had a spear, the Trojan had none (9053–60). Heroes are also constructed from the most unlikely materials. Even hapless Margariton, whose death incites Hector to enter his last battle, appears as a much more aggressive and courageous warrior in the *Laud* (compare 10471–88 with 21.123–25; p. 174).

Villain hatred is the other side of hero worship, and the poet practices it too. Paris is as base throughout the *Laud* as his brother Hector is noble and, much more clearly than in the *Historia*, he is identified as the root cause of the fall of Troy. When the Greeks assemble at Athens to attack Troy, the poet adds a long lament for the destruction to come (3352–80). He opens by fixing blame directly on Paris (3352–55), then regrets that Apollo did not drown him on his way to get Helen (3360–66), and closes by asserting that Troy would still be standing were it not for 'Paris ffals a-voutrye!' (3380).[22] The digression is in the poet's characteristic voice; instead of imitating Guido's formal and moralizing rhetoric, he involves himself personally in the story, cheering on the good and cursing the bad, like the narrator of *King Horn* or *Havelok*. His most extreme hatred is reserved for the traitors Antenor and Aeneas. Just as Hector can only be killed by treachery, the city falls only before deceit:

> 3it was it neuere wonne with fyght,
> With the Gregeis, ne with ther myght;
> Hit was be-trayed falsly—Alas!—
> With Antenor and Eneas. (4703–06)

In recounting how the two go to Priam with their false plan, the poet stresses their hypocrisy (17288–89) and lets his emotions explode: 'The deuel hem mot In helle senke!' (17290). Elsewhere Aeneas is branded as 'fals' (17239 and 17309), and his 'wickednesse' and 'gret felnesse' are excoriated (17555–56). Antenor, for his part, is called a 'lyther schrewe' (17631), 'lyther thyng' (17940), and 'lyther fende' (18023), and once is introduced as 'The fals traytour—the deuel him cheke' (17689). Such a narrator forces the reader to become as involved in ancient history as he would be in a contemporary romance.

The Laud as a Hector Romance

In the best study yet written on the Middle English romance, Dieter Mehl asserts that one of the few generalizations possible about the *genre* is that 'in England the word "romance" often implied some particular hero in whose praise the romance was written.'[23] The *Laud*-poet clearly intends his work to be the romance of Hector. After listing other romance heroes, he announces his subject:

> But of the worthiest wyght in wede
> That euere by-strod any stede,
> Spekes no man, ne in romaunce redes
> Of his batayle ne of his dedis. (27–30)

Even though the poet also declares that he will tell the whole story of the war, there is no doubt but that Hector will be its star. The new *Manual of the Writings in Middle English* is accurate in calling the Laud a 'Hector-romance,'[24] and its being so demonstrates both the poet's debt to the Middle English romance tradition and his skill at reshaping the *Historia* on a large scale.

Throughout the *Laud*, Hector's role is given special attention; he is Troy's principal hero and with him go the fortunes of the city. Again and again, the poet reminds us of how fearsome a military force Hector is by stressing his overwhelming physical might. Priam's desire that Hector lead the Trojans in revenge against Greece, because he is superior to his brothers in 'arms and deeds of courage' (6.93–94; p. 59), becomes eight lines of romance cliches extolling him as 'hardi, strong, & bolde' and praising his 'strengthe & myght,' his 'hardinesse' and 'doughtinesse' (2299–2306). A new prologue added in the *Laud* before the Greeks sail for Troy claims that Hector is the worthiest man ever to ride a horse, as well as the boldest ever born; five times within a few lines it uses the word *strong* like a epithet to describe him (3253–70).[25]

The poet constantly expands the *Historia* to describe his hero's great deeds in more detail. One example that may stand for innumerable others occurs during Guido's fourth battle. Hector tries to capture Menelaus, but is frustrated when 'a countless number of warriors advanced at once to his aid. For this reason, when he had let him go, [Hector] attacked the Greek troops with his men, killed them, and on account of his might and that of his men, the Greeks were forced to flee and the Trojans pursued the flying Greeks' (17.119–23; pp. 154–55). This simple incident becomes a heroic encounter of epic proportions in the *Laud*, beginning with the Greeks coming against Hector:

> On Ector alle thei gan leye,
> Many a body he did ther dye,
> Many a man to dethe gos,
> For thei lette him of his purpos;
> He sclees hem & falles that he reches,
> Delful strokes he hem be-teches,
> He maymed hem and ouer-al slees,
> That he hadde neuere more pees,
> Many a man he ther spilles. (6995–7003)

The Greek rout that follows is immediate and complete; and although the verse that describes it is loose and visually imprecise, it does contain a good sample of the poet's energetic similes:

> The Gregeys ffleis ouer dales & hilles,
> As faste as thei may ride,

> Toward her tentis on eche a side.
> Ector affter euere chases,
> At eche a lepe his stede vnbrasis,
> Thei fledde him as hare doth hound;
> Men my3t haue filled a gret dromound
> With bodijs that he sclow chasand,
> And euere he folowed manassand.
> He swar here deth by bok and belle,
> He nolde neuere sese hem to qwelle. (7004–14)

Guido's account is not directly contradicted, but the *Laud*'s focus remains entirely on Hector: there is no hint during this single-handed rampage that the rest of the Trojan army did anything more than cheer.

In addition to Hector's military might, the poet develops another, gentler side of his hero: the thoughtful opponent of war and needless slaughter. In the debate over war with Greece in Book 6, Guido gives Hector a long speech in opposition; but when his advice is ignored, we hear no more about it. The *Laud*-poet remembers, however, and later recalls Hector's wise counsel in an original lament to Priam:

> Haddest thow don be Ectores rede,
> Then haddest thow not be dede.
> Now comes thi sorwe and thi wo,
> Alas, thi Ioye schal ouer-go! (3603–06)

When Hector accepts Achilles's challenge to single combat, a further addition reveals Hector's concern for those killed in battle: 'For we do euel and mychel synne,/Off mannes blod that we don spille' (8412–13). Proof of both Hector's greater mercy and importance in the *Laud* occurs during the debate on what to do with the captured Thoas. In the *Historia*, Priam demands death for the prisoner but is opposed by Aeneas, while Hector is said only to have 'quite approved the advice of Aeneas as praiseworthy' (18.26–27; p. 155). In the *Laud*, Aeneas openly asks for Hector's support (7187–88), which is given in direct discourse (7189–94). Priam's reply is specifically to Hector, not to Aeneas as in the *Historia* (7195–98). As a coda, the *Laud* adds lines that vividly portray the fear felt by Thoas, Priam's lurid desire for revenge, and Hector's mercy:

> Kyng Thoas herte be-gan to qwake,
> He wende to be hanged al nake;
> But Ector wolde he were saued.
> Priamus wolde that Troye hadde be paued
> With hethen hond and euery a membre;
> That he hadde bended or Septembre,
> If he my3t haue had his wille;
> But Ector wold not lete him spille,
> And thus hadde thei that conseil ent. (7213–21)

The player of only a supporting role in the *Historia*, Hector has once again been made the star of the *Laud*.

The *Laud*'s emphasis on Hector is so pronounced that his praises continue to be sung even after death. To Penthesilea's reproach of Pyrrhus because his father had killed Hector, the poet adds lines that celebrate the Trojan champion (16839–43). Another such expansion is more bizarre. Smitten with love for Polyxena, Achilles takes to his bed and laments: 'Alas for me, because I, whom the bravest and stoutest of men could not conquer by any means, whom not even the very brave Hector, who surpassed the bravest of all, could conquer, am now overwhelmed and cast down by the sight of one frail girl!' (23.137–41; p. 185). The brief parenthetic reference to Hector is much expanded in the *Laud*:

> And he that was so mychel of myght,
> The strengest that was In any fyght,
> Ector of Troye, that doughti man,
> That price & honour of alle men wan,—
> That alle the men that stalworthe wore
> He ouercome with strokes sore,
> Alle that were styff & strong
> That doughti kny3t to dethe throng;
> I knewe neuere non that hadde that myght,—
> That was so strong ne dou3ti wyght,—
> A3eyn him that my3t stonde,
> Whil he leued In this londe—
> And 3it he with alle his fforce
> Ne my3t ouercome my carful corse! (12059–72)

It would be hard to find a more inappropriate context or a more unlikely speaker for such a eulogy, but the poet has found another opportunity to honor his idol.

In the medieval history of Troy, Achilles appears as a sneaking murderer while Hector is by far the best knight at the war. The *Laud* enthusiastically endorses this dichotomy, as we might expect, and intensifies the contrast between brave, honorable Hector and cowardly, ignoble Achilles. Guido describes a battle between Hector and Achilles that would have caused the death of one or both had they not been separated (17.91–95; pp. 149–50). In the *Laud* Diomedes is named as peace-maker, and to him is attributed a much less ambiguous view of the fight's probable outcome:

> But Diomedes was ful sicur,
> Hadde he Achilles lefft In that beker,
> That he scholde haue had no pouste,
> Ne qwik with lyff ne grace hadde be. (6189–92)

Shortly thereafter, and much earlier than in the *Historia*, Achilles admits that Hector can only be defeated by treachery. Speaking before his men, Achilles describes the Trojan's military superiority (6291–304) and insists that they have only one hope: 'Iff we myght be so quaynte and scly,/That we vn-armed come him by' (6307–08).

   Soon all the Greeks believe that Hector can only be stopped dishonorably. The council during which thoughts of treachery against Hector are first expressed is greatly expanded from a little over half a page in Griffin's edition (p. 151; 17.1–21), and only twenty-eight lines in the faithful *Destruction of Troy* (7346–73), to one hundred and thirty lines in the *Laud* (6363–492). Hector's ability is given in such detail that he begins to seem superhuman—almost a force of nature:

> It was neuere man ȝaff suche strokes;
> Off a man were mad of okes,
> Off Marbil gray and grete stones,
> And yren and stele were alle his bones,
> He wolde hem al to-cleue—
> By him that made Adam and Eue! (6385–90)

In Guido the Greeks give Achilles the task of eliminating this nonpareil, which he is to accomplish 'not so much by means of his strength as by means of his ingenious cleverness' (17.14–15; p. 151). The *Laud* eschews such euphemisms. Agamemnon moans that without some 'quayntise' (6431) they will never succeed, and he berates the warriors for not killing Hector 'With som tresoun and ffelonye' (6450). The final Greek charge to Achilles is equally direct:

> Opon thi strengthe truste thow nought,
> But on thi wit and on thi scleyght,
> And holde the euere fro him on heyght;
> Whan thow him sees in a myscheef,
> Than schaltow him dedly greef
> By thi strengthe and thi wit. (6480–85)

   After that council, the *Historia* does not mention treachery against Hector again until the fatal attack itself, but the *Laud*-poet carefully establishes a pattern of cowardly action by Achilles and thereby shows himself to be not only Hector's partisan but also seriously concerned with dramatic causation. In the very next battle, without altering the substance of Guido's narrative, the poet contrasts Greek villain and Trojan hero. While Hector is victorious in battle (6511–26), Achilles holds himself back and hopes to find Hector at a disadvantage, just as 'ffische is dreven to the bayte' (6529). Then to Guido's simple description of Achilles being wounded by Hector and rescued by Diomedes (17.47–51; p. 152), the poet provides an important addition. Men may here compare the might of each champion, he says (6616); Hector had been fighting the whole day (6617), while Achilles kept himself out, waiting 'To stele on him as a theff,/When he fond him at myscheff' (6619–20). Yet despite his weariness, the Trojan is still able to get the best of Achilles, whose slyness has this time failed.[26]

As Hector's end approaches, the poet begins to mix his praise with laments (e.g., 9969–9992). Everything about the hero's death is expanded and made more emotional, including Andromache's ominous dream and her attempt to keep Hector from battle the next day. In the *Historia* the dream is reported with distant objectivity: 'Andromache, therefore, since she was terrified at this vision, burst into floods of tears and ventured that very night to reveal that vision to Hector in bed where she was lying with him' (21.45–48; p. 172). Compare this with the *Laud*'s dramatic rendering:

> By her lord In hir bed sche lay:
> A dredful dreme that lady dremed,
> That In hir sclepe sche cried & scremed.
> The while sche was In hir sclepe,
> Ector ȝaff to hir good kepe,
> Sche was sore & sche was dredful,
> To wakyn hir it was nedful;
> He waked hir & seide: 'swetyng,
> Thow art ful ferd In thi sclepyng.
> Whi fares thow thus? what ayles the?
> Whi art thow ferd? what may this be?' (9996–10005)

Andromache's unexplained cries and Hector's anxious concern create a terrifying and effective scene reminiscent of the way the Queen's awful dream is narrated in *Sir Orfeo*.

The *Laud*-poet gives more attention to everything surrounding Hector's death, especially the hero's own exploits. From the time Hector learns that his natural brother Margariton has been killed, and thus enters the fighting, until he is himself killed and brought back to Troy takes less than two pages in Griffin's edition of the *Historia* (pp. 174–75), and is closely translated in eighty-six lines by the *Destruction* (8588–8673); the *Laud* expands the scene to four hundred and sixty-four lines (10509–972), most of which chronicle the prowess of Hector, which is never greater than just before his death. The episode opens with a fine description of the revenge-seeking Trojan champion advancing to battle past his fleeing countrymen. Guido's brief account of Hector's fighting (21.134–40; p. 174) becomes an extended catalogue of marvelous deeds (10553–10638). No one is strong enough to withstand Hector: he would have killed all the Greeks had he not been fated to die (10678–684) and takes on 10,000 at once (10689–90). When we last see the Trojan champion in action, he has already killed two thousand Greeks and thus earned the reputation of being 'non erthely man' (10896). In contrast, we get an original and rather sarcastic glimpse of Achilles, 'that lordly sire,' who dares not meet Hector (10573–76).[27]

The actual death scene is once again faithful to the basic historical truth of the *Historia* (Hector dies at the same time, in the same way, by the same man), but the poet continues to glorify his hero. While defending his men, Hector attacks a Greek king who had killed or wounded many Trojans (10897–10904). The king begs for mercy (a detail not in the *Historia* but possible to infer from its account of the capture), and, in the highest tradition of knightly chivalry, Hector accedes (10907–10). As Hector puts his shield on his back to lead off the captured king, Achilles seizes what he knows will be his only chance for success ('he scholde neuere to dethe him do,/But he myȝt that tyme come there-to' [10933–34]) and kills the undefended Hector from behind. The dishonor of skulking Achilles is much stressed by the poet (10921–40); for it has been his argument from the beginning that the greatest knight in history could only have fallen from the blackest treachery. After his hero's death, the poet adds his own lament for the 'gode knyȝt,/That no man myȝt withstande In fight' (10987–88). Never was there a better 'knyȝt of chiualrie,' but death defeats all and on this earth nothing may last (10987–11016).

The Limits of the Laud as a Hector Romance

Because of the *Laud*-poet's commitment to the truth of his history, 'Hector-romance,' though accurate, is finally an incomplete description of his work. Despite a special interest in Hector, the poet fulfils his promise in the prologue to present the whole story of Troy (the 'werre sothe alle plenere' [66]). He declares he will tell not just the stories of Hector and Achilles, but those 'of alle the gode lordes echon;/And of alle here dedis schal lakke non' (95–96). Although Hector is continually glorified in the *Laud*, the poet's respect for historical truth is such that he retains episodes that bring discredit on his hero. Merion's defiant insults to Hector for trying to plunder the armor of Patroclus are preserved despite their harshness:

> thow wolff, thow art wel grede!
> Wenestow wynne that wyght rauyne,
> Certes his harneys schal neuere be thyne. (5008–10)

Hector's role is greatly expanded in the *Laud*, but invention is always controlled by the demands of historical truth. The *Laud*-poet is much more like a medieval author retelling a Biblical story (who may dramatize and color but not fundamentally alter) than a writer of romance (who may change his material almost at will). It is obvious to all that the *Laud*-poet is no slavish translator of Guido, but it is much harder to see his dedication to preserving the true history of the Trojan War.

One student of the *Laud* has claimed that after the death of Hector, the poet becomes bored with his material and renders it mechanically and with extensive condensation.[28] Our previous discussion of Hector's prominence in the *Laud* might lead us to accept unhesitatingly such a judgment, but the evidence simply will not support it. In keeping with his method of focusing on the war itself, the poet eliminates the Greek returns, but his work continues for 9,000 lines after the death of Hector with no evidence of diminished enthusiasm. He continues to expand battle description and to add original romance detail, such as a passage describing how the wounded knights comforted themselves with hunting during a long truce (13565–74). His passion for promoting the magnificence of his material seems to increase. After the truce just mentioned, he includes a long assertion that never 'Sithe Eue bare Caym and gode Abel' (13696) has there been a greater battle than the one he is about to describe (13687–722). These warriors fought every day for a month, and there is not a knight living today who could do that!

The most important new development in the *Laud* after Hector's death is his replacement by another hero; the poet does not lose heart after the death of Hector, rather he gives it to another warrior. Once Hector has fallen an astonishing metamorphosis occurs: Achilles goes from skulking coward to the story's principal hero, and much care is now devoted to recording and expanding his exploits. One reason for this, surely, is the poem's romance design, which demands there always be a hero of some sort, even if he has to be a Greek. Yet this begs the question of why, if the *Laud* really is a Hector romance, the last part of the story needs to be included at all—why not end with the dramatic death of his principal hero as Chaucer does in the *Troilus*? The poet continues, and with no loss of interest, because whatever the *Laud*'s romance coloring it remains fundamentally a history and thus committed to telling all that happened at Troy.

The poet begins the rehabilitation of Achilles in the battle following the death of Hector. The *Laud* adds a passage that specifically notes Achilles's absence, but then it goes on to claim that had he been present, he would have taught the Trojans 'to synge a sori sang' (11749–54). From then on Achilles is given the kind of special attention and emphasis previously lavished on Hector. Much is made of the damage his withdrawal from the fighting for love of Polyxena causes the Greek effort. To Guido's factual information that Agamemnon requests a truce because of the destruction of his army (26.145–46; p. 201), the poet adds the Greek commander's fear, expressed in direct speech, that all will be lost unless Achilles returns immediately: 'But Achilles on vs rewe,/Ther schal not skape of vs a Grewe!' (13944–48). When Achilles does re-enter battle, his military value is confirmed. The *Laud* gives an original speech to Troilus in which he reports to Priam that the city's troops had thoroughly routed the Greeks—until Achilles's arrival:

> That Ilke knyght him-selff alone
> Maked oure men to fle echone

> For any thyng that we coude do,
> And made vs lese oure worschepe so. (14305–08)

The *Laud*-poet makes even more fundamental changes to show his new favorite in a positive light. Guido's long criticisms of Homer for praising such a knight as Achilles, who can kill only by fraud, are eliminated (26.265–93 and 340–42; pp. 204–06). The poet elsewhere ignores similar rhetoric as inessential to the history and wearying for his audience, but in this case he has also tampered with one of the prosecution's main exhibits: the killing of Troilus. In the *Historia*, the Myrmidons, on Achilles's orders, surround Troilus, kill his horse, wound him repeatedly, tear off his helmet, and generally exhaust him before Achilles ambles into administer the *coup de grace* (26.226–64; pp. 203–04). In the English version, however, the Myrmidons seem to surround the Trojan only so that none of his companions will come to his aid; Troilus remains unwounded until the arrival of Achilles, who himself cuts off the knight's helmet, drives him from his horse, and slays him (14839–92). This episode reveals how far the *Laud*-poet will stretch Guido's facts to exalt his heroes.[29] Yet there are definite limits to his changes. Achilles's dragging of Troilus's body, with 'schame & vylony' (14897), despite its implied blame of the Greek, is retained in the *Laud* as a historical fact. The poet's glorification of Achilles, as with Hector, reaches an apotheosis at his death. The *Laud* adds a long lament for the fallen hero (15439–52) and much expands the description of his tomb (15505–18).

The special attention given Achilles finally comes to an end, as does the glorification of Hector, giving way to praise of other heroes: Penthesilea and Pyrrhus. We have previously seen the development of the Amazon warrior in battle; the same kind of attention is also granted Pyrrhus, the son of Achilles. The *Laud* is written in the form of romance, and so it tends to focus on individual heroes, but the poet's principal commitment is not to any one hero, not even Hector, but to the whole, true history of Troy.

The Laud as History

Because the *Laud*-poet is infatuated with heroes and delights in bloody battle description, because he has no sense of historical anachronism and deliberately designs his poem to appeal to a romance audience, his very real historical seriousness has been ignored. One of the first to write on the poem, Dorothy Kempe, declared that the poet 'does not profess to be more than a "gestour," consequently he is at less pains to give verisimilitude to his tale,' and a recent article by Paul Strohm on several Middle English Troy narratives reveals that this view is still alive: 'With little sense of obligation to be faithful to his sources and a strong interest in presenting the deeds of Hector, the *Laud*-poet was free to omit some of Guido's more elaborate historiographical flourishes in favor of a more action-filled narrative with a single hero close to its center.'[30] Strohm's plausible description of the *Laud* is fundamentally misleading because it does not recognize the diligent historian at work behind the romance facade. The *Laud*-poet, in common with the other Middle English translators of Guido, sought to produce the specific, if limited, kind of history defined in my first chapter: a detailed and factual record of the events at Troy based on the eyewitness journals of Dares and Dictys. To the *Laud*-poet, 'Guido's more elaborate historiographical flourishes' are simply rhetorical decoration which can be replaced by his own romance style without compromise to essential historical truth. Contrary to Strohm's claim, the poet feels a deep obligation to preserve this truth as he has received it from Guido's *Historia*. He reshapes and rewrites his source, but always strives to conserve and pass on its record of real events.

As we have already seen, the *Laud* does not begin to approach the word-for-word faithfulness of the *Destruction*; the *Laud*-poet is often a careless translator and reshapes battles and his heroes' exploits shamelessly. In addition, much of Guido's material is completely missing; Atwood lists sixty-three 'principal' omissions, and he is conservative.[31] But if the poet's cuts are severe, they are not capricious. He succeeds in making the story more unified, and thus simpler for a listening audience, by focusing on the facts of the war itself and drastically reducing anything not directly connected to it. The largest single omission is the Greek returns, which is completely excised; similarly, the story of the Argonauts, which opens the work, is severely pruned. A second class of omissions includes Guido's learned and rhetorical digressions. Guido's condemnations of women, seasonal descriptions, account of the rise of idolatry, references to classical literature, and geographical discussions disappear from the *Laud* almost without a trace, along with the *Historia*'s catalogues of ships and principal characters and even most lists of battalions and their leaders. Much more insistently than the author of the *Destruction*, the *Laud*-poet retells the history in his own words and in his own style; yet poetic freedom is never allowed to become historical license.[32] However gaudily dressed or dramatically presented, Guido's historical record always remains beneath.

The historian guides the poet in reshaping the *Historia*, and he carefully preserves important factual information from passages omitted in the interest of narrative excitement. Early in the history, Guido ends his account of the vessel built for the Argonauts with a learned digression: he notes that some think this was the first ship to reach distant places by sail and so scholars call any large ocean-going ship an Argo (1.158–62; p. 9). The poet characteristically eliminates this piece of pedantry, but he does inform us that the ship was large and called *Argon* after its builder

(336–40). Such narrative skill combined with historical scrupulousness is still present near the end of the poem, after the death of Hector. The construction of the Trojan Horse is given much more briefly than in the *Historia* (30.78–99; pp. 230–31), yet the essential facts remain: the horse was made of brass and so built that a thousand men could hide within it (17995–18004). Guido's rhetorical flights, such as his famous seasonal descriptions (one even lies behind the opening of the *Canterbury Tales*), are usually eliminated as well, again without sacrifice of important historical information. The seventh book of the *Historia* opens with one of the shortest such descriptions:

> The sun had already completed its course between the Hyades and the Pleiades, and since it was in the sign of Taurus, the month of May was adorning the fields of the country with various flowers, and the trees, growing green with new leaves, were giving promise of fruits to come by the profusion of their blossoms. (7.1–5; p. 67)

Though all of Guido's verbal decoration is gone in the *Laud*, the information that the month was May is kept (2714) to prove the care and deliberation behind the poet's excisions.

The poet's artistic command of his material and his commitment to preserve its historical truth are both revealed in certain felicitous rearrangements of the story. Robert Lumiansky has discussed the postponement, but not elimination, of an early scene describing the relationship between Troilus and Briseida.[33] Lumiansky is certainly correct that the poet's chief motive here is to remove anything that might take attention away from his hero, Hector. However, since the poet later combines this omitted scene with another than concerns the lovers, we may conclude two other things about his method: as a historian, he wishes to preserve all the facts in his source; as a poet, he knows the love story will be better understood if presented in larger, more coherent units. Similarly, the description of Ilion is removed from Guido's account of the rebuilding of Troy and saved to be used, along with other postponed material, in a lavish description of the Chamber of Beauty (9449–568). In this new location, the information can be introduced dramatically in connection with the poem's central hero, for the Chamber is where Hector recuperates from his war wounds.

The *Laud* frequently contains passages not found in its source. These additions do not come freely from the poet's creative imagination, but are further examples of his historical seriousness. With Griffin's edition of the *Historia* in hand, we can see that the gaps thus filled are merely examples of Guido's woolly narrative style, but the *Laud*-poet must have considered them real *lacunae* which, from his deep knowledge of the history, he sets about to repair. The largest group of these supplements has already been examined: The transformation of Guido's vague summaries of battle into specific and concrete action. Let us now note two briefer examples. When the Greek warrior Thoas is captured by Troy, Guido's Aeneas opposes Priam's desire to put him to death for the practical reason that the Greeks may retaliate if a Trojan is later taken (18. 4–27; p. 155). The *Laud*-poet, however, remembers that Thoas had killed Cassibilans, one of Priam's natural sons (15.457–61; p. 140), and so he adds an original passage in which Aeneas recalls that killing to explain the king's unreasonable passion to kill his prisoner:

> He saw the kyng hadde wratthe I-tane
> For the dethe of Cassibalane,
> The kynges sone, he loued best;
> For wratthe him thoght his herte brast. (7139–42)

At the end of Guido's Book 18, Antenor is captured, and when his son Polydamas rushes up to rescue him, night ends the battle with Antenor in enemy hands (18.149–157; p. 159). The *Laud*-poet translates the episode closely (7884–901), but then, obviously feeling the story to be incomplete in the *Historia*, he adds a long passage on the bereft son's wakeful sorrow all that night and his arming the next morning to lead his men against the Greeks in revenge (7902–16). In the stories of both Thoas and Polydamas, the poet goes beyond his source, but only to provide material that makes the history more complete and understandable to his audience.

The *Historia* contains many characters who make only brief and widely scattered appearances. The *Laud*-poet takes pains to explain these figures and their place in the story. In so doing, he again reveals his comprehensive knowledge of the history and constant desire to present its full truth. In the midst of a long passage following the first destruction of Troy, Guido refers in passing to the fate of Laomedon's daughter Hesione, who 'was made a harlot subject to the lust of Telamon' (5.5–6; p. 43). To this phrase the *Laud* adds lines that look forward and remind us that the issue of this forced union will be the hero Ajax Telamon, fated to do great things in the second war at Troy (1747–54). Ajax Telamon is not mentioned by Guido until much later (8.157–161; p. 84), and his parentage goes unreported until his meeting with Hector at the end of Book 15. The poet also proves himself a conscientious historian in his presentation of Creusa and Aeneas. Early in the poem, he follows Guido in identifying Creusa as the wife of Aeneas (5.66–70; p. 45), but replaces the *Historia*'s injunction to turn to the *Aeneid* for more detail with a foreshadowing passage informing us that Aeneas will later be traitor to Troy (1877–80). At the end of the poem, while Hecuba is blaming Aeneas for his betrayal of Priam, the *Laud*-poet alone, unlike Guido or his other Middle English translators, recalls the family relationship and has Hecuba list as one of Priam's benefits to Aeneas that 'He ȝaff the his doghter to wyue/Be-ffore alle men that were on lyue' (18321–22).

Two other examples are of special importance because they prove the

poet knows well even those sections of the *Historia* he chose not to
translate. While reporting the Greek decision to spare Andromache's
children after the fall of Troy, the *Laud* omits Guido's information that
Pyrrhus wants them dead but adds this about one of the sons:

> And sithen was on a kyng In Grece,
> Off riche londes & riche fece,
> Off alle the londes kyng Pirrus
> And of the londes of kyng Pelleus. (18453–56)

The ascension to the throne of Thessaly by Laomedon, the son of Hector
and Andromache, is told along with the Greek returns at the end of the
Historia, though none of this is included in the *Laud*. The poet's
knowledge of Laomedon's destiny supports my earlier contention that
the truncation of the *Historia* in the *Laud* comes not from carelessness
but from a deliberate decision to concentrate on the siege itself. He is
nevertheless familiar with what has been left out, and he uses it when
appropriate—to tell us about Laomedon's fate, as we have just seen, or
about the later exile of the Trojan traitors, Aeneas and Antenor (18599–
606). In the *Historia*, this story occurs in Book 21, another part of Guido
that is omitted in the *Laud* but whose information is known to the poet.

At times the *Laud*-poet seems to have left his source altogether.[34] His
version of Guido's eleventh and twelfth battles (26.1–46; pp. 197–98)
contains the most extensive and puzzling additions I have been able to
find in the poem. The two battles occupy 220 lines in the *Laud* (13323–
542); this compares with a mere 78 lines in the closely translated
Destruction (9864–9941) and only 103 lines in Lydgate, who is famous for
his prolixity (4.2029–131). At a first reading, the *Laud* and its source may
appear to be describing totally different events; but despite some real
differences to be examined below, there is basic agreement in factual
substance. Both works describe the eleventh battle as major and a Greek
defeat. Both consider the twelfth also an important battle and describe
how Diomedes kills many Trojans only to suffer the retribution of
Troilus, who then upbraids him over Briseida. Both have Menelaus
unsuccessfully attacking Troilus and being carried to his tent. Both then
show Agamemnon riding up with other Greek leaders to take revenge,
which is accomplished but only at the price of being wounded. Finally
both have Agamemnon, fearing further loss to his men, ask the Trojans
for a six-month truce, which is granted by Troy with some reluctance.

Despite this underlying similarity, the poet has changed his source in
many ways. The first class of differences we have encountered before:
expansions that add detail and narrative energy to Guido's mere
summaries. Preparations for the eleventh battle and a general overview of
it are given at much greater length in the poem (13323–44), and, as usual,
the poet is especially apt at describing the bloody violence of war:
'Knyghtes falle, and stedis stray,/The dede bodyes on hepe lay' (13343–

44). In the same battle, Troilus's extraordinary rampage against the Greeks in revenge of his brother's death is also much expanded (13345–54). Interestingly enough, the poet seems wary of the *Historia*'s claim that Troilus killed 1,000 knights that day (he says only that Troilus slew 'many knyghtes'), but he gives Troilus's revenge more narrative reality through greater length and detail. The *Laud* ends its account of the eleventh battle with an original description of the two sides returning home, eating, and falling asleep in utter exhaustion, all of which also emphasizes the ferocity of battle (13369–78).

The *Laud*'s account of the twelfth battle also begins with romance additions: the shame of the defeated Greeks and their eagerness for revenge is developed at length, and we see their banners as they march out and the initial clash (13379–402). The fight that develops between Troilus and Diomedes follows the *Historia* closely, but once again the information is more dramatically presented in the poem. Instead of Guido's third-person summary, we watch from Troilus's perspective as Diomedes slaughters the Trojans as told in the poet's racy style: 'He pared her chekes al aboute,/That al here tethe fellen oute' (13407–08). The encounter between Troilus and Diomedes is more concerned with chivalric honor here than in Guido because of the addition of Troilus's spoken challenge to Diomedes and the Greek's spirited acceptance (13419–26). The subsequent fight between Menelaus and Troilus is only slightly longer (13445–64), but to the *Historia*'s vague statement that Agamemnon entered the battle with others, the *Laud* provides specific names (13465–82). Finally, the poet expands the epilogue to this battle with a long passage on the wounds of Menelaus and Diomedes, a simple deduction from the narrative, and he gives more details concerning the truce negotiations (13513–42).

So far the poet's method and motive are clear: his narrative is made more exciting and dramatic, while Guido's historical facts remain constant— the *Laud* is both poem and history. However, I have chosen to discuss these two battles in such detail because they are exceptional in containing other additions that seem to have absolutely no warrant in the *Historia*. These include the arrival of Menelaus and Diomedes, who slay many Trojans, in the eleventh battle (13355–61); and in the twelfth battle, the serious wounding of Troilus by Telamon (13483–90), Paris's slaughter of the Greeks (13491–96), the wounding of Agamemnon by an unknown knight and not by Troilus (13497–500), and the Greeks being driven to their tents in defeat (13501–12).

Despite their number, these additions do not significantly alter the general shape of the two battles and just possibly they come in part or whole from corruptions in the poet's text of Guido. All of them, except for the wounding of Troilus, are similar to the expansions discussed above. They are merely extreme attempts to bring Guido's generalities to life. The introduction of Diomedes and Menelaus serves to render effectively

Guido's vague 'and a very hard-fought battle was waged between them'
(26.4–5); similarly, Paris's heroics in the twelfth battle provide some
concrete proof for Agamemnon's feats of complete defeat (26.36–42). The
same fears, which are stated but not further explained in the *Historia*, also
justify the description of the Greeks falling back to their tents, a passage
based on a similar episode in the *Historia* following the eleventh battle
which the *Laud* had omitted (26.9–12). This leaves only the inexplicable
scene in which Troilus is unhorsed by Telamon. I can find no reason for
such a brief and capricious addition, and, if there is not some textual
problem, it should probably be attributed to that carelessness which the
Laud-poet, more than either of the other Middle English translators of
Guido, is prone to. But, however free, the *Laud*-poet never allows himself
to lose control completely. Having for some reason added the unhorsing
of Troilus, he remains consistent a few lines later: Agamemnon's
wounding is not attributed to Troilus, as in Guido (26.38–40), but to an
anonymous assailant.

 The number of changes in the eleventh and twelfth battles is very much
an exception. Generally the *Laud* demonstrates a remarkable fidelity to
Guido. The poet wants to make his story appeal to a general romance
audience, but he is careful that it remain history. Although battle scenes
are the most common subject for expansion in the *Laud*, the poet is not
automatically prolix in matters military. When warfare is described in
sufficient detail in the *Historia*, as it is during the Greek landing at Troy
(*Historia*—14.86–120; pp. 120–21; *Laud*—4251–4318) or in one of the
early battles (*Historia*—15.549–92; pp. 143–44; *Laud*—5675–5770), the
Laud's version approaches the closeness of translation found in the
Destruction. Moreover, the poem often, though not always, reproduces
numbers and names in its source closely. Despite differences in style and
emphasis, a reader with the *Historia* before him can always find the same
basic story in the *Laud*. The poet has no desire to invalidate the truth of
the *Historia*, his aim is only to retouch it so that it might appeal to his
special audience. Like all the Middle English historians of Troy, the
author of the *Laud* is both historian and poet. The popular and often
sensational accent of the poet must not keep us from recognizing the
capable intelligence of the historian.

V

John Lydgate's Troy Book: *History as Learned Rhetoric*

We have little idea who wrote the *Destruction of Troy* or the *Laud Troy Book*, each of which survives in only a single manuscript, nor can we date either one with certainty. In addition, there is no proof that the *Destruction* or the *Laud* ever had the slightest influence on any other work. John Lydgate's *Troy Book* is a complete contrast. Lydgate tells us the exact hour on which he began it, and over twenty manuscripts of the poem remain extant, along with a print of 1513 by Pynson and one of 1555 by Marshe.[1] Though nominally a monk of Bury St. Edmunds, Lydgate was as much a court poet as Chaucer and was near the center of both the political and literary life of England in the fifteenth century. The *Troy Book* itself was commissioned in 1412 by Prince Hal, who became Henry V long before the eight years had elapsed that it took Lydgate to complete his history. Lydgate's *Troy Book*, along with Caxton's *Recuyell of the Historyes of Troye*, became the standard English source for the medieval history of Troy through the Renaissance, and it has been shown to have been a source for John Pikeryng, Thomas Kyd, Christopher Marlowe, and Shakespeare, among others.[2] Like the other Middle English historians of Troy, Lydgate is committed to preserving the true record of the past and faithfully transmitting it to his own time. In addition, he brings a strong intelligence, considerable learning, and high rhetorical ambition to the story of England's ancient ancestors.

What I have just said, however mild the praise, will seem absurd to many. We have all been taught from our first medieval survey that Lydgate's works form the Valley of Poetic Despair, and their only function is to connect the two Delectable Mountains of Chaucer and Shakespeare. Lydgate is still commonly regarded as no better than 'a voluminous, prosaic, driveling monk' or 'a dull, long-winded and metrically incompetent poet.'[3] In the last few years, however, three books by eminent medievalists, Walter Schirmer, Alain Renoir, and Derek Pearsall, have stoutly defended Lydgate against his detractors—both those who have and those who have not actually read him.[4] The three studies have demonstrated Lydgate's intelligence and real, if limited, literary skills, which are those of a craftsman rather than those of a great poet. Schirmer discusses Lydgate in the context of his own time; Renoir demonstrates his role as a transition to the Renaissance; and Pearsall makes clear that his work is criticized more because the function and fashion of poetry have changed than because of unforgivable defects in his ability. Lydgate so completely satisfied the tastes of his own age that he must inevitably seem more and more irrelevant to later periods.

Today the *Troy Book* is scorned for the same reason it was once honored: its uncompromising desire to preserve entire the factual truth of ancient history. This modern judgment is unfair to Lydgate and forces ignorance on us. Without fundamentally altering Guido's historical record (however much we might wish otherwise), Lydgate adds his own literary decoration. Often his elaborations are merely conventional, but there are some impressive surprises: the *Troy Book* has a real, if embryonic sense of history, and though one of Lydgate's assumed offices (historian, rhetorician, moralist, or scholar) is usually performed at the expense of the others, there are moments in which all work in harmony and we realize how good the monk can be.

The Poetry of the Troy Book

Lydgate, like Guido's other Middle English translators, desires to present the factual material of the *Historia* in a form that will make the ancient history appeal to a contemporary audience. In place of the narrative energy of the *Laud* or the precision of the *Destruction*, he uses formal rhetoric to add interest to the history. Lydgate's style consists largely of a continuous expansion of his source along the lines recommended by the rhetorical manuals of his day—an approach that derives in part from Chaucer and was much admired in the Renaissance. Lydgate's rather mechanical decoration of his source suggests his limitations as a poet, but it also testifies to his commitment to history. He will amplify his source, yet do nothing to compromise its factual truth.

Of the three Middle English historians of Troy, Lydgate is the only one to discuss seriously his stylistic goals. At the beginning of the *Troy Book*, he specifically praises Guido for his 'souereinte of stile' (Pro. 373). After commending him for preserving the historical substance of Dares and Dictys (Pro. 354–59), Lydgate singles out Guido's exterior rhetorical decoration as the source of the modern reader's pleasure:

For he enlvmyneth by crafte & cadence
This noble story with many fresche colour
Of rethorik, and many riche flour
Of eloquence to make it sownde bet
He in the story hath ymped in and set,
That in good feythe I trowe he hath no pere,
To rekne alle þat write of this matere,
As in his boke ȝe may beholde and se. (Pro. 362–69)

At the end of his poem, Lydgate modestly insists that he himself is incapable of reaching Guido's stylistic heights and that he has been content to transmit only the matter of the history (5.3491–93 and 5.3540–43). In fact, Lydgate, alone among the Middle English translators of the *Historia*, not only preserves Guido's formal rhetorical passages but also expands them, and he even adds original ones of his own.

A major influence behind the fresh colors and rich flowers with which Lydgate decorates the *Troy Book* is Chaucer. Lydgate always defines himself as a follower of Chaucer, and the older poet is responsible for much that is good in the *Troy Book* as we shall shortly see; but Lydgate's rhetorical prolixity is also Chaucerian—the monk's earnest attempt to reach the high, sonorous style Chaucer introduced into English poetry. The unfortunate effect Chaucer sometimes had on Lydgate can be seen in a description of the season when the Greeks sail to the first destruction of Troy. Lydgate replaces Guido's passage (4.55–68; pp. 34–35) with an imitation of the opening of the *Canterbury Tales*, itself ultimately derived from elsewhere in the *Historia*, and the result is simply horrendous:

Whan þat þe soote stormis of Aprille,
Vn-to þe rote ful lawe gan distille
His lusty licour, with many holsom schour,
To reise þe vertu vp in-to þe flour;
And Phebus was ascendyng in his spere,
And on þe brest smote his bemys clere
Of þe Ram, ful colerik at al,
Halvynge in ver þe equinnoccial;
Whan May kalendis entre in for-sothe,
And Zephirus, ful agreable and smoþe,
Þe tendre braunchis enspireþ & doþe springe,
And euery busche is lusty blossumynge,
And from þe hil þe water is revolvid
Of snowys white, þat Phebus hath dissoluyd,
And þe bawme vapoureth vp a-lofte
In-to þe eyre of þe erbes softe,
Þe Rotis vertu, with colde of wynter hid,

Hath hool his myȝt and his force kyd,
Oute of þe erþe in erbe and euery tree
Schad in þe braunchis his humydite,
Areised only with þe sonnys hete,
And with þe moysture of þe reynes swete;
Whan siluer welles scheden oute her stremys
In þe ryuers, gilt with þe sonne bemys,
And Flora had with newe grene ageyne
Hir lyuere schad vp-on euery playn,
And nyȝtyngales, þat al þe wode rong,
Ful amorously welcomed in hir song
Þe lustry sesoun, fresche and desyrous,
Namly to hertis þat ben amerous,
And þe see is calme and blaundisching
From trouble of wynde or wawy boilyng,
And from tempest is smoþe to eskape— (1.3907–39)

The length of this passage alone suggests Lydgate's problem. Chaucer's eighteen-line sentence, a stylistic tour-de-force, becomes a lung-bursting and monotonous thirty-three lines in the *Troy Book*. The precise, sensual images of the General Prologue are submerged in murky rhetorical conventions: Chaucer's open-eyed and unforgettable nightingales, for example, are here no more than another conventional detail of spring (1.3933–36). By itself the passage is awkward, but with Chaucer's model in our ears it becomes intolerable. Lydgate's real devotion to Chaucer betrays him and proves the point he himself so often makes: in comparison with his master's poetry, his limps always behind.[5]

Such comparisons between Chaucer and Lydgate are unfair if carried very far, however, because the aims of the two are finally so different. Derek Pearsall has noted that, unlike Chaucer, Lydgate is never touched by the complexity of the human experience he narrates; instead he automatically responds to conventional stimuli by churning out the stock rhetorical response: 'it is in this realm, in the treatment of narrative as a series of "themes" for amplification, that the *Troy Book* achieves whatever significance it can be said to possess. It is when the narrative allows him to write more or less separate poems in conventional rhetorical moulds that Lydgate is at his best.'[6] Although Chaucer usually reshapes his material on all levels to create a new and greater work, as in his transformation of Boccaccio's *Filostrato* to produce *Troilus and Criseyde*, Lydgate in the *Troy Book* achieves his goal by the addition of mere surface decoration and detachable rhetorical passages. The procedure of each poet is appropriate to his chosen goal: Chaucer is writing fiction, however, historically based, and is therefor relatively free to transform or invent events and characters (the original meeting at Deiphobus's house and his complex Pandarus, for example); Lydgate

sees himself as a historian. Supplementary and obviously detachable
rhetoric may be added to make the subject more appealing, but fundamental alteration of the history is impossible.

Medieval rhetorical manuals, with their mechanical instructions for
developing a literary topic, may seem to offer little insight into the poetic
achievements of great writers like Chaucer or the *Gawain*-poet, but they
are more exact guides to the achievement of Lydgate's *Troy Book*. Pearsall
calls special attention to Lydgate's rhetorical exercises on the themes of
women and the seasons and to his passages of mythological information
and moral instruction.[7] Pearsall concludes that the poem's amplifications
'bear a strikingly close relation to the eight devices of amplification
recommended by Geoffrey of Vinsauf, in his *Poetria Nova*, or for that
matter to those of a more recent writer, Brunetto Latini, Dante's teacher.'[8]

Lydgate often expands the rhetorical passages he finds in the *Historia*
and thus continues the ornamented style for which he praises Guido and
which his own audience obviously demanded.[9] Speeches especially call
forth the monk's tendency toward rhetorical elaboration. For instance,
Cassandra's speech warning the Trojans of the ruin that Paris's marriage
to Helen will cause is formal and elevated in the *Historia* (7.465–85;
p. 79), and it is even more so in the *Troy Book* (2. 4195–239). Lydgate takes
one section of the address ('Ah, unhappy Helen, a terrible seductress
indeed, how many griefs you will produce for us!' [7.482–83; p. 79]) and
develops it thus:

> Allas, allas! I seie to þe, Eleyne,
> Vnhappy woman, causere of oure peyne,
> Hard & vnȝely, and also graceles,
> Vnwelful woman, disturber of oure pes,
> Þou haste vs brouȝt in meschef & in were,
> Kyndled a brond to sette vs alle a-fere! (2.4231–36)

This easy, mechanical expansion reveals Lydgate's limitations as a poet,
but he succeeds in adding stylistic decoration to his source without
contaminating its historical truth.

Lydgate, like the *Laud*-poet, expands Guido's passages on knights and
chivalry, but there is a difference in their interests. The *Laud*'s concern is
always battle itself, the bloodier and more violent the better, but knighthood in Lydgate's *Troy Book* is most often an occasion for pageantry and
rhetorical set-pieces. For example, the *Historia* notes the beginning of
the first formal battle in a short sentence: 'When all the battalions on both
sides had been formally set up, each side went out to the open plain to
fight' (15.194–95; p. 133). The *Laud* expands this passage: first with
descriptions of the warriors' martial equipment (4943–49), then with lines
that insist on the violence on the field (4955–63). Lydgate's expansion of
the same scene is somewhat different:

And in þis wise forþe þe Grekis goon
In-to þe feld, with pompe ful royal,
With thensygnes and tokenes marcial,
Han take her ground, passingly arrayed;
And on her stondardis, richely displaied,
Brode baners and many fresche penoun—
Ageyn þe wynde þat made a hidous soun,
And riȝt dredful, pleinly, for to here—
And þer men seie many crestis clere,
And many tuft of gold & siluer schene,
Meynt with feþris rede, white, & grene,
And deuyses wonder merueillous,
And of folkis þat wern amerous
Þe tokenes born to schewen openly
How þei in loue brenten inwardly
Som hiȝe emprise þat day to fulfille. (3.716–31)

Lydgate continues for twelve more lines that describe the trumpets
sounding for battle, the horses' reaction to them, and all the Greeks and
Trojans in their appointed places for the start of hostilities (3.732–43).
The passage in the *Troy Book* is stately and emblematic and avoids the
actual fighting. It reads more like an account of a tournament or a pageant
than the beginning of a deadly war.

Lydgate's amplifications of his source often show real intelligence and
craft, even by modern standards. The usual accusations of uninspired
prolixity and Pearsall's judgment that Lydgate expands Guido 'like a
candy-floss machine' are too harsh.[10] Amplification and rhetorical
elaboration might be more appropriate terms for what Lydgate has
accomplished, and they suggest one reason for the wide popularity
enjoyed by the *Troy Book* through the Renaissance. Ulysses's argument
that Achilles should return to the war (4.1701–1805) has been cited by
Schirmer as an example of that prolixity in the *Troy Book* which impedes
the narrative.[11] True, Lydgate's version is longer (105 lines) than the same
passage in either the *Destruction* (36 lines; 9707–42) or the *Laud* (80 lines;
13047–126), but the extra lines are not wasted. Ulysses shamelessly
flatters Achilles and warns that his great fame may be tarnished by the
withdrawal, thus effectively presenting the traditional characterization of
Ulysses as an eloquent, wily, and politic rhetorician and of Achilles as a
proud and touchy warrior, quick to take offense.[12]

Achilles's answer to Ulysses also shows Lydgate's skill. In the *Historia*,
the Greek hero ends his reply by asserting, 'I would prefer that my
reputation for valor be extinguished rather than my person. For even if
right conduct is praised sometimes, oblivion suddenly swallows it up'
(25.214–17; p. 195).[13] Lydgate expands the passage into a meditation on
worldly transitoriness, one of his favorite themes:

> I nat purpose in þis werre or strif
> For to iuparte any more my lif,
> For leuer I haue þat palled be my name
> Þan to be slayn, & han an Idel fame;
> For worþines, after deth I-blowe,
> Is but a wynde, & lasteth but a þrowe;
> For þouȝ renoun & pris be blowe wyde,
> Forȝetilnes leith it ofte a-syde
> By lengþe of ȝeris and obliuioun,
> Þoruȝ envie and fals collucioun.
> Þe laude of knyȝthod & of worþines,
> Of wysdam eke, & of gentilnes,
> Fredam, bounte, vertu, & swiche grace,
> Forȝetlines can dirken and difface;
> And, þer-with-al, malys and envie
> I-serid hath þe palme of chiualrie
> By fals report. (4.1867–83)

These lines can be criticized because the voice we hear is clearly not that of Achilles, the nominal speaker, but that of John Lydgate, rhetorician; yet the result, whatever its dramatic inappropriateness, is competently professional—an example of what Pearsall calls Lydgate's 'solemn and powerful eloquence.'[14] The *Troy Book* has few moments of great poetry but much solid craftmanship like this.

Solemnity is not Lydgate's only poetic mode, however; as a true Chaucerian he can also imitate his master's playful attitude toward the verbal 'colors' both found so important. The *Historia* matter-of-factly notes the arrival of evening on the day when Achilles first sees and falls in love with Polyxena (23.128; p. 185), but Lydgate has fun with this detail:

> Þe longe day þus went he to and fro,
> Til Phebus char lowe gan declyne
> His golden axtre, þat so cler doth shine,
> —Þis to seyne, þe sonne wente doun. (4.626–29)

Even more unexpected are Lydgate's clumsy but appealing transformations of Guido's tired anti-feminist tirades.[15] The originality of these passages shows that Lydgate is no mere mechanical translator of Guido. During his accounts of Medea and Helen, Lydgate gives what he claims are Guido's strong denunciations of women's falsity (1.2072–96; 2.3536–631), and then he insists he is sorry to have to repeat such sentiments because he himself is a defender of women (1.2097–135; 2.3555–68). One critic cites these passages as proof of Lydgate's incompetence at structuring his narrative, but, as the editor of the *Troy Book* notes, Lydgate is actually having a little misogynistic fun at Guido's expense.[16] In both instances cited above, Lydgate has actually expanded Guido's original attacks and made them more colorful. Moreover, his supposed defenses of women are often wildly exaggerated to comic absurdity. At one point, he asserts that since women are so 'good and parfyte euerchon,' he believes that not one is untrue; even though they may take new lovers, they are not to blame: women must provide for themselves if men refuse, and, since it is not fitting for them to be alone, it is not wrong if they have more than one man (1.2105–14).

Although few of Lydgate's lighter touches are totally successful, they do indicate his desire to carry on the witty sophistication of Chaucer, and they anticipate the salacious humor with which the Renaissance will treat certain aspects of the Troy story, as in Thomas Heywood's *Troia Britanica*. For example, Lydgate asserts that Jason went to Medea's bed 'to trete of som holynes' and once there practiced the rites of Venus secretly, 'not openly as ypocrites preye'; the poet then concludes that he is too 'dul for to comprehende/Þe obseruaunce of swiche religious' (1.3545–81). Not the least of the delights of this passage is to see the monk of Bury using to such comic advantage the very word (dull) that his critics have so often comtemptuously flung at him.[17]

Even some of Lydgate's most scholarly additions are laced with humor: he ends his discussion of Idolatry with the affair of Mars and Venus and their discovery in bed by Vulcan (2.5803–25). In a parody of his usual moral earnestness, Lydgate unexpectedly finds Vulcan to be the guilty party because of his violent jealousy and then offers some cheeky general advice for such situations:

> God forbede þat any man accuse
> For so litel any woman euere:
> Where loue is set, hard is to disseuere;
> For þouȝ þei don swyche þing of gentilles,
> Passe ouere liȝtly and bere noon hevines
> Liste þat þou be to wommen odyous. (2.5814–19)[18]

The mockery continues as Lydgate states that he has put Vulcan last in the list of pagan gods because of his inexcusable waking of the lovers (2.5820–25). Although Lydgate's humor, like a politician's, is welcomed more for the relief than for its quality, it does suggest that the monk is cleverer and more self-aware than is usually thought.

When we go beyond Lydgate's rhetorical set-pieces and consider the style of the *Troy Book* as a whole, we find that it is generally formal and abstract with little of Chaucer's verbal precision or the concrete imagery and narrative enthusiasm that can be found in the two other Middle English histories of Troy. The *Troy Book* rarely comes alive as literature. Nevertheless, Lydgate often adds details that clarify the vague descriptions in his source and show the seriousness with which he regarded his task of putting history into verse. For instance, Guido briefly notes the arrival of fresh Trojan troops during the Greek landing: 'The countless number of the Trojans who had not yet arrived at the battle directed themselves impetuously toward the Greeks' (14.153–54; p. 122). Lydgate's version is much longer:

> But þanne in hast, doun fro Troye toun,
> Of worþi knyʒtes freschely armyd new,
> With diuises of many sondri hewe,
> With-out abood, schortly to conclude,
> Þer cam doun so gret a multitude,
> Eche his armys depeint vp-on his schelde,
> Þat in her comyng gletereth al þe felde
> Of her armwre and þe sonne briʒt. (2.8234–41)

These lines are certainly loose and conventional, without the energy of battle description in the *Laud*, yet the added detail does allow us to visualize the scene more clearly. Later in the *Historia*, Achilles fully realizes the suffering his absence from the war is causing the Greeks when the 'tumultuous confusion' of their cries reaches his tent (26.176–80; p. 202). Lydgate's version includes an original and striking visual image: he says the sounds reached Achilles 'Of hem þat laye ageyn þe hote sonne,/With mortal woundes ʒeldinge vp þe breþe' (4.2508–09).

Lydgate also allows himself more extensive re-arrangement to heighten the impact of a scene. One example occurs during the fall of Troy. The *Historia*'s narrative gives a general description of the Greek rampage, during which 20,000 are killed, and then describes Priam's flight to Apollo's temple where he falls on the altar to await his death (30.179–200; p. 233). Lydgate's retains all of Guido's information, but he creates dramatic contrast by describing first Priam's terrible awakening and flight to the temple (4.6312–41), then the general slaughter of his subjects (4.6342–60), and finally Priam again, now at prayer by the altar (4.6361–65). The horror of this night is effectively increased by Lydgate's original bracketing of the general ruin by Priam's individual terror. The poet has modified his source only slightly, but to good effect: the importance of this scene has been impressed on his readers' memories.

Lydgate's amplifications of quieter passages to introduce more sentiment into the poem are also effective. His version of Achilles's long lamentation on the troubles he has brought on himself by falling in love with Polyxena (23.137–54; p. 185) is made more moving by the addition of many original touches (4.653–712). The return of the Trojans to the city with the body of the slain Hector is underdeveloped in the *Historia* (21.177–79; p. 175), but, because Hector is as interesting to Lydgate as he is to the *Laud*-poet, his death is commemorated in the *Troy Book* with the addition of a graceful and melancholy passage:

> And after þat, whan it drowe to eve,
> Þei of Troye, with gret reuerence

> Dide her labour and her dilligence
> Þe ded cors to carien in-to toun
> Of worþi Hector, whan Titan wente doun.
> And to þe temple dolfully þei wende;
> And of þat day þis was þe woful ende—
> I can no more—but þus þe longe nyʒt
> In heuynes, as it was skil and riʒt,
> I wil hem leue, and ageyn returne
> To my mater to help hem for to morne. (3.5412–22)

This selection of verses will have convinced no one that Lydgate is a great poet, nor is that my intent. The *Troy Book* is most valuable for its non-literary qualities—Lydgate's moral and intellectual concerns which will be discussed below—but we must not neglect the work's solid craftsmanship and the rare but genuine moments of good, effective poetry.

The Classical World in the Troy Book

Another class of additions in the *Troy Book*, more interesting than these strictly rhetorical elaborations, contains original passages of classical material.[19] Much of this is simply Lydgate's desire to show off how much he has read, but some of his additions have a more serious purpose. Chaucer taught Lydgate to see the classical past as different and distant from his own time, and the monk, in his turn, desires to create a believable picture of the ancient world for his readers. The *Troy Book* reveals the beginnings of a genuine sense of historical perspective that is not found in any of the other Middle English histories of Troy.

   Although Lydgate's direct knowledge of classical literature is not as impressive as his many references to it would suggest (most of his Vergilian material, for example, seems to have come from Chaucer), Schirmer correctly asserts that he was 'widely read' and possessed 'a degree of learning which was remarkable for his time.'[20] The monk is certainly proud of what he knows of the ancients and never misses an opportunity to display his erudition. The *Destruction* and *Laud* both begin with Christian prayers, but the *Troy Book* opens with long invocations to Mars, Othea (supposed goddess of Prudence), and the Muses (Pro. 1–68). Such displays of learning again show Lydgate to be the most like Guido of the three Middle English historians of Troy: he supplements the *Historia* with classical material as Guido himself had supplemented Benoît; the other historians, whatever their actual knowledge, rarely stray beyond what is provided in the source.

   In his study of the minor sources of the *Troy Book*, E. Bagby Atwood

concludes that Lydgate's direct classical knowledge comes principally
from Ovid, who is also Chaucer's favorite.[21] The *Metamorphoses*
especially provides Lydgate with information such as Iphigenia's role in
the sacrifice to Diana at Aulis (2.6215–37) and additional details about the
pagan deities added to Guido's digression on idolatry (2.5559–825).
Atwood shows that Lydgate also used medieval authorities for classical
information: Isidore of Seville and Fulgentius (or, more probably, one of
the later mythographers) contribute to descriptions of the pagan gods and
to the Judgment of Paris. Atwood finds no influence of Benoît, Dares, or
the other English translations of Guido in the *Troy Book*, but he thinks it
likely that Lydgate knew Statius's *Thebaid*. Other scholarly information
in the *Troy Book* has been shown to come from contemporary sources like
Jacobus de Cessolis's *De Ludo Scaccorum*, or John Trevisa, and later I will
demonstrate the influence of Christine de Pisan's *L'Epistre Othea*.[22] The
Troy Book also contains evidence of Lydgate's knowledge of the past that
need not be assigned to a specific source. Guido's brief reference to Brutus
prompts the monk to mention Silvius and the giants from whom Britain
was won (1.831–36); and while describing Priam's rebuilding of Troy, the
poet modestly insists he lacks the proper terms because he never read
Euclid: 'Þat þe maister and þe foundour was/Of alle þat werkyn by squyre
or compas' (2.554–56). This list of minor sources shows the relatively
scholarly nature of the *Troy Book*, yet what Atwood says about Ovid is true
for all of Lydgate's classical additions: 'Lydgate's borrowings from Ovid
are nearly always in the nature of added details; that is, very rarely do they
tend to modify or contradict the narrative of Guido.'[23] As with his
rhetorical additions, Lydgate's intent is to fill out the *Historia* and renew
it for his audience, while being careful to preserve its historical
authenticity.

Chaucer is the most important influence on all aspects of the *Troy Book*,
and he contributes much to its account of the ancient world.[24] Lydgate
adds Chaucer's mythical Lollius to his list of writers on Troy (Pro. 309),
calls Guido's Briseida Criseyde, and twice describes Penthesilea as the
Queen of Femynye (4.3759, 4070), a title not in the *Historia* but taken
from the *Knight's Tale* (A 866, 877). Chaucer's influence also goes beyond
this kind of minor and superficial detail. He taught Lydgate a new way of
seeing the past. In a pioneering study, Morton W. Bloomfield has argued
that Chaucer, especially in his later works, reveals a genuine 'sense of
history' that is an important element of his art.[25] Bloomfield shows that a
new concern with history—a greater attention to past, present, and
future—arose in the fourteenth and fifteenth centuries, and is demonstrated in '(1) a more accurate sense of chronology and (2) a sense of
cultural diversity.'[26] Chaucer's sense of history, seen especially in his
treatment of the past, is developed far beyond that of most of his contemporaries and is often highly sophisticated, according to Bloomfield.
Troilus and Criseyde, for example, contains passages that reveal a genuine

appreciation of historical development and cultural variety (e.g., 2.29–49), and throughout the poem Chaucer deliberately plays with the differences between past and present time and culture.[27]

My intent here is to demonstrate that Lydgate had read Chaucer carefully and that he understood the older poet's achievement in creating a sense of history. In the *Troy Book*, Lydgate also strives to present a believable picture of the ancient world, although he does not exploit the differences between past and present to create the complex dramatic and thematic tensions achieved by Chaucer. The monk's practice is more mechanical and in keeping with his other additions to the *Historia*: he limits himself to self-contained passages which remind the reader that he is being told about ancient events.[28] What I am suggesting is far from the usual view: Renoir describes the *Troy Book* as overwhelmingly hostile to classical antiquity, especially to its poets and religion, and Pearsall notes Lydgate's 'contempt' for pagan religious practices which causes the narrative to wither.[29] Lydgate is certainly not soft on paganism, but he has more interest in its customs and greater respect for them than has been recognized. Of course, by any objective standard the *Troy Book* is a thoroughly medieval work and its picture of the ancient world no more historically accurate than Chaucer's, but it is futile to judge the efforts of either by modern standards. Every age views the past through the filter of its own beliefs and practices so that its histories, when read by a later generation, tell us more about the time in which they were written than about the past. Therefore we must try to understand Lydgate's achievement from the perspective of his own era. Although no modern reader would be convinced, Lydgate makes great efforts to give contemporary readers the sense that the Trojan War took place in an ancient and alien culture. This special effort to create a convincing ancient world is clearly seen in comparison with the two other English translations of Guido. The *Destruction* contributes nothing to the *Historia*'s sense of history, and the *Laud Troy Book* adds the most specifically medieval elements to Guido's work without any sense of anachronism.

Some of the classical decoration that appears in the *Troy Book* is not uncommon in Middle English literature. Many dawns are associated with Phoebus and Aurora (e.g., 3.1–18; 3.3097; 3.3313; 3.3324; 3.4894; 4.1655; 4.2050; 4.2422), and Antropos claims more than one doomed warrior (e.g., 3.966–67; 4.2401–23; 4.4270–86). Helen's grief for Paris is compared to that of other classical ladies who loved and lost (4.3654–79), and the general sorrow at Troilus's death leads Lydgate to insist that even Boethius, Statius, and Ovid—famous for the descriptions of the sorrows of such as Niobe, Oedipus, and Dido—could not have done justice to the city's woe (4.3008–45). This is the sort of superficially learned decoration found throughout late medieval poetry, but Lydgate's careful descriptions of ancient secular customs are exceptional.

In his account of the rebuilding of Troy, Lydgate describes Priam's organization of knightly tournaments (2.789–97). Since today we know these are medieval activities, the lines may at first seem another example of the naive chronology of the Middle Ages; but the learned opinion of Lydgate's time held that knighthood had begun under Jupiter and Saturn, who were regarded as historical kings of Crete (Lydgate refers to this belief at 2.789–800). Moreover, Lydgate's statement that knighthood, far from being a Christian institution, was dedicated in both Troy and Crete to the honor of Mars (2.790–92; 2.800) must have given the audience of the *Troy Book* a powerful sense of the different culture of Troy. Similarly, after describing the knighting of Pyrrhus with golden spurs, 'As was þe maner' (4.4005), Lydgate insists on the ancient nature of the ritual: 'Like þe custom of þe Grekis lawes/And þe rytis vsede in þo dawes' (4.4009–10).

In his account of the rebuilt Troy, Guido notes the opinion of some that comedy and tragedy were first performed in the city (5.192–94; p. 49). Lydgate elaborates this single sentence with the traditional definitions of the two genres (2.845–59), and he then adds a remarkable passage, based on the informed opinion of his day, describing the manner in which ancient tragedy was 'rad or songyn':

> In þe theatre þer was a smal auter
> Amyddes set, þat was half circuler,
> Whiche in-to þe Est of custom was directe;
> Vp-on þe whiche a pulpet was erecte,
> And þer-in stod an awncien poete,
> For to reherse by rethorikes swete
> Þe noble dedis, þat wer historial. (2.863–69)

After discussing the theme of Fortune in the tragedies, he returns to the performance of the poet:

> And whil þat he in þe pulpit stood,
> With dedly face al devoide of blood,
> Singinge his dites, with muses al to-rent,
> Amydde þe theatre schrowdid in a tent,
> Per cam out men gastful of her cheris,
> Disfigurid her facis with viseris,
> Pleying by signes in þe peples siȝt,
> Þat þe poete songon hath on hiȝt. (2.897–904)

We are then told that the actors mimed the actions and emotions of the poet's words exactly (2.905–16).[30]

Throughout his description, Lydgate stresses the non-medieval nature of these performances. The poet is 'awncien' and, though he reads from a pulpit, it is pointed to the East 'of custom.' The heroes win the laurel of Mars before their lives are ended by the Parcae and particularly by Antropos (2.873–80). For our purposes, it is not necessary to discover

Lydgate's immediate source for these lines or to wonder if tragedy really did begin at Troy! We should simply recognize that Lydgate has gone to a great deal of trouble to create a scene that could not fail to give his audience a sense of historical distance and impress them with the strangeness of ancient customs.

Later in the *Historia*, Achilles tries to convince the other Greeks that the war is folly. He argues that Helen is just not worth all the trouble, and he advises Menelaus and the Greeks to forget her: 'Obviously there are in different parts of the world many noble women from whom King Menelaus can choose not just one but two or more for a wife' (24.95–97; p. 188). In the *Troy Book* the speech is considerably changed by the addition of a passage on marital law that has no support in the *Historia*. Achilles first advises Menelaus to choose another wife and then continues:

> Siþen þat he, with-oute gilte or synne,
> May be þe law from Eleyne twynne:
> For of dyvos causis ben y-nowe,
> Poruȝ-oute þe worlde of euery wiȝt I-knowe,
> Of avoutri for þe foule vice.
> For to lawe is no preiudice,
> Pouȝ Menelay iustly hir for-sake,
> Whan so hym list, and anoþer take
> Pat shal him bet boþe queme & plese. (4.1049–57)

This passage so annoys the editor of the *Troy Book*, Henry Bergen, that he scolds Lydgate for having the cheek to pretend to a historical sense: 'Thus for some unknown reason Lydgate, to whom like most old writers anachronisms meant nothing, forsakes Canon for Roman law.'[31] Lydgate, of course, was aware of the Church's grounds for divorce, or annulment as it is now called, but here he is trying to describe the customs of pagan Troy. The passage is a good example of his strengths and weaknesses in portraying the ancient world. Although his knowledge is faulty and his identification of past eras imprecise (he seems to equate the practices of classical Rome with those of Troy), he does provide his audience with a description of laws, and thus a civilization, totally different from his own. Bergen's outrage proves that Lydgate is usually blamed for his modest successes as well as for his faults.

Bloomfield notes that in the *Knight's Tale* Chaucer reveals his awareness of cultural diversity between past and present by his use on at least three occasions of the clause 'as was tho the gyse' or a similar phrase.[32] Such phrases are also common in the *Troy Book* and are especially important because, in the author's own voice, they clearly draw attention to the antiquity of the history. Chaucer's use of distancing phrases in the *Knight's Tale* is almost always in reference to pagan religious ceremonies, but Lydgate, with no support in the *Historia*, uses them for

secular customs as well. When Ulysses and Diomedes come to Troy as
ambassadors, Lydgate explains at some length that, although they had not
made previous arrangements, they were not refused entrance:

> For þo dayes paraunter was nat vsid
> To haue no conduit for embassatrie;
> Þe custom was to no man to denye,
> As I suppose, entre nor passage,
> Ʒif it so wer he come for massage. (2.6746–50)

Elsewhere, Guido describes a silver image given to Jason by Medea,
'which she said was constructed by means of binding spells and by virtue
of great craft,' (3.146–47; p. 26). Lydgate's version, in addition to a
reference to astrology, carefully explains the antiquity of these images:

> for ful longe a-goon is,
> Whilom whan þei were flouryng in her ages,
> Þat þei vsede to make suche ymages,
> As dide þe kyng called Tholome. (1.3006–09)[33]

The historical perspective of the *Troy Book* is perhaps more obvious in
a second group of additions that describe paganism and its rites. Lydgate's
increased appreciation of the past does not mean that he is more
sympathetic to false religion: Guido's discussion of idolatry in Book 10 is
considerably expanded in the *Troy Book* (2.5404–940), and Lydgate adds a
totally original passage that curses each of the classical gods by name
down to Naiads, Dryads, Satyrs (4.6930–7035). These changes have two
effects: the falseness of paganism is given more stress, but so is the reality
of the gods (by euhemerism) and the evidence of their worship in the
ancient world.[34]

Lydgate's changes in the *Historia*'s many descriptions of funeral rites
provide the clearest illustrations of his attempt to create a believable
classical world in the *Troy Book*.[35]

The burials of Achilles and Paris are good examples of his method. In
both cases, Guido, perhaps reacting against the ornate and historically
suspect descriptions in the *Roman de Troie*, ignores the ceremonies and
insists that it would be superfluous and impede the narrative to describe
the tombs (27.63–64, 173–75; pp. 208, 211). The *Destruction* briefly
describes the tombs of Achilles (10583–85) and Paris (10780–83), and notes
that the latter was buried 'With Sacrifice and solenité suche as þai vsit'
(10786). In accord with the general tone of his poem, the *Laud*-poet adds
the kind of splendid detail often found in medieval romance, with a
special emphasis on rich decoration. The sepulchre of Paris:

> A tombe was made of precious stones,—
> To lay him In, bothe body & bones,—
> Off riche werk, of fair facture:

> Off saphires, gold, & riche asure;
> Hit was richer then other fyue;
> I may not al the werk discryue,
> Ne halff the richesse that ther was on
> Off riche gold & precious ston. (15881–88)

The *Laud*'s description of Achilles's tomb is even longer (15505–18); but in neither of these accounts is there even a hint, like the brief one in the *Destruction*, of ancient, pagan rites.

Commenting on these two passages in the *Troy Book*, Derek Pearsall claims they are two instances in which Lydgate's use of the brevity-topic indicates genuine shortening: 'both [passages] concern pagan burial rites, in which Lydgate takes a good deal less interest than Guido.'[36] But Pearsall is wrong, perhaps because he has not compared the *Troy Book* with the *Historia* (Guido does not mention pagan rites at all at this point), or perhaps because his judgment is based on what Lydgate says he is doing and not on what he does do in fact. Concerning the burial of Paris (4.3722–35), Lydgate claims he cannot fully present 'al þe ritis and þe guyse/Þat þer wer made in her peynym wyse' (4.3729–30) nor 'Her peynym ritys supersticious' (4.3735). The important point to note here is that Lydgate has changed the focus of the passage, which in the *Historia* dealt only with the tomb, so that it now concerns pagan rites. Although Lydgate claims to neglect these rites, the phrases he uses in his dismissal draw attention to the ancient, non-Christian nature of the ceremonies.

Lydgate takes a similar approach in his account of Achilles's burial, and here also his claimed omission concerns funeral rites while Guido just refers to the tomb. With the rhetorical device of *occupatio* so effectively used by Chaucer, Lydgate insists he will not give all the details of the ceremony, but he then proceeds to describe at length, with stress on their antiquity, the rites he will be unable to tell us about (4.3251–61). Although it eliminates the humor, this passage is almost certainly based on the account of Arcite's funeral in the *Knight's Tale* (A2882–966)— another poem that is set in ancient times and strives to create a sense of historical distance and cultural diversity.

We have seen how carefully Lydgate modified his source in order to present a convincing picture of the ancient world, and yet the final effect of this very real achievement is not entirely successful. Even in his own era, a few men—like Petrarch—demonstrate a feeling for the past that makes Lydgate's efforts seem crude and unsophisticated.[37] Although he is no antiquarian, Chaucer uses his sense of historical perspective as an element in poetry whose complexity is far beyond anything produced by the monk of Bury. Lydgate's inability to equal his master does not, however, mean that he could not understand him. Unfortunately, Lydgate was forced by circumstances to exercise this knowledge in poetry, a form in which his talents, as he continually reminds us, were modest. In happier times, he would, I think, have made an excellent scholar and could have lectured well on Chaucer. Nevertheless, his achievement, however limited, is real: Lydgate understands Chaucer's sense of history and works hard to include the same perspective in his Trojan poem. If he does not equal the accomplishments of Renaissance historians, he at least anticipates them, and we must honor his ambition. In this case, Lydgate's additions, far from being mindless examples of prolixity, represent a serious and systematic effort to make the ancient world understandable to his readers.

Lydgate's Historical Fidelity

Although Lydgate has some understanding of the new historical perspective that would become one of the intellectual achievements of the Renaissance, his basic view of the historian's job is more limited. Like the other Middle English translators of Guido, he sees his task as preserving the eyewitness truth of the *Historia*—getting right all its facts and details. The care which Lydgate takes to transmit the factual truth of his source has been insufficiently recognized and, when recognized, misinterpreted. Style is never allowed to interfere with truth, and nothing essential to the history is omitted in the *Troy Book*; its additions are also superficial. At whatever cost to his poetic success, Lydgate is determined to retain all the historical matter of Guido's *Historia*. This fidelity is for him the mark of the true historian.

In a review of Alain Renoir's book on Lydgate, Jerome Mitchell claims that a 'glance at [Guido's] *Historia Troiana* suffices to show that [Lydgate] was not honor-bound to translate everything in his source.'[38] The imprecision of this statement makes it technically correct (Lydgate does not, of course, translate *everything*), but a second glance will show how diligently the monk labored to preserve the material of the *Historia*. Nevertheless, even those who are prepared to recognize Lydgate's fidelity often ascribe it only to incompetence. Pearsall complains that while it is common for medieval authors to claim that they are following their source exactly, the 'difference with Lydgate is that in his case the statements are true, for he makes no attempt to re-order or re-interpret the narrative, no new "sens" of the old "matiere," nothing remotely approaching Chaucer's reappraisal of the Troilus story.'[39] Elsewhere Pearsall concludes that Book 3 of the *Troy Book* is 'something of a disaster' because of its interminable battles, though he wearily accepts that this must be so: 'It is against Lydgate's nature to omit anything.'[40] Yet this is unfair. Lydgate's commitment to history, not his nature or inferiority to Chaucer, is the cause of his fidelity. The monk believes that his job is to keep alive the factual truth of the past:

But thoruȝ writyng þei be refresched newe,
Of oure auncetrys left to vs by-hynde;
To make a merour only to oure mynde,
To seen eche thing trewly as it was,
More bryȝt and clere þan in any glas. (Pro. 166–70)

In the prologue to the *Troy Book*, Lydgate insists that he will follow the *Historia*, 'as nyȝe as euer I may' (Pro. 375), and in general he keeps his word. His few reductions are inconsequential and usually consist of information that has nothing to do with the war itself, such as Guido's discussions of Mediterranean geography. More reduction than elsewhere occurs in Book 5, where Lydgate admits that his great task has exhausted him ('For almost wery, feint & waike I-now/Be þe bestes & oxes of my plow' [5.2927–28]), but nothing essential to the history is lost and even here an addition is possible: Thetis's speech begging Pyrrhus to spare her father is longer and much more emotional in the *Troy Book* than in the *Historia* (5.2568–76). The story of Troilus and Criseyde suffers some reduction, but Lydgate resists the temptation to eliminate a portrait of Criseyde, even though he says she has been described better by Chaucer:

And but I write [the portrait], I mote þe trouþe leue
Of Troye boke, and my mater breue
And ouer-passe and nat go by and by
As Guydo doþ in ordre ceryously. (2.4687–90)

The omissions and reductions that occur sporadically throughout the *Troy Book* are all like the ones just discussed: they are few, they form no pattern, and they are not the result of any consistent purpose. In no way do they compromise Lydgate's fidelity to the *Historia*.[41]

Lydgate's additions to the *Historia*, as we already know, are more extensive than his reductions, but they also do not affect the substance of the history. The monk's added rhetorical, moral, and learned passages almost always have some basis in the *Historia* and, like Guido's own additions to Benoît, they are usually detachable from the factual narrative itself. Lydgate's practice of decorative addition is not a sign of his automatic prolixity or carelessness; instead it is a conscious principle of translation in the *Troy Book*.[42] We will remember that in the prologue, Lydgate describes Guido's achievement in the *Historia* and thus defines the ideal of history writing toward which he himself strives. Guido, he says, is faithful to the substance of the true history received from Dares and Dictys— '& cast hym nat transmwe/In al the story a worde as in sentence' (Pro. 356–57)—yet Guido is also free to exercise his 'passyng excellence' of style in literary adornment:

For he enlvmyneth by crafte & cadence
This noble story with many fresche colour

Of rethorik, and many riche flour
Of eloquence to make it sownde bet. (Pro.362–65)

Even Lydgate's constant and general expansion of the *Historia*, a line-by-
line amplification resulting from both his famed prolixity and stylistic
ambition, does not make him unfaithful to Guido. Battle scenes are often
expanded in the *Troy Book* because, as Lydgate several times states
directly, he finds Guido's accounts too general and lacking in detail (e.g.,
3.3596–98; 4.2586–88; 4.4262–64). In fact, Lydgate does not usually add
the missing detail, he simply repeats Guido's information using more
words. For example, Guido's brief description of one part of a battle
(17.34–39; p. 152) is expanded into twenty-two lines by Lydgate (3.2792–
813). Nothing has really been changed except the space used. Here and
elsewhere, Lydgate's narrative remains as distant and abstract as Guido's
original, without the precise visual imagery found in the *Destruction* or
the *Laud*'s crude enthusiasm.

Expansion of non-battle scenes in the *Troy Book* is no more purpose-
ful. Guido, describing a certain council called by Priam, says merely,
'When they had come and were standing before him . . . ' (18.8; p. 155).
Lydgate expands this thus:

And whan þei wern to his paleis come,
Þis lordis han þe riȝte weye nome
Vn-to þe kyng, with-Inne his closet;
And whan þe hussher haþ þe dore shet,
And eueryche hadde, liche to his degre,
His place take, and his dewe see. . . . (3.3117–22)

This is no improvement or real change; it is simply meaningless
prolixity—and faithfulness to Guido. Here as throughout the *Troy Book*,
Lydgate takes the obvious in his source and makes it even more obvious.
At the beginning of his eight-year labor, he had vowed to follow Guido as
closely as he was able, and in the final book he humbly announces that his
task is complete. He has no more Latin to translate

After Dites, Dares, nor Guydo,
And me to adden any more þer-to
Þan myn auctours specefie & seyn,
Þe occupacioun, sothly, wer but veyn,
Lik a maner of presumpcioun. (5.3361–65)

For all his rhetorical ambitions and original moral and learned passages,
Lydgate, like the other Middle English historians of Troy, never betrays
his basic devotion to the complete historical record of Troy.[43]

The moral lessons of the *Troy Book* have long been recognized as a distinctive feature of the poem, but their importance tends to be exaggerated. Walter Schirmer describes the poem as 'a historical work containing all the moral and political lessons which history was expected to teach,' and John Studer claims that 'Lydgate takes every opportunity to draw a moral from his story and frequently thrusts one into it: In a word, he has *moralized* the story of Troy.'[44] These conclusions are misleading because they fail to indicate how superficial, *ad hoc*, and contradictory Lydgate's lessons are, and how secondary they remain to the factual record. Studer's claim that 'at times, the narrative is no more than a framework of moral instruction' ignores the monk's devotion to the history.[45] Lydgate's moral lessons, like his rhetorical and learned additions, are important as his special contribution to the received material; they make up his poetic *style,* but they always remain separate and detachable from the factual narrative itself, which contains the historical *substance.*

Lydgate's frequent lessons are never original or complex. One large group contains no more than the poet's automatic responses to certain traditional situations; these are similar to the proverbial lessons in the *Historia* but are usually more elaborately developed. Guido condemns the terrible sin of avarice in priests while describing Antenor's corruption of the one who guarded the Palladium (30.39–47; p. 229). Such a lesson probably had a special appeal to the monk of Bury, and he expands this passage (translated by the faithful *Destruction* in 14 lines [11768–81] and totally missing in the *Laud*) to 59 lines (4.5833–91). Often it seems that almost anything will trigger Lydgate's moralizing, no matter how inappropriate the occasion.[46] During his account of the rebuilding of Troy, Guido briefly mentions one of the city's inventions: 'games of dice which lead suddenly to quarrels on account of the unexpected losses and momentary profits of the little cubes' (5.190–92; p. 49). Lydgate is inspired to turn this into a much longer sermon on the vicissitudes of gambling (2.828–41). More appropriate, but similarly mechanical, is a long, original set-piece on Ire and Anger (2.1067–94), called forth by Priam's first thoughts of revenge against the Greeks and begun in Lydgate's highest declamatory style:

> O hatful harm, whiche most is for to drede!
> Kyndled so long, o spark of old hatred,
> Rote of debate, grounde of envie and Ire,
> With newe flawme hertis for to fyre! (2.1067–70)

Lydgate's specifically political lessons are also quite conventional and serve to decorate the historical narrative rather than subject it to any very searching analysis. Pearsall says that the poet offers good advice, but 'it is all too general to be any more than a public expression of private morality' and 'far too commonplace to have any particular topical import.'[47] V. J. Scattergood similarly refers to the advice in the *Troy Book* as 'decent, sensible and commonplace.'[48] Thus Lydgate expands and recommends the generosity shown by Aeëtes ('he þat was of fredam a merour') in welcoming the Argonauts to Colchis (1.1345–73) and by Agamemnon in distributing the booty plundered at Tenedos:

> For who þat can with larges first be-gynne,
> Ne failleþ nat after wel to spede
> Þoruȝ help of men, whan þat he haþ nede:
> For loue folweþ fredam comounly. (2.6496–99)

Negative political cliches also appear as Lydgate solemnly warns against such evils as Envy and Discord (e.g., 3.2342–54; 4.4502–37). These lessons are perfectly proper, generosity is a good thing in a ruler and discord bad for his realm, but they have as little practical application as Guido's proverbial advice. The lessons in the *Historia* can only be applied in retrospect, while Lydgate's invoke a general moral ideal (do the good and avoid the bad) that is both impossible to achieve completely and of dubious efficacy.

What lessons the *Troy Book* does offer are, like those in the *Historia*, not allegorizations; they arise instead from the literal story itself. For example, the poet follows Guido in blaming Paris for the rape of Helen because it is wrong to steal another man's wife; he does not, however, turn Helen into a symbol of Worldly Delight whom Paris desires at the peril of his immortal soul. Such an allegorization is possible for Lydgate in another kind of work—it is, in fact, the interpretation of Paris's action he presents in *Reson and Sensuallyte*—but it would not be appropriate in the *Troy Book*. Similarly, Lydgate does not use the rape, as Gower does in the *Confessio Amantis* (5.7579–90), as only one of many illustrations of a certain wrong (sacrilege) which itself is only a small part of a systematic treatment of all seven deadly sins. For Gower's purposes a different episode would do almost as well as Paris's raid, but Lydgate is committed first to the historical narrative, not to the morality. The rape of Helen is a crucial episode in the whole history of the Trojan War, and he provides the moral lesson only in passing.

If Lydgate does not allegorize the history, neither does he exploit England's Trojan heritage in any special way. Renoir finds a 'violent nationalism' pervading the *Troy Book* 'from beginning to end,' which causes Lydgate to present the Trojans as if they can do no wrong.[49] Lydgate certainly cheers on the Trojans, and especially Hector, while denigrating the Greeks, but he is not as consistently one-sided or passionate as Renoir's observation suggests. The monk frequently points out what he considers to be the faults of Priam and Hector, some of which are not in his source, and he adds a long passage early in the work in which

Jason contrasts the dishonorable refusal of Laomedon to allow the Argonauts to land at Troy with the noble hospitality the Greeks would offer in a similar situation (1.1036–78). Even more revealing is Lydgate's refusal to draw contemporary moral lessons for England from the story of its ancient ancestors—a common device in medieval English literature as witness Gower's *Vox Clamantis*.[50] Although Lydgate is aware that Britain was founded by Trojans—he translates Guido's reference to it (1.832–36) and even earlier describes Henry V as ruler of 'Brutys Albyoun' (Pro. 104)—in the *Troy Book* the connection is only a historical fact and not an excuse for claiming that Troy has special moral advice to offer its descendants.

Because the moral lessons in the *Troy Book* are disconnected, not part of an over-all scheme or interpretation but particular responses to individual events, they easily fall into self contradiction. Pearsall notes that Lydgate's condemnation of the falseness of men to women goes oddly with earlier attacks on the falseness of women and that the poet both approves and scorns dependence on popular opinion,[51] but the greatest contradiction in the *Troy Book* is the poet's attitude to the story itself. The war is a comfortable subject for the *Laud*-poet, and he glories in its action and brutality, but Lydgate's response is more ambiguous. The contradiction between Lydgate, peace-loving monk, and Lydgate, court poet for Henry V (who, we are told, deserves the palm of knighthood 'For worþines and for hiȝe victorie,/As thou þat art drad on se & lond' [Lenvoy. 16–17]) is never resolved. As a monk, Lydgate sincerely hates war and argues that the story of Troy leads one to pacificism. Schirmer notes the poet's 'deeply ingrained love of peace' and discusses these added passages of anti-war sentiment.[52] Lydgate's hatred of war is found throughout the *Troy Book*; two speeches, an early one in which Priam argues that peace is to be preferred over fighting (2.1243–70) and a late one in which Achilles tries to persuade the Greeks to end the war (4.960–1134), are much expanded in the *Troy Book*. One of Lydgate's longest additions in support of peace is an elevated condemnation of Mars for the murder, treachery, and total ruin he has brought to Troy (4.4440–537). The work ends with hope that 'cruel Mars shal no more manace' and that Henry V will bring peace between England and France (5.3399–442).

Yet these admirable sentiments do not completely square Lydgate the court poet. The *Troy Book* is full of chivalric pageantry, and the poet adds or expands accounts of feasting, weapons, armor, and battle itself. More confusing still are his presentations of the warriors as heroes worthy of imitation. Hector is the poem's chief ideal, and, although his prudence and virtue are constantly stressed (e.g., 2.237–56) and contrasted to the cruel violence of Achilles, he is also described as the mightiest and most deadly fighter at Troy (e.g., 2.8487–96). Moreover, though he elsewhere criticizes Priam's rashness and eagerness for revenge, Lydgate turns Guido's factual description of the new king besieging a castle (5.49–53;

p. 44) into an admiring portrait of his knightly exploits in which 'liche a conquerour' he strives to win 'worschip and honour' (2.208–30). Lydgate's confused attitude toward war can be seen again in the figure of Mars. The god is condemned for the ruin he brings to Troy, but he is also more respectfully invoked at the beginning of the poem (Pro. 1–37): 'Now help, o Mars, þat art of kynȝthod lord,/And hast of manhod the magnificence!'

Although Lydgate keeps and expands Guido's proverbial advice, no trace remains of the *Historia*'s deep pessimism. Instead of Guido's despair before the extent of human ignorance, instead of his laments that all men are helpless puppets of fate who must inevitably fall to the forces of chaos and violence, Lydgate offers a facile optimism based on a simple material justice. At the end of the *Troy Book*, Lydgate argues that the lesson of his poem is that all is transitory and unstable on this earth ('Be exaumple of Troye, like as ȝe may se,/Þat in þis lif may haue ful surete'), and thus one should trust only in Christ (5.3544–92).

In the narrative itself, however, he often takes a more worldly view. For example, to Guido's factual description of Achilles's death, Lydgate adds several passages that gloat over the ignoble end of Troy's greatest enemy and find it a clear and uncomplicated working out of justice:

> And riȝtfully, of resoun as it sit,
> Þus was þe fraude & þe falshede quit
> Of Achilles, for his hiȝe tresoun:
> As deth for deth is skilfully guerdoun
> And egal mede, with-outen any fable,
> To hem þat be merciles vengable. (4.3195–200)[53]

At many other places in the *Troy Book*, Lydgate adds original passages in which he describes the hand of God intervening directly in human affairs to punish wrongdoing: for example, sacrilege (5.674–80) or adultery and murder (5.1142–47 and 5.1467–87).[54] Prudence is the most consistent lesson taught in the *Troy Book*, yet, here again, Lydgate's concern is practical not spiritual. Those who are prudent will succeed in this world, but those who practice willfulness (for instance, Laomedon and Priam) must inevitably fail (e.g., 2.73–142; 2.1243–94; 2.1797–899; 3.1303–22; 4.4606–722).

Willard Farnham long ago found this same kind of 'crude moral didacticism' in a later work by Lydgate, his *Fall of Princes*.[55] In the *Fall* also Lydgate argues that vice is punished and virtue rewarded—not abstractly or in the terms of Christian salvation, but through material prosperity or ruin on this earth. Farnham demonstrates that the *Fall* uses the 'simplest and most materialistic formula of tragic justice,' and, though the work is an important, if clumsy step toward Elizabethan Tragedy, that it contains no sense of the complexity of human guilt.[56] We can now see that Lydgate expresses this same conception of direct justice as early as the *Troy Book*, yet it does not there achieve even the limited success that Farnham finds in the *Fall*. The *Fall of Princes* is fundamentally a moral work, designed to be a mirror for princes, and is thus free to choose and shape its stories in support of didactic ends. In contrast, the *Troy Book* is restrained by its commitment to Guido's true historical record. One of the reasons the moral lessons just discussed appear so intermittently in the *Troy Book* is that not many of its stories can be made to reveal a justice of any kind. Lydgate is a compulsive moralizer, but his respect for history kept him from adjusting events to produce morals in the *Troy Book*, and few of his additions go much beyond simple literary decoration.

Fortune in the Troy Book

Lydgate's special approach to the history of Troy is shown in miniature by his use of Lady Fortune. In this figure, we see Lydgate's learning and his tendency to decorate the history with rhetoric and moralization. Alone among the Middle English historians of Troy, Lydgate personifies the vague and malignant *fata* and *fortuna* of the *Historia*, and he also adds many original references to the goddess of chance. These additional passages, like his moral lessons, reveal the monk's attempt to find order and meaning in the story of Troy, though the result is once again relatively superficial and even contradictory. Norton-Smith's comments on the *Fall of Princes* are also true for the *Troy Book*: 'The poet's insights into the concept of Fortune and human motivation are inconsistent and eclectic. They are scarcely combined into an intelligible pattern.'[57] As another critic notes, Lydgate is a prime example of those minor medieval writers who become 'obsessed' with the theme of Fortune and then 'fall prisoner to it.'[58]

We can distinguish three views of Fortune in Lydgate's *Troy Book*. One sees the goddess as little more than chance, a view close to the historical pessimism found in Guido's *Historia*, and Lydgate frequently expands such passages from his source. The 'envious course of the fates,' which, 'for no cause,' impels Laomedon to turn away the Argonauts in the *Historia* (2.7–15; p. 11), becomes a personified picture of random Fortune in the *Troy Book*:

> For sche was cause, God wotte, causeles,
> Þis gery Fortune, þis lady reccheles,
> Þe blynde goddesse of transmutacioun,
> To turne her whele by reuolucioun
> To make Troyens vniustly for to wene
> Þat Grekys werne arived hem to tene.
> So þat þe cause of þis suspecioun
> Hath many brouȝt vn-to destruccioun. (1.753–60)

The poet makes it clear here that the Trojans are not themselves to blame for the subsequent evils since all comes about 'for no þing but þat Fortune wolde/Schewen her myȝt and her cruelte' (1.776–77).

Lydgate reinforces Guido's pessimistic view of Fortune with original passages of his own that stress the random fickelness of the goddess's actions. When he comes to Troilus's death, the poet declares:

> whan Fortune haþ a þing ordeyned,
> Þouȝ it be euere wailled and compleined,
> Þer is no geyn nor no remedie
> Þouȝ men on it galen ay & crye. (4.2683–86)

The same helplessness before irrational Fortune is expressed at the death of Ajax (4.3502–09). Lydgate's longest original discourse on Fortune, prompted by the destruction of Laomedon's Troy, is equally despairing (2.1–72). Fortune is called the 'false lady of transmutacioun,' and her actions are shown to be as fickle as those of Chaucer's Fame (2.31–46).

Lydgate is not entirely satisfied with the random Fortune he inherited from the *Historia*, however. The English monk is a practical, optimistic moralist and cannot long sustain Guido's blind determinism. Instead, he searches the story for useful remedies against the goddess and her power. At one point, Guido notes that 'hearing of the adverse fortunes of other men is pleasing and delightful' (6.27–28; p. 57). This worldly insight is replaced in the *Troy Book* by a more practical sentiment that reveals much about the monk: the story of Troy's fall will be pleasant to those who hear it, says Lydgate, because 'be example þei may be war & lere' (2.1890). In short, there are useful lessons to be learned. Therefore, in addition to Guido's view of Fortune as irrational and irresistible, the *Troy Book* also contains more moralistic conceptions of the goddess. In an original passage discussing Medea's growing love for Jason, Lydgate insists that Fortune attacks only the unwise: this false lady of transmutation 'enhasteth þinges to foolis ful greable' that afterward cause their ruin (1.2258–62). A few lines later, the poet repeats his view that only fools are Fortune's victims:

> As sche þat can with a benigne eye
> Fully of folis parforme the entent,
> Wher-þoruȝ þei be in gret meschef schent
> At þe ende, and can no crafte teschewe
> Þe vnwar harme þat at hir tail doþ sewe— (1.2266–70)

In this view, Fortune is still irrational, but not omnipotent—she controls only those who commit themselves to her. The result is a simplified version of the *Consolation of Philosophy* in which Boethius learns to despise Fortune because, though she controls all worldly things (even partial goods like fame), her gifts are unstable. When Priam decides to revenge his injuries on the Greeks, Guido laments the 'unhappy quirk of fate' which incites him, but admits that 'these impulses are not in the control of man' (6.8–12; p. 56). Lydgate's version is less resigned. We should, he insists, learn from the 'example of Priamus' (2.1879) not to trust in Fortune: 'Perfor, no man haue noon affyance/In Fortune, nor in hir variaunce' (2.1873–74). Disaster does not come to the Trojan king by chance, rather it occurs because he deliberately chose to submit himself to the unstable goddess:

> For sothly, Priam, þou wer to rekeles,
> For to comytte þi quiete and þi pes,
> So dredfully, duryng by no date,
> To cruel Fortune or to fikel fate;
> Whos maner is, of costom comounly,
> Þat whan a man trusteth most souereynly
> On þis goddesse, blind & ful vnstable,
> Þan sche to hym is most deceyueable. (2.1857–64)

Elsewhere in the *Troy Book*, Lydgate adds other passages that present Fortune as a more optimistic force. Here she is not to be feared as uncontrollable, nor despised as worldly, but seen as the simple working out of divine justice in earthly, material terms. In these additions, Lydgate insists that fortune is a rational force used directly by God to punish the wicked and reward the good—in short, men get exactly the Fortune they deserve. Pickering notes that this conception becomes influential in the Renaissance, and it is certainly an example of the 'crude moral didacticism,' which Farnham sees as Lydgate's contribution to Elizabethan tragedy.[59] Whatever its historical importance, this third depiction of Fortune, which C. S. Lewis calls 'common to vulgar Pagans and vulgar Christians alike,'[60] fits oddly with the other presentations of the goddess in the *Troy Book*, and is a good example of Lydgate's irrepressible efforts to find moral lessons in the history.

This optimistic view occurs in a virtually original passage during which Agamemnon, after recalling the injuries that Fortune with her 'cher fraward & dowble countenaunce' (4.3272) has done the Greeks, continues on to insist that satisfaction lies within the power of the Greeks themselves:

> Now semeth me þat it shal be sene
> Ʒif any manhod in ʒoure hertis be,
> Or knyʒtly force, in aduersite
> For tendure by vertu of sufferaunce,
> Til of his deth ʒe take may vengaunce,
> And manly quyte þis outragous offence,
> Whan tyme cometh to make recompence. (4.3278–84)

Here Fortune is seen to be neither hateful nor irrational, but the true measure of a man. Such a conception goes against both Boethius and

Guido, of course; it removes the latter's pessimism and elevates what the former considers to be false goods of Fortune into man's final aim. As with some of his other moral lessons, Lydgate's advice concerns the achievement of material prosperity and success rather than genuine virtue or Christian salvation.

Throughout the *Troy Book*, Lydgate seems to want to replace Guido's pessimism with practical advice on how to win good fortune for oneself, but his success is incomplete. A final attempt to sum up the lessons of the *Troy Book* contains each of Lydgate's three views of Fortune in succession with no suggestion that the poet himself is aware of any confusion.[61] He begins by claiming that the history shows the changeability and irrationality of Fortune: 'in her cours mutable,/Selde or nat feithful ouþer stable' (5.3547–48). This is essentially Guido's view, which emphasizes the goddess's random malignancy ('Many worþi causyng for to dye' [5.3560]) and finds nothing but uncertain wretchedness in human life:

> For þer is nouþer prince, lord, nor kyng,
> Be exaumple of Troye, like as ȝe may se,
> Þat in þis lif may haue ful surete. (5.3576–78)

Then Lydgate moves on to a second view, which is his version of Boethius's remedy against Fortune in the *Consolation of Philosophy*. Do not put your faith in worldly things, he cries, but trust only in Christ:

> Þerfore, to hym þat starf vppon þe rode,
> Suffringe deth for oure alder goode,
> Lyfte vp ȝoure hertis & þinke on him among. (5.3579–81)

However, it soon becomes clear that this is no call to the devout and ascetic life. Christ is to be relied on not because he brings salvation or true spiritual happiness, but because he has immediate, practical control over Fortune:

> For be ȝe neuere so myȝti nor so strong.
> With-oute hym al may nat availle;
> For he can ȝif victorie in bataille
> And holde a felde, shortly to conclude,
> With a fewe ageyn gret multitude. (5.3582–86)

This is Lydgate's third view of Fortune: she is the agent through which God punishes the wicked and rewards the good in simple, material ways: he makes 'worþi kynges for to regne longe,/And tirauntis sodeynly oppresse' (5.3588–89). Before ending with prayers for the success, on earth and heaven, of his patron, Henry V, Lydgate expresses sentiments that would comfort any man who is prosperous in the world. Fortune is not random or wicked, but just: 'in his hond power [God] reserueth/Eche man taquite liche as he disserueth' (5.3591–92).

Lydgate's contradictory views of Fortune seem to come in part from his inability to accept Guido's pessimism and in part from his genuine prolixity; he always values the number of examples over their compatibility. We must always remember, however, that Lydgate's primary concern in the *Troy Book* is historical accuracy. Although the temptation to moralize is constant with him, such impulses are never allowed to distort the historical record; they always remain supplementary and decorative, lacking consistent principle but testimony to Lydgate's familiarity with a wide range of conventional sentiments.

Prudence and the Death of Hector

Lydgate's attempts to counter Guido's pessimism are clearly seen during one of the most significant moments in the medieval history of Troy: the death of Hector. This episode shows Lydgate at his best as poet, historian, and moralist. Without significant change of the facts in his source, he effectively uses his learning to give the event meaning. As an antidote to the random and destructive forces of *fortuna* and *fata* inherited from the *Historia*, Lydgate advocates the virtue of prudence. The death of Hector in the *Historia* is merely a chance of war, but Lydgate, relying on Christine de Pisan's *L'Epistre Othea*, gives Hector a fatal moral flaw—and he thus provides the reader with an explanation of the tragedy.[62]

The *Epistre Othea*, subtitled *L'Epistre Othea de deesee que elle envoya a Hector de Troye quant il estoit en l'aage de quinze ans*, was written by Christine de Pisan in about 1400 and includes one hundred classical stories, each presented in three parts.[63] The first part, the Text, is a four-line narrative that is the actual letter of Othea, supposed goddess of Prudence, to Hector; the second part, the Gloss, elaborates and explains each episode in prose and then provides a practical lesson for the knight supported by a quotation from a philosopher; the third part, the Allegory, concerns 'goostli knyghthood' (the soul's fight against the Devil [cf. pp. 7–8]), and it draws the spiritual significance of the story with quotations from Scripture and a Doctor or Father of the Church. Unlike Guido and Lydgate, Christine is not writing ancient history or even telling a story; instead she is part of the allegorical tradition of Troy, and the brief classical narratives serve merely to justify the religious lessons, her real concern. The one hundred Texts are isolated episodes and have little narrative or chronological continuity, but the Allegories follow sequences that illustrate the Seven Deadly Sins, the Ten Commandments, and the like. The allegorical level so dominates the literal that Christine is able to use the story of Vulcan's discovery of Mars and Venus to point an unusual moral: 'þe good spirit schuld kepe him from þe watches of þe feende' (p. 70). The popularity of the *Epistre* in England is indicated by the three independent translations produced before 1550.

In addition to its specific influence on the death of Hector, to be discussed shortly, the *Epistre* affects the entire *Troy Book* and seems responsible for the poem's emphasis on the value of Prudence. Lydgate's first invocation is to Mars; his second is to Christine's creation. 'Othea, goddesse of prudence,/This wirke texsplyte that ʒe nat refuse . . .' (Pro. 38–39). Moreover, the value of Prudence—one of the four cardinal virtues Christianity took over from classical antiquity and added to the three theological virtues—is Lydgate's most important practical lesson in the poem. He modifies his source to stress that the specific fault of both Laomedon in expelling the Argonauts and Priam in seeking war with Greece is a willfulness that ignores prudence (1.957–58; 2.1797–899). During most of the poem, Hector is the complete opposite. Repeatedly portrayed as the paradigm of all chivalric virtue (e.g., 3.480–91),[64] his special virtue in the *Troy Book* is his unshakable prudence (e.g., 2.1129–37; 2.2231–33). All suddenly changes just before his death. Like the author of the *Laud*, Lydgate gives special emphasis to Hector throughout his poem, but for the monk Priam's eldest son is a moral exemplar as much as a military hero, and so it is natural that the cause of the hero's death is found in a moral failure.

Although Hector is Troy's greatest champion and his death foredooms the city, Guido's account of his end is surprisingly brief:

> Hector in the meantime had rushed upon a certain Greek king, had seized him and was trying to drag him in captivity away from the troops. He had cast his shield over his back so that he might more easily snatch the king away from the troops. For this reason he displayed his unprotected chest in battle since he lacked the defense of his shield. When Achilles realized that Hector did not have the protection of his shield over his chest, he took a very strong lance, which Hector did not observe, and rushed upon him and wounded him mortally in the abdomen, so that he fell dead from his horse. (21.165–73; p. 175)

In the *Troy Book* the same passage is expanded to a full sixty-eight lines (3.5332–99). Lydgate begins its version with a long, original description of the Greek king's armor that stresses its bejewelled splendor and richness (3.5334–43): 'Of whos array, whan Hector takeþ hede,/Towardis hym faste gan hym drawe' (3.5344–45). Hector does not take the king prisoner, as in the *Historia*, but immediately slays him (3.5346); the Trojan then carries the body away 'To spoillen hym of his riche array' (3.5352). The plundering is an addition in the *Troy Book*, although earlier Guido had stressed Hector's desire for the armor of the dead Patroclus (15.212–17; p. 134).[65] To drive home Hector's lapse, Lydgate departs from the narrative to present a short sermon against covetousness that begins in his best rhetorical style: 'But out! allas! on fals couetyse!' (3.5354–72). Hector's desire for booty is seen as undermining the chivalric ideals of which he is usually the exemplar:

Þe etyk gnaweþ be so gret distresse,
Þat it diffaceth þe hiȝe worþines,
Ful ofte sythe, of þies conquerours,
And of her fame rent aweie þe flours.
Desyre of hauynge, in a gredy þouȝt,
To hiȝe noblesse sothly longeth nouȝt,
Nor swiche pelfre, spoillynge, nor robberie
Apartene to worþi chiualrye:
For couetyse and knyȝthod, as I lere,
In o cheyne may nat be knet y-fere;
For kouþe it is, þat ofte swiche ravyne
Hath cause ben and rote of þe ruyne
Of many worþi—who-so liste take hede—
Like as ȝe may now of Hector rede,
Þat sodeinly was brouȝt to his endynge
Only for spoillynge of þis riche kyng. (3.5357–72)

At first glance, we would seem to have another example of Lydgate's crude moralism, his belief that history shows the good are rewarded and the wicked punished in simple, material ways. Hector has sinned and so he must die. Nevertheless, this particular event is actually presented with unusual felicity and logic. Hector's greed is not punished directly or from above; it simply makes him careless. In order more easily to spoil the dead warrior, Hector 'reklesly' casts his shield on his back and thus provides Achilles with an opportunity to attack (3.5373–82). Lydgate laments this foolishness on the part of a knight who had previously symbolized prudence and discretion: 'Allas, why was he þo so rekeles!/þis flour of knyȝthod, of manhood pereles' (3.5383–84). Hector's failure to live up to his ideals costs him his life.

Lydgate's discovery of a moral failure in Hector in no way excuses his slayer. Later in the *Historia*, Achilles is blamed for the cowardly attack on Hector, but in the death scene itself Guido shows only his manly resolve to avert the Greek rout by killing Hector or dying in the attempt. The *Troy Book*, however, describes Achilles's efforts to conquer Hector by craft. In an original passage, 'cruel and venemous' Achilles lies in wait for Hector until, driven by hate and envy, he sees a chance 'couertly' to slay him (3.5385–95). Lydgate adds a lament to his source that underlies the tragedy to Troy of Hector's loss (3.5423–502). Once again, and despite his fatal lapse, Hector's surpassing chivalric excellence is stressed (3.5468–74).

Little critical attention has been paid to this episode in the *Troy Book*, and none of it recognizes what Lydgate has done. Hinton discusses only the sermon against covetousness and finds it an example of Lydgate's mindless moralizing: the sermon 'jars with his characterization of Hector as the "flour of chiualrie," of course, but what a chance to give Prince Hal a moral lesson!'[66] Renoir considers the scene another instance of Lydgate's preference for the Trojan champion over the Greek. The death 'is presented as practically accidental,' and the bias is clear: 'Whereas Hector is the hero, Achilles is definitely the villain of the affair.'[67] The essential similarity of the two scenes in the *Historia* and *Troy Book* may explain these failures to note Lydgate's changes. Despite the general truth of Renoir's argument, in this scene Hector is not completely chivalric, but displays a flaw that causes his death. Hinton's reading also misses the point. Far from contradicting the portrait of Hector as the 'flour of chiualrie,' Lydgate's sermon on covetousness attempts to explain his death in terms of chivalric ideals. Lydgate is not satisfied with Guido's presentation of the death as a meaningless act of war. His desire to go beyond the simple pessimism of his source and to find a coherent explanation for the tragedy leads him to Christine's *Epistre* and to her Othea, supposed goddess of Prudence.

The episodes that concern Hector's death (LXXXVIII–XCII) are the closest the *Epistre* comes to sustained and continuous narrative. LXXXVIII describes Andromache's vision of Hector's impending death; although LXXXIX concerns Babylon, the lesson sets the tone for Hector's death by arguing against trust in the protection of the world; XC shows Hector ignoring Andromache's warning; XCI and XCII portray the fatal outcome. In the Text of XCI, Othea tells Hector to avoid death by keeping his arms about him in battle. The Gloss, which presents the practical lesson, reinforces this message: 'it is seyde to the good knyght that he shulde not in batayle be discouered of his armes. For Hermes seyeth þat deeth farith as the strok of an arowe and lyf fareth as an arowe sette to shotte' (p. 110). This passage may have caused Lydgate to give greater emphasis than Guido to the recklessness of Hector in his last battle (3.5373–83). The Allegory presents the spiritual lesson of the episode: 'the good spirite shulde kepe his wittes cloos and not voyde' (p. 110). Lydgate, however, refuses to follow the *Epistre* this last step; he has no interest in providing a Christian message not directly connected to the literal meaning of the narrative.

The next section, XCII, deals with the death itself. The Text and Gloss explain that Hector is killed because his covetousness offers Achilles an opportunity to attack him unarmed. The following is the Gloss in its entirety:

> Polibetes was a ful myȝti king, þe which Hector slowe in þe bataile aftir many othir greet deedis þat he hadde doon þat day. And because þat he was armyd wiþ faire armys & riche, Hector coveited theim & stouped doun vppon his hors necke for to dispoile þe body. And þanne Achilles, þe which suwed aftir him with hole will to take him discouerte, smote him beneþe for faute of his armure & at a strook killed him, of whom it was greet harme for a worþier knyȝt was nevir girde wiþ swerde of

þe which þe stories makiþ mencion. And þat such couetises
may be noyous in such places, it shewith bi þe seid caas.
Therfore þe philozophre seith: Disordinat covetise ledeth a
man to deeth. (p. 111)

The Allegory draws the spiritual lesson of the incident: 'þe good spirit
shoulde haue no covetise to no maner of worldly thing' (p. 111). We are
told that Innocent III says that 'covetise is as a fire þat may not be
staunchid,' for the covetous man is never satisfied, but always desires to
have more: 'Euer he setteþ his ende in as myche as that he tenteth to haue
more and not to that þe which he hath' (pp. 111–12). Thus: 'Covetice is þe
wey to þe goostly deeth and ofte tymes to bodily deeth. Therfore þe apostil
Seint Paul seith: Radix omnium malorum est cupiditas' (p. 112).

This section has obviously contributed much to the death of Hector in
the *Troy Book*. Lydgate has replaced the prisoner in the *Historia* with
Christine's account of Hector plundering a slain king's rich armor, and
the poet attributes Hector's death to the covetousness found in the
Epistre. The praise of Hector's worthiness and the description of Achilles'
stealth, both in the Gloss to section XCII, have inspired similar passages
in the *Troy Book*. Nevertheless, Lydgate is careful not to destroy the
historical validity of his principal source. In both the *Historia* and *Troy
Book*, the story is essentially the same: Hector dies because he puts his
shield on his back in order to deal with a captured Greek king, giving
Achilles an opportunity to ambush him. Both works, unlike the *Epistre*,
omit the name of the Greek king, specifically mention Hector's misplaced
shield as permitting Achilles's attack, and describe Hector as leading the
captive away from battle rather than dealing with him in the press.
Lydgate thus uses the *Epistre* primarily to provide an explanation of the
Historia's historical facts, but he does not significantly change them.

Although Lydgate borrows from the *Epistre*'s Gloss on the death of
Hector, he rejects its allegorization as inappropriate for a historical work.
The Allegory to XCII stresses the insatiability of covetousness, and while
Lydgate does touch on this quality in his sermon, his main argument is
that covetousness defaces chivalric honor (3.5357–69). Christine's
Allegory, as we have seen, uses Hector's desire for the dead king's armor
to argue the broader moral that one should not covet any wordly thing.
Covetousness is said to cause 'goostly deeth' as well as 'bodily deeth.'
Ignoring abstract and spiritual allegorization, Lydgate will only go as far
as the Gloss and show that covetousness like Hector's may be 'noyous in
such places.' Lydgate's concern is history and knighthood, not Christian
salvation; he does not examine the state of Hector's soul or its possible
'goostly deeth', but he limits himself to arguing that Hector's failure to
live up to the ideals of chivalry causes his physical death. Although the
Epistre is in a different tradition from the *Historia* and the *Troy Book*,
Lydgate shares its celebration of prudence as a chivalric virtue, and

Christine's concern with spiritual knighthood may have influenced his own idealistic, if secular, conception of that vocation. More importantly, Lydgate uses the *Epistre* to provide an explanation for Hector's tragic death without subverting the historical truth, as he saw it, of Guido's *Historia.* In the *Troy Book,* Lydgate attempts to balance at least four roles: historian, rhetorician, scholar, and moralist. In most cases, the first of these roles is performed at the expense of the other three, but during the death of Hector all are successfully combined to satisfy the reader both dramatically and intellectually. During this important moment in his history, Lydgate's ambition and ability are one.[68]

PART THREE

THE LITERARY TRADITION

VI

The History of Troy in Middle English Poetry

Episodes from the medieval history of Troy are found throughout Middle English literature, though these are usually brief and mixed with material from other traditions. John Gower's *Confessio Amantis* is a good example. Material about Troy is only part of the *Confessio*, and of those stories that do concern the city, some are from the *Historia*, while others are taken from classical sources or from medieval allegorizations of myth like the *Ovide Moralisé*.[1] For Gower, the medieval history of Troy is only one of many sources of information to be used in his moral history of the world. A significant appearance of the historical tradition occurs at the beginning of *Sir Gawain and the Green Knight*. Alfred David has argued convincingly that the traitor mentioned in lines 3–4 ('Þe tulk þat þe trammes of tresoun þer wroȝt') is Aeneas himself, and this identification has also been made by Norman Davis.[2] If so, the poet is referring not to the *pius* hero of the *Aeneid* but to the Aeneas in the medieval history of Troy, who, along with Antenor, betrays the city to the Greeks.

A purely romance tradition that deals with the story of Troy also exists in Middle English literature. *The Seege or Batayle of Troye*, which survives in four quite different versions in as many manuscripts, is a popular, exciting story that provides some revealing contrasts to the medieval history of Troy.[3] The *Seege or Batayle* claims Dares as its ultimate source, but much has been changed and added. We can read Guido's *Historia* and its three Middle English translations side-by-side and find the basic historical material virtually the same in each, despite differences in style and approach. The case is far different with the *Seege or Batayle*. Its source appears to be some version of the Latin *Excidium Troiae*, but if we read that work along with the four Middle English romances very little is alike from text to text. Clearly, none of these poets feels any obligation to preserve the factual truth of his source, but each, like an Arthurian romancer, adapts the given material with great freedom. In contrast, the author of the *Laud Troy Book*, who apparently wished to appeal to the same popular audience, never goes so far as to compromise the historical accuracy of his material. It is ironic that, although many elements of the classical story of Troy not in the *Historia* are found in the *Seege or Batayle*, in the Middle Ages only the tradition from Guido carries the weight of authority. The *Seege or Batayle* might be entertainment for the common folk, but its crude, unlearned approach disqualified it from claiming the attention of any serious audience.

Chaucer's Troilus and Criseyde

Troy is the principal subject of one undoubted masterpiece in Middle English—Chaucer's *Troilus and Criseyde*. Although the medieval history, contributes much, the *Troilus*'s great achievement is possible only because Chaucer feels under no obligation to reproduce the history accurately or in full. Because he uses it only selectively, he avoids the sheer bulk of factual material which oppresses and eventually over-whelms each of the Middle English translators of Guido. Chaucer also has no hesitation in contaminating the historical record with his own pseudo-historical additions or with material from the non-historical tradition. Nevertheless, he expects his readers to know the complete history of Troy, and he manipulates that knowledge to create and deepen the tragedy of the lovers. Benoît's *Roman de Troie* seems as much a source for the *Troilus* as does Guido's *Historia* (another indication that Chaucer does not take the role of historian too seriously), but the Latin work has a much greater influence on the *Troilus* than has previously been recognized. Guido's primary gift to the Middle English historians is simple fact, but he provides Chaucer with more: a distinctive way of seeing and presenting the history of Troy. Although the *Historia* contributes relatively few details to the plot of the *Troilus*, Chaucer seems to have found much that he could use in other, less superficial aspects of the work—especially its deep pessimism and unusual narrative stance.

Chaucer as Historian in the Troilus

It has become a critical commonplace that much of the effect of *Troilus and Criseyde* comes from the narrator's presentation of himself as a historian.[4] To we who are fresh from considering the faithful translators of the *Historia*, this idea comes as something of a surprise. In the *Troilus*, Chaucer is certainly not a historian like Lydgate or the authors of the

Destruction and *Laud*. The narrator makes it clear early in the poem that he does not intend to reproduce the whole history of Troy. For that he refers the curious reader to more complete authorities:

> But how this town com to destruccion
> Ne falleth naught to purpos me to telle;
> For it were here a long disgression
> Fro my matere, and yow to long to dwelle;
> But the Troian gestes, as they felle,
> In Omer, or in Dares, or in Dite,
> Whoso that kan may rede hem as they write.[5]

The 'matter' of the *Troilus* is but a limited part of the full history, only the love story, as Chaucer tells us again at the end of the poem:

> And if I hadde ytaken for to write
> The armes of this ilke worthi man,
> Than wolde ich of his batailles endite.
> But for that I to writen first bigan
> Of his love, I have seyd as I kan,—
> His worthi dedes, whoso list hem heere,
> Rede Dares, he kan telle hem alle ifeere. (5.1765–71)

To create the *Troilus*, Chaucer drew on many works that are not part of the historical tradition; this material is not merely decorative or supplemental, as in Lydgate's *Troy Book*, but occupies the very center of the poem. Chaucer's principal source is, of course, Boccaccio's *Filostrato*, itself a self-proclaimed personal and not a historical work.[6] The poet's most extensive additions to Boccaccio are from Boethius's *Consolation of Philosophy*; he also uses Ovid and, much less, Vergil—two writers specifically identified by Guido as good poets but untrustworthy historians. To take one example, Chaucer depends on Ovid for the story Pandarus tells of Paris's love affair with Oenone (1.652 ff.), an amatory episode during Paris's career as a shepherd described in the *Heroides* but entirely ignored by Guido. In order to reinforce themes in his narrative, Chaucer also includes material that directly contradicts the medieval history. In the *Historia*, Calchas deserts to the Greek side before the war, while at Delphos to discover from Apollo who will win (10.268–300; pp. 98–99). Chaucer, however, follows the story in Boccaccio and has Calchas leave from Troy itself during the war (1.64–91). He obviously feels under no obligation to give the 'historical' truth, even on such an important matter, because Calchas's departure from the city creates an effective parallel with Criseyde's later going over to the Greeks. Yet, even here, the medieval history seems to have some effect; Chaucer stresses more than Boccaccio that Calchas's foreknowledge comes from an 'answere' of his god who is called 'Apollo Delphicus.'

Despite his differences from the medieval historians of Troy, Chaucer works hard in the *Troilus* to *seem* like a historian, and he succeeds in giving the story a historical plausibility and depth not found in the *Filostrato*. Boccaccio's Troy is not very convincing as an ancient locale and is used primarily as a transparent disguise under which he can write about his personal affairs. The *Troilus*, however, reveals that 'sense of history' identified by Bloomfield, which Lydgate attempts to imitate in his *Troy Book*.[7] Again and again Chaucer insists that his is an old and true story and that, like the Middle-English historians of Troy, he is inventing nothing but is instead scrupulously reproducing an ancient, authoritative author. Much of this is a deliberate literary pose, which Chaucer manipulates for complex effects, but the *Troilus* does seem to have been accepted in its own time as genuine history, at least by some. Elsewhere I have shown how the anonymous author of the brief prose *Sege of Troy* on one occasion deserts his principal source, Lydgate's *Troy Book*, to follow Chaucer's account of Calchas.[8] It is even possible, and I think quite likely, that the *Troilus* was the actual inspiration for the three Middle-English translations of Guido that have been the major subject of this study. The *Destruction of Troy* and the *Laud Troy Book* both seem to have been written within a few years of the *Troilus*, perhaps as specific responses to Chaucer's challenge to turn to Dares and Dictys for the full story of Troy: 'Whoso that kan may rede hem as they write' (1.147). Lydgate, whose debt to the *Troilus* is acknowledged throughout, admits that the ability to read Dares and Dictys was limited in England. King Henry accordingly commissioned the *Troy Book*:

> By-cause he wolde that to hyȝe and lowe
> The noble story openly wer knowe
> In oure tonge, aboute in euery age,
> And y-writen as wel in oure langage
> As in latyn and in frensche it is. (Pro. 111–15)

For all his knowledge and use of the medieval history of Troy, Chaucer handles it freely. In a study of the sources of *Troilus and Criseyde*, Karl Young demonstrates how frequently Chaucer supplements Boccaccio with historical details from Benoît and Guido.[9] Yet even though these additions are of great importance to the poem, they are rarely scrupulous or exact. The *Troilus* contains little sustained historical narrative and gives only the illusion that it is reporting history. Troilus's military exploits as described by Pandarus to Criseyde (2.190–203) and the account of his triumphant ride after routing the Greeks (2.612–44) read like descriptions in Benoît or Guido, but both are actually Chaucer's inventions. The *Troilus* has sometimes been called the first novel; in its use of the medieval history of Troy, however, it is most like a historical novel— factual events provide the background but not the substance of the poem. There is no reason to doubt that Chaucer shared the contemporary belief in the medieval history of Troy, but he does not let this get in the way of producing a great poem. Chaucer seems to have relied on Benoît more than on Guido for material about Troy, though the two are often so close that it is impossible to tell which is the source for any single episode; Benoît's spectacular romance and the sober Latin history are interchangeable for his permissive purposes.[10]

Chaucer has no intention of producing a history of the entire Trojan war; but he does expect the reader to be familiar with the history, and he manipulates that knowledge to deepen the experience of his poem. Although it remains in the background and does not overwhelm the principal story, the war permeates the *Troilus*, as it does not the *Filostrato*, even during the height of the love affair. In a speech for which there are only hints in Boccaccio, Pandarus, while first trying to help the love-struck Troilus, pretends to believe that fear of the Greek siege has brought on his care: 'God save hem that biseged han oure town,/That so kan leye oure jolite on presse,/And bringe oure lusty folk to holynesse!' (1.558–60). Likewise, when Pandarus, trying to whet his niece's curiosity, tells Criseyde that he knows something that will make her happy, her immediate response is: 'Now uncle deere, . . . telle it us,/For goddes love; is than thassege aweye?' (2.122–23). Even later, ready to be summoned to Pandarus's house to meet Criseyde, Troilus has an excuse prepared in case he is missed. He is waiting at Apollo's temple for the god 'to telle hym whan the Grekes sholden flee' (3.544).

Chaucer's use of the history of Troy goes beyond mere setting or authenticizing detail: it helps to create the mood and moral of his poem. John McCall has shown how the love story and the war are made parallel in the *Troilus*: 'Chaucer adapted the tragedy of Troy as a suitable background for the tragedy of Troilus, and . . . he made the characters, careers and fortunes of the two parallel and even analogous.'[11] When the love story prospers, references to the war are positive or fade out altogether, according to McCall, but as fate catches up with Troilus and Criseyde we are again reminded of the unhappy destiny of the city. The turning point for both foreground and background action is the exchange of Criseyde for Antenor: 'The change of the city's fortune, which comes with the capture and exchange of the traitorous Antenor, is simultaneously the occasion for the change of Troilus' fortune and an anticipation of Criseyde's betrayal.'[12] We can extend McCall's valuable argument and assert that the reader who knows the medieval history of Troy will find that Chaucer uses it to anticipate future events and to produce a sense of inevitable doom even at the happiest moments. An apparently casual statement that Criseyde 'fairer was to sene/Than evere were Eleyne or Polixene' (1.454–55) reminds the reader familiar with the *Historia* of the disasters these two women brought on the men, Paris and Achilles, who loved them. In Book 3, when Pandarus tells Troilus that his meeting with Criseyde has been arranged, the happy knight vows to be true with this asseveration: 'And if I lye, Achilles with his spere/Myn herte cleve' (3.374–75). The statement is made unselfconsciously by Troilus, but the effect is chilling to those who have read Guido. This is exactly the terrible end that is soon to meet the exuberant lover.

Guido's *Historia* is, of course, an odd work to propose as a major influence for Chaucer since modern scholarship has insisted for almost seventy years that its contributions to the *Troilus* amount to no more than a few minor details.[13] But there is something strange here. Chaucer certainly knew Guido well: he calls him one of the upholders of Troy in the *House of Fame* and uses the *Historia* as his principal source for the tale of Medea in the *Legend of Good Women*.[14] In addition, Chaucer is much more interested in the history of the war than Boccaccio, and he supplements the *Filostrato* with Benoît, Ovid, the rather obscure Joseph of Exeter, and even Theban material from Statius.[15] Since he makes such wide use of these other writers, we may well ask why he apparently chooses virtually to ignore the standard history of Troy, even though it was familiar to him. I believe that because modern scholars have not really understood Guido, they have failed to recognize his important contributions to *Troilus and Criseyde*. I suggest that Chaucer did understand the *Historia* and, whether it was actually before him or only in memory (I suspect the latter), he saw possibilities for his poem in Guido's historical pessimism and distinctive narrator.

Chaucer's Debt to Guido's Historia

In addition to the general influence on the *Troilus* of the medieval history of Troy (most of which probably came from Benoît's *Roman de Troie*), Chaucer owes a large, special debt to Guido delle Colonne's *Historia Destructionis Troiae*. I do not claim that the *Historia* is a source in the usual and most superficial sense of that term. Chaucer is not indebted to Guido for a plot or a certain number of lines; the process is deeper and more subtle. The *Historia* gave Chaucer a way of looking at the story of Troy and some suggestion on how to write about it.

In recent years, no character in Chaucer's *Troilus and Criseyde* has stirred more interest than its disembodied narrator. Talbot Donaldson has described his double role as historian and participant, and Morton Bloomfield shows that one source of the tensions in the *Troilus* is this same duality: 'an historian who knows the outcome in conflict with his sympathies as an artist and man.'[16] Chaucer had experimented with narrative voices before, but in the *Troilus* he breaks fresh ground. His previous narrators are unprepossessing characters lost in strange dreams who, while physically present in the story, have little understanding and only limited emotional involvement. The narrator as historian is a new development and so is his intense, often frantic concern for the characters and their fate. Despite the importance and originality of this complex figure, however, no one has yet explored his origins. I suggest that the beginnings of Chaucer's narrator in the *Troilus* can be found in Guido's *Historia* and that the deep pessimism which informs his history exerted a strong and unrecognized influence on Chaucer's tale of Troy.

It will be useful here to review briefly the conclusions reached in our study of Guido in the first chapter. We found that the *Historia* contains a series of emotional laments, far different from anything in Benoît, in which the narrator does not assess blame or discover ultimate meaning but is reduced to weeping before the human ignorance and impotence revealed in the history. These laments are possible only because of the narrator's distant, historical perspective; he knows the end of the story. A fundamental pessimism concerning man's ability to foresee the consequences of any action results from the conflict between the ignorance of his characters and the narrator's own omniscience. In the *Historia* there is no sense of God's guiding hand or any other logic to be found in the ruin and carnage of the Trojan War; instead the vague and malignant forces of *fata* and *fortuna* hold sway. Given such a story, the only lessons Guido's narrator dares to offer are conventional proverbs—truisms which beg rather than solve the questions raised and which, like his laments, are possible only because he sees the outcome of events. Faced with Troy's tragic history of human ignorance, Guido's narrator is helpless to offer more than tears or proverbs.

Turning to Chaucer's *Troilus*, we find a similar narrator, one who also sheds tears and who claims his very verses weep as he writes (1.7). The narrator in *Troilus* so involves himself with the love story that at one point he wonders why he has not sold his soul for one such night of bliss (3.1317–20), and in the last two books he repeatedly defends Criseyde while sharing the sorrows of Troilus. Alternatively, Chaucer's narrator, like Guido's, finds objective fact a refuge from the pain and complexity of his material. Near the end of the *Troilus*, as Donaldson has shown, the historian's voice is suddenly present in the formal portraits of Diomedes, Criseyde, and Troilus (5.799–840), as well as in the flat, precise account of Hector's death (5.1548–61).[17] The double perspective of the narrator is clearly seen just after Troilus, helped as always by Pandarus, finally embraces Criseyde. Chaucer quickly moves from intimate involvement to historical and bookish objectivity and back again:

> Criseyde, which that felte hire thus itake,
> As writen clerkes in hire bookes olde,
> Right as an aspes leef she gan to quake. (3.1198–1200)

In only three lines the narrator has twice crossed the expanse of time and space that separates him from his story. Effects like this were undreamt of by the plodding Guido. Nevertheless, the basic design is fully present in his *Historia*: a narrator who looks back through time and agonizes over disasters as they begin to unfold for characters whose stories have, in fact, ended centuries ago.

The *Troilus* and the *Historia* share other stylistic similarities. Chaucer seems to have adapted Guido's use of proverbs to his more complex purposes in the *Troilus*. According to B. J. Whiting, 'Chaucer uses a greater proportion of proverbs and sententious remarks in the *Troilus* than in anything else he wrote.'[18] Most are uttered not by the narrator after the fact, but by the baffled characters themselves. Yet the effect is similar, Chaucer like Guido uses proverbs to show how little man can know.

Perhaps the greatest user of proverbs in the *Troilus* is Pandarus. Chaucer's Pandarus is at the center of the *Troilus*, and he is radically changed from Criseyde's pale cousin in Boccaccio. He is a man of action, an arranger who uses language to manipulate others. He is full of plans and advice, but, like his proverbs, his wisdom is superficial and dangerously relative. Proverbs, like analogies, do not by themselves, prove anything, as the use of them in Guido shows, but Pandarus applies them as universal laws. In Book One, he quotes two versions of 'A fool may often guide a wise man' (1.630 and 635) to get Troilus to accept his advice; in Book Four he repeats the saying, 'A new love drives out the old' (4.415, 422–24, 427) to convince Troilus that he will soon forget Criseyde. Both proverbs may be true in some circumstances; in the *Troilus* neither is ever true. Pandarus's views on a number of subjects are contradictory, as Charles Muscatine has shown;[19] he ignores consistency and grabs whichever argument or proverb most helps him at the time. Chaucer's other characters do likewise. Criseyde convinces herself to dare to love Troilus with the proverb 'he which that nothing undertaketh,/No thyng acheveth' (2.807–08), but opposes Troilus's plans to prevent her going over to the Greeks with the opposite sentiment: 'hastif man ne wanteth nevere care' (4.1568).

This transfer of proverbs to the characters themselves creates a powerful tragic effect because they, unlike Guido's narrator, cannot look back at a completed story and apply the appropriate truism. Instead, events that mock their wisdom and activity overtake them: 'thi proverbes may me naught availle' (1.756), says Troilus to Pandarus early on, and time proves this so. In his last, pitiful scene, Pandarus realizes that all his ingenuity has come to naught. 'My brother deere, I may do the no more' (5.1731), he admits to Troilus; and then, finally, 'I kan no more seye' (5.1743). They are his last words in the poem.

Despite differences of style and aim, Guido and Chaucer find the same pessimistic lesson in the history of Troy: man is fundamentally ignorant and unable to foresee the consequences of his actions.[20] This theme appears early in the poem, just before Troilus's scorn of lovers is transformed into hopeless subjection to Criseyde:

> O blynde world, O blynde entencioun!
> How often falleth al the effect contraire
> Of surquidrie, and foule presumpcioun;
> For kaught is proud, and kaught is debonaire.
> This Troilus is clomben on the staire,
> And litel weneth that he moot descenden;
> But al day faileth thing that fooles wenden. (1.211–17)

And Troilus does not fall alone. From the Greek camp, Criseyde, her plans to return unrealized, looks regretfully back to Troy and defines the human condition:

> On tyme ypassed wel remembred me;
> And present tyme ek koude ich wel ise;
> But futur tyme, or I was in the snare,
> Koude I nat sen; that causeth now my care. (5.746–49)

If the reader feels superior to her folly, and many recent critics seem to, it is only because for us, as for Guido's narrator, the Trojan future is already past. But all is not so simple in the midst of events. The problem, as Guido showed Chaucer, is time and perspective. Criseyde especially has reason to complain. Beginning with her father's sudden desertion and continuing through his equally unexpected demand for her return, the future always comes to her as a surprise. There really is nothing unreasonable about the plans Criseyde makes to return to Troy after the exchange of Antenor (anymore than there is anything unreasonable about Laomedon's decision to expel the Argonauts) except that they are made in ignorance. In another time or place one of her schemes might easily have worked, or a final peace might really have been just around the corner as she claims to have heard (4.1345 ff.). Later, Chaucer emphasizes how little anyone in the midst of human events really knows: he goes far into the future to narrate Criseyde's eventual surrender to Diomedes (5.1037–99) before coming back in time to describe Troilus at the walls of Troy on the tenth day awaiting his beloved's return. Troilus confidently expects to see Criseyde (at one point he actually thinks he has [5.1158]), but we are already far ahead of him and have been shown how the tragedy will end. The *Troilus*, even more than the *Historia*, is a story of deception, blindness, error, and ignorance. All ends badly, but no one sees until it is too late.

Chaucer's conception of Fortune is certainly more Christian than Guido's, but the present tendency by such as D. W. Robertson and Ida Gordon to blame the lovers' misfortune on their own selfish errors is too glib and misses the point.[21] Chaucer's characters are not saints or followers of Lady Philosophy, but fleshly and attractive beings caught up and destroyed by tragic events. When it comes to controlling the affairs of this world, they and all men are helpless. In this sense, Troilus's long soliloquy on Fortune in the fourth book, which argues for something close to predestination, is not merely ironic. He knows much of the Boethian advice about these questions (put your trust in eternal rather than in material things), but such an answer is no help in dealing with practical matters.[22] The older critics were right to stress the doom and destiny that overhang Troy. Chaucer's subject, as our study of the *Historia* helps us see, is not the Christian questions of Free Will or ultimate moral responsibility (one reason he may have chosen a pagan setting) but the helplessness and ignorance of human beings.

Boccaccio has really nothing like this, and Chaucer's special intent seems most clear in his additions to the *Filostrato*. A principal example occurs in his version of the exchange of Antenor for Criseyde which seals the fate of both the city and the love affair.[23] The Trojans act reasonably, if ungallantly, in giving over Calchas's daughter to regain one of their chief leaders. They have no way of knowing what disastrous consequences will follow, any more than does Laomedon when he sends away the Argonauts, and Chaucer's lament is like those in Guido:

> O Juvenal, lord! soth is thy sentence,
> That litel wyten folk what is to yerne,
> That they ne fynde in hire desir offence;
> For cloude of errour lat hem nat discerne
> What best is; and lo, here ensaumple as yerne.
> This folk desiren now deliveraunce
> Of Antenor, that broughte hem to meschaunce.

> For he was after traitour to the town
> Of Troye; allas, they quytte hym out to rathe!
> O nyce world, lo thy discrecioun! (4.197–206)

Chaucer here expresses a pessimism as complete as Guido's. Finally, not even genuine knowledge is a sure guarantee of control. Cassandra's truths are disbelieved here as in the *Historia*. When we are first introduced to Criseyde, she is listening to the story of Thebes, whose seer Amphiorax 'fil thorugh the ground to helle' (2.105). The wisdom of the Trojans' own seer, her father, is also incomplete, as Robert apRoberts has shown: 'Calchas, who knows of the destruction of Troy, does not understand what part of his action in seeking the exchange [of Antenor for Criseyde] is to play in bringing about that doom.'[24] Furthermore, he does not foresee that he is rescuing his daughter from Troy only to have her ruined by Diomedes.

The *Troilus* is unlike anything else in the Chaucer canon. On the one hand, it is the only one of his works in which human sexual love is shown as attractive (by contrast, an anthology of sexual scenes from the *Canterbury Tales* would be nasty, brutish, and short). On the other hand, the poem has a deep sense of man's ignorance and pitifulness, a pessimism announced early ('Fro wo to wele, and after out of joie') and never very far from the surface. I have tried to show that we have grounds for believing that Guido's *Historia* taught Chaucer to see the Troy story this way and its unlikely materials helped to inspire a masterpiece.

Henryson's Testament of Cresseid

The only fifteenth-century poem written in Great Britain that begins to rival the moral and artistic complexity of Chaucer's *Troilus* also has Troy for its setting—Robert Henryson's *Testament of Cresseid*. Henryson must have known the medieval history of Troy in some form (perhaps through one of the Middle English translations of Guido), but he does not seem to have made explicit use of the *Historia*. Nevertheless, the Trojan history can contribute much to an understanding of the *Testament*, especially of the roles of Troilus and Criseyde, and the poem addresses one of Guido's central concerns: his pessimism concerning human ignorance and impotence.

In form and intent the *Testament* is even further away from the medieval history than is the *Troilus*. Henryson has no hesitation in changing 'historical' facts for thematic purposes, and so here Calchas is not a priest of Apollo (which is his office in the *Historia*) but of Venus and Cupid, appropriate deities for the father of the much-loved Criseyde.[25] Chaucer keeps the history very much in the background of the *Troilus*, but the *Testament*, in addition to a narrower narrative scope than Chaucer's poem, contains not one scene actually from the historical tradition.

By having his narrator go out of his way to question the reliability of historical poetry, Henryson shows himself no true Trojan historian. The narrator claims as his source not only the *Troilus*, but also another book which tells of the 'fatall destenie/Of fair Cresseid, that endit wretchitlie' (62–63). Having two authorities prompts him to wonder about the truth of both:

> Quha wait gif all that Chauceir wrait was trew?
> Nor I wait nocht gif this narratioun
> Be authoreist, or fenȝeit of the new
> Be sum poeit, throw his inuentioun
> Maid to report the lamentatioun
> And wofull end of this lustie Creisseid,
> And quhat distres scho thoillit, and quhat deid. (64–70)

This is a view of poetry we have not seen before, one that looks toward the wider possibilities of poetic history in the Renaissance. Henryson admits what Chaucer cannot: a poet is not always to be completely believed because his work may be 'fenȝeit of the new' or come merely from his 'inuentioun.' Chaucer, still firmly in the medieval tradition, feels obliged to insist that he is accurately following ancient authority on the subject of Troy, despite the complex effects he creates with the role of historian. While not truly one of the Middle English historians of Troy, he must *seem* to be one. But Henryson is willing to admit directly that the story of Troy may be contradictory or even that some of it may spring from the creative mind of a poet. The medieval history of Troy is becoming contaminated, and in the Renaissance it will finally disappear as an independent and self-contained tradition. Nevertheless, although not used directly, it still has great influence on the *Testament*. With our knowledge of the history, we can see that Troilus's role in the poem is less positive than has previously been believed and that, in the figure of Cresseid, Henryson finds a solution to the problems of human ignorance and limitation that haunt Guido and Chaucer.

Although no two readers of the *Testament of Cresseid* agree in their judgments of the heroine (the degree of her guilt or innocence, the justice of the punishment she receives from the gods, or the extent to which her suffering leads to self-knowledge), the verdict on Troilus is unanimous. Every critic who has considered him insists that Troilus is a positive and benevolent figure. His distribution of alms to the unrecognized beggar Cresseid in sorrowful memory of their lost love has been universally considered the magnanimous action of a true and admirable chivalric lover. Cresseid's own view has not been challenged: 'O fals Cresseid and trew knicht Troylus' (546, 553, and 560). Charles Elliott, in his edition of Henryson, describes Troilus as '*trew*, noble, worthy, gentle, and *fre*, the ideal warrior, successful yet not without "magnificence." '[26] Denton Fox calls him 'noble, generous, and sensitive.'[27] John MacQueen argues that when Troilus appears 'his act of disinterested charity reasserts to the full the power of moral virtue which Cresseid had previously discarded' and sees in their meeting a contrast between Virtue and appetite.[28] In an early study E. M. W. Tillyard refers to the 'great generosity' of Troilus.[29] Douglas Duncan and Sydney Harth, whose readings of the poem agree on absolutely nothing else, also both insist on Troilus's 'generosity.'[30]

Our knowledge of the medieval history of Troy forces us to question the usual view of Troilus. His triumphant entrance as a conquering warrior is undercut by our realization of the imminence of both his death and the final fall of Troy, and his brief meeting with Criseyde is described so that he comes to represent all the helpless ignorance both Guido and Chaucer find in the story of Troy. Even though he is an admirable paradigm of pagan chivalry, Troilus exemplifies a system of worldly values, the limits of which the Christian reader can recognize and which Cresseid learns, however haltingly and incompletely, to reject as delusive and empty. Contrary to the usual view, it is Cresseid, not Troilus, who is capable of lasting nobility and true generosity.

Troilus is introduced in a way that insists on the contrast between his noble estate and Cresseid's wretched one:

> That samin tyme, of Troy the garnisoun,
> Quhilk had to chiftane worthie Troylus,
> Throw ieopardie of weir had strikken doun
> Knichtis of Grece in number meruellous;
> With greit tryumphe and laude victorious
> Agane to Troy richt royallie thay raid
> The way quhair Cresseid with the lipper baid. (484–90)

The medieval histories of Troy, however, reveal that this heroic entrance is deceptive. If Troilus is now chieftain of the city, Hector must already be dead and Troilus's own end fast approaching. The victory over the Greeks from which Troilus is here returning is but a temporary stay of Troy's fall. Troilus's military success will soon suffer a cruel and complete reversal when he is treacherously slain by Achilles and then, according to the medieval history, dragged around the walls of Troy. With the death of her two principal heroes, Hector and Troilus, the city cannot long stand.

When we recall this historical context, the worldly fortunes of Troilus and Cresseid no longer seem so disparate. For the moment they are beggar and knight, but he is shortly to join her in debasement and death. Both must fall from Fortune's wheel; and, although Cresseid suffers more extended humiliation, she is thereby given the opportunity to profit from her calamity. Upon his high horse, Troilus seems totally unaware of the gathering fates that mean his doom; he is like the other characters at Troy who never foresee the disasters that will overtake them. Cresseid, without saying anything directly critical of her former love, has already begun to sense the dangers in his values. Henryson uses verbal parallels to contrast the two characters. In the passage just quoted, the poet refers to Troilus's 'greit tryumphe and laude victorious' and describes him as riding 'richt royallie.' In her Complaint, Cresseid uses similar language when she considers the world she has lost: gone are her 'greit royall renoun' (424) and her 'greit triumphand fame and hie honour' (434). She then warns the ladies of Troy and Greece by the example of her misfortune to 'Be war in tyme, approchis neir the end' (456). Both Troilus and Cresseid are indeed approaching their end: Cresseid responds to this reality with a slowly increasing understanding of the world and of herself; but Troilus, insulated by his glory and high station, is oblivious to it.

During the meeting of the former lovers, Troilus's generosity—so often insisted on by the critics—is sincere but superficial. More important for the meaning of the poem are his self-absorption and inability to escape from the dead past. He is a symbol of the human ignorance described by Chaucer and Guido. When he comes upon Cresseid, he does not recognize her because leprosy has so transformed

her body, but something about the beggar woman does trigger his
memory:

> 3it than hir luik into his mynd it brocht
> The sweit visage and amorous blenking
> Of fair Cresseid, sumtyme his awin darling. (502–04)

Poor Troilus. His fidelity to the memory of Cresseid is touching and
everything we might expect of a chivalric lover; and yet, gently but
without sentimentality, Henryson shows that it is not nearly good
enough. Without denying the poignancy of the situation (Henryson's
genuine sympathy replaces the helpless laments in Guido and Chaucer),
the poet insists on the delusion. Troilus remembers a woman who no
longer exists, and yet he cannot recognize the truth of the person standing
before him. Like the aged narrator earlier in the poem, Troilus is unable
to deal with the passage of time and is therefore conquered by it. The
problem, as Guido showed Chaucer and Chaucer showed Henryson, is
time and perspective. Troilus's love for Cresseid has been made foolish by
time like the narrator's observances to Venus. For example, 'fair' is one
word that no longer has any relevance whatsoever to Cresseid. The gods
had promised that her 'sweit visage' would be 'ouirspred with spottis
blak,/And lumpis haw appeirand in thy face' (339–40) until it was 'sa
deformait' (349)—and this has now become fact (393–96). Likewise her
'amorous blenking' is gone because they vowed to have her 'cristall ene
mingit with blude' (337). By portraying Troilus's attachment to Cresseid
as foolish, Henryson has turned the faithfulness for which the knight is
famous against him. However falteringly and unwillingly, Cresseid will
change and learn while Troilus remains frozen in attitudes that circumstances have made absurd.

Henryson gives a whole stanza to the explanation of how Cresseid is
recalled to Troilus's mind:

> Na wonder was, suppois in mynd that he
> Tuik hir figure sa sone, and lo, now quhy:
> The idole of ane thing in cace may be
> Sa deip imprentit in the fantasy
> That it deludis the wittis outwardly,
> And sa appeiris in forme and lyke estait
> Within the mynd as it was figurait. (505–11)

Marshall Stearns has shown that Henryson is here using a tradition of
psychological analysis that ultimately derives from Aristotle.[31] He
concludes that 'the resulting delusion of the "wittis" or rational thought
is caused by Troilus's passion for his beloved, and in his mind he sees the
"Idole" or image of fair Cresseid in the "forme" or bodily likeness that it
was "figurait" or imagined.'[32] The words Henryson chooses in this
passage are designed to give a more censorious portrayal of Troilus's

delusion than Stearns is willing to grant. The word *idole* has a more negative sense than just 'image,' for Fox notes that according to the *OED* its use in Middle English is only in reference to religion.[33] Troilus's real tragedy is that his pagan circumstances and almost inevitable lack of perspective make idolatry of one kind or another the only religion he can know. Stearns defines *fantasy* as 'imagination,' and Fox agrees while also suggesting 'memory.'[34] The *MED*'s article on *fantasie* indicates the term was most frequently used to describe a delusive, false, and illusory figment of the imagination. Chaucer seems almost always to employ the word in this way, especially in the *Troilus* (e.g., 2.482; 3.275, 1032, 1504; 4.1470; 5.261, 329, 358, 461, 623, 1523), and Henryson follows the older poet in this as in so much else when he insists that the process *deludis* Troilus's wits.

The extent and nature of Troilus's ignorance becomes clear in the next stanza:

> Ane spark of lufe than till his hart culd spring
> And kendlit all his bodie in ane fyre;
> With hait fewir, ane sweit and trimbling
> Him tuik, quhill he was reddie to expyre;
> To beir his scheild his breist began to tyre;
> Within ane quhyle he changit mony hew;
> And neuertheles not ane ane vther knew. (512–18)

This passage is clearly designed to echo the description of Troilus's love-longings throughout Chaucer's poem and the brief mention of them at the beginning of the *Testament* (45–49).[35] Even at this late date the lover has learned nothing. Because we have seen the real and horrible sickness of Cresseid, Troilus's amorous suffering for a phantom seems all the more foolish and irrelevant. He does not see what has happened to Cresseid and does not realize what is soon to happen to himself or to Troy.[36] The other leper lady's advice to a suffering Cresseid would be even more appropriate to Troilus in his love pangs: 'Sen thy weiping bot dowbillis thy wo,/I counsall the mak vertew of ane neid' (477–78).

During Troilus's brief appearance in the *Testament*, his knightly pride, glory in victory, love-longing, and wealth make him an exemplum of those who trust in earthly things. Troilus's reputation for generosity derives from his gift of money to the leper Cresseid, but possessions are not necessarily the root of all good. We recall that Cresseid had previously come to realize that earthly wealth 'away as wind it weiris' (467). The dangers of trust in wordly goods is one of the lessons most commonly drawn in the Middle Ages from the story of Troy. Lydgate refers to it at the end of his *Troy Book* (5.3544–78), and Chaucer advised his readers that they should 'repeyreth hom fro worldly vanyte' and follow Christ rather than seek 'feyned loves' (5.1835–48).

When Troilus impulsively gives great alms to Cresseid, he does not do so only from disinterested charity, but in large measure from remembrance of his past sexual love. Yet here and elsewhere Henryson helps the reader avoid any temptation to harsh moralization. When Troilus first hears the leper band, before specifically recalling Cresseid, he indeed feels 'pietie' (496). Troilus is an ideal pagan knight and has real virtues; but for Henryson and his audience these virtues are finally insufficient and even selfish. Troilus might well have shown benevolence to any beggars, but the extent of his generosity here is due to 'pietie' for his lost love (519), as the lepers are quick to realize (529–32).

Troilus ultimately plays a minor role in Henryson's poem. He occupies only a few lines and is presented as a static figure unable to respond adequately to the tragedy around him. His dramatic importance, however, lies in the contrast he provides to Cresseid: it is her *Testament*. Both suffer, but only she profits. From this point of view, we can argue that Henryson used Cresseid to provide an answer to the pessimism and sense of doom found by Chaucer and Guido in the story of Troy.[37] Whatever her faults, the suffering she endures is extreme and capricious—like the disasters that befall Laomedon and Priam. Those who have found pessimism in Henryson himself or talk of his 'dark moral vision' in the *Testament* are confusing the problem with its solution.[38] As Henryson knew it, the story of Troy, like that of Troilus and Cresseid, was already a dark tale of human ignorance and misery. Far from inventing or adding to its bleakness, he searches for some solution. He is too sophisticated to provide us with a happy ending or with Cresseid's salvation, but he does show her regaining a measure of control over her own destiny. Henryson shows Cresseid's growth without violating her characterization in Chaucer as a vain woman unable to accept direct responsibility for her own actions.[39] She does achieve a high level of self-understanding, but only after a long and psychologically accurate process. In addition, the *Testament* continually leads its Christian audience to see the lessons of Cresseid's story more clearly than she herself is able to do. Fox has argued that Cresseid not only improves morally but actually attains Christian knowledge and salvation.[40] On the contrary, the sureness of Henryson's art refuses such a forced result. The *Testament* is careful to remain faithful to its pagan setting (it maintains Chaucer's 'sense of history') while demonstrating the need, also felt in the world of the *Knight's Tale*, for Christ's mercy to replace the strict justice of the gods.[41]

When Cresseid first confronts her leprosy in a mirror, her reaction is pure self-pity and blame of 'our craibit goddis' (347–57). Her long Complaint in the hospital (407–69) is more philosophical, and, as we have seen, her recognition there of the transitoriness of earthly pomp and pleasure helps the reader, but not herself, to realize Troilus's limitations. Yet even here Cresseid attempts to avoid personal responsibility. Using herself as a mirror to warn others of the passing of worldly delights is an advance over the mirror of vanity in which she first saw her deformity, but she substitutes a universal horror ('As I am now, peraduenture that ჳe/For all ჳour micht may cum to that same end' [458–59]) for a personal one and thus avoids having to admit her own particular culpability. Her Complaint describes the vanity of this world in terms that would have been meaningful to Henryson's contemporaries, and yet she is not herself Christian and ends blaming the random agent whom Guido and Chaucer describes as ruling Troy: 'Fortoun is fikkill quhen scho beginnis and steiris' (469). In so doing she echoes the old and foolish narrator who early in the poem argues that the guilt for her lust lies with Fortune and not with herself (85–91).

Cresseid does not remain trapped in self-pity and blame of others forever; the poem itself, if not the narrator, finds a way out. She is informed that the warrior who has given her money is Troilus, and in her long speech of reaction she makes a truly significant advance toward self-knowledge (546–74). From its beginning, this complaint is directed against herself: 'O fals Cresseid and trew knicht Troylus!' (546). She goes on to laud Troilus extravagantly as a true and noble lover (e.g., 547 and 554–57). The reader now knows this to be excessive praise occasioned by her limited perspective, but it is an appropriate measure of her moral growth. She will not blame Troilus, and she no longer need excuse herself. Now she is able to realize that it was her choice to be under Fortune's sway: 'Sa efflated I was in wantones,/And clam vpon the fickill quheill sa hie' (549–50). At the end she reaches a noble acceptance of herself and her actions: 'Nane but my self as now I will accuse' (574). Her advance has been forced and reluctant, but she has succeeded in traveling a great distance. As a pagan, however, she is incapable of a truly Christian view of her past and can only see her fault in human terms—she has been untrue to a loyal lover. With its perspective, Henryson's Christian audience has all along understood the issues involved more fully than Cresseid. For example, near the end of her second complaint, Cresseid provides a warning:

> Louers be war and tak gude heid about
> Quhome that ჳe lufe, for quhome ჳe suffer paine.
> I lat ჳow wit, thair is richt few thairout
> Quhome ჳe may traist to haue trew lufe agane. (561–64)

Although she remains, as she must, on the level of sexual love, Henryson makes her echo the end of Chaucer's *Troilus*:

> For he nyl falsen no wight, dar I seye,
> That wol his herte al holly on hym leye.
> And syn he best to love is, and most meke,
> What nedeth feynede loves for to seke? (5.1845–48)

Cresseid dies thinking of Troilus and Diomeid and of her treatment of each (589–91), but in her testament she, like Theseus in the *Knight's*

Tale, approaches, if never actually reaches, a Christian understanding. She recognizes the ultimate worthlessness of the physical and consigns her body to rot (577–78). In the disposal of her goods, she shows herself capable at last of the proper use of Troilus's gifts. She now has the ability to give charitable and not just amorous love, and she leaves her posses- sions to the leper folk (579–81). She falls back into her human, pagan world by leaving a ring to Troilus and her soul to Diana (582–88), but it is she and not Troilus who has, however tentatively demonstrated *caritas.* Henryson has found an answer to the pessimism of the medieval history of Troy by showing that man is not merely a helpless victim of fate. Although Troilus, like the other characters of Chaucer and Guido, remains ignorant and impotent, Cresseid does not. True, she suffers greatly (Henryson has no doubt that this is a hard world), but she is not destroyed morally. Instead she comes to a real measure of self-knowledge and self-control. Henryson is no easy optimist, but he does believe that the doom that visits Trojan and Greek alike in the medieval history can be resisted and that all need not be despair.

Henryson clearly shows the difference between Troilus and Cresseid in the response of each to her death. She dies thinking of others, and especially of him; he is informed of her end and can think only of himself. After learning that her former lover was the generous almsgiver, Cresseid faints and 'with siching sair and sad' (540) gives her moving speech of regret and self-recognition. This scene is repeated ironically when Troilus learns of her death, for he also faints and speaks 'siching full sadlie' (601); but he is capable only of self-pity: 'I can no moir;/Scho was vntrew and wo is me thairfoir' (601–02). In contrast to Cresseid, who had left her body to the worms, he continues his commitment to material pomp and display by building her a marble tomb with gold letters (603– 09). His message is directed to 'fair ladyis' as was her Complaint (452); yet even at this late date he has learned nothing and can offer no lesson except the flat and misleading facts of her life:

> Lo, fair ladyis, Cresseid of Troy the toun,
> Sumtyme countit the flour of womanheid,
> Vnder this stane, lait lipper, lyis deid. (607–09)

These lines reveal the sadness of an honest heart's baffled emotions and prevent us from coming to a severe final judgment. If Cresseid's epitaph is the last word on Troilus's limitations, it is also the expression, pure and naive, of the pain that his limitations force upon him. Henryson forces us to look steadily at the results of error, but he never asks us to deny human sympathy. The poet's Christian orthodoxy moves us beyond simple justice and the inexorable doom of the medieval history to a full and complex mercy for chastened whores and even for noble knights.

NOTES

NOTES

I. The Medieval History of Troy: Guido delle Colonne

[1] For a general discussion of Dares and Dictys see R. M. Frazer's introduction to his translation of them in *The Trojan War* (Bloomington, 1966), pp. 3–15. Also useful is Nathaniel Griffin, *Dares and Dictys: An Introduction to the Study of Medieval Versions of the Story of Troy* (Baltimore, 1907). The Latin text of Dares was edited by Ferdinand Meister (Leipzig, 1873) and that of Dictys by Werner Eisenhut (Leipzig, 1958).

[2] For a more favorable view see Robert Lumiansky, 'Dares' *Historia* and Dictys' *Ephemeris*: A Critical Comment,' *Studies in Language, Literature, and Culture of the Middle Ages and Later*, ed. E. Bagby Atwood and Archibald Hill (Austin, 1969), pp. 200–09.

[3] Frazer, *Trojan War*, p. 6.

[4] Benoît de Sainte-More (Maure), *Le Roman de Troie*, ed. Leopold Constans, Société des anciens texte français, 6 vols. (Paris, 1904–12).

[5] Guido de Columnis (delle Colonne), *Historia Destructionis Troiae*, ed. Nathaniel Griffin, Mediaeval Academy of America Publication No. 26 (1936; rpt. New York, 1970). Some recent general discussions of Guido not cited below include: Raffaele Chiàntera, *Guido delle Colonne* (Naples, 1956); Carlo Dionisotti, 'Proposta per Guido Giudice,' *Rivista di Cultura Classica e Medievale* 7 (1965) 453–66; Santino Caramella, 'L'Umile Tragedia di Guido delle Colonne,' *Accademia degli Arcadia Letteraria Italiana Atti e Memorie*, Ser. 3, vol. 4, fasc. 4 (1967), Studi in onore del Alfredo Schiaffini, pp. 106–11; and Hugo Buchthal, *Historia Troiana: Studies in the History of Mediaeval Secular Illustration* (London, 1971). The title *Historia Destructionis Troiae* is apparently not authorial but scribal (see Griffin, pp. xv–vi); nevertheless, while I used the short title *Historia* for convenience only, Gùido himself several times refers to his work thus in his text.

[6] For a discussion of this hypothesis see Alfred L. Kellogg and Waller B. Wigginton, 'How Dares Collaborated with Dictys,' in *Chaucer, Langland, Arthur:*

Essays in Middle English Literature (New Brunswick, New Jersey, 1972), pp. 146–54.

[7] *An Apology for Poetry*, ed. Geoffrey Shepherd (Manchester, 1965), p. 110.

[8] Nathaniel E. Griffin, 'Un-Homeric Elements in the Medieval Story of Troy,' *Journal of English and Germanic Philology*, 7 (1907–08), 36–38.

[9] The histories of Troy are classified as romance in popular surveys like George K. Anderson's *Old and Middle English Literature from the Beginnings to 1485* (New York, 1962), pp. 131–33; and, more surprisingly, by Lumiansky in Vol. I of the new *A Manual of the Writings in Middle English*, ed. J. Burke Severs (New Haven, 1957).

[10] Alain Renoir in 'Thebes, Troy, Criseyde, and Pandarus: an Instance of Chaucerian Irony,' *Studia Neophilologica*, 32 (1960), 14–17, has shown how often these works and their redactions were thought of and even bound together.

[11] For a masterful survey of this material see George Cary, *The Medieval Alexander*, ed. D. J. A. Ross (Cambridge, 1956).

[12] For a recent survey of this subject see Antonia Gransden, *Historical Writing in England c. 550 to c. 1307* (Ithaca, N.Y., 1974).

[13] Galbraith, *Historical Research in Medieval England* (London, 1951), p. 2. Here is the original in Gervase: 'Historici autem et cronici secundum aliquid una est intentio et materia, sed diversus tractandi modus est et forma varia. Utriusque una est intentio, quia uterque veritati intendit. Forma tractandi varia, quia historicus diffuse et eleganter incedit, cronicus vero simpliciter graditur et breviter. "Proicit" historicus "ampullas et sesquipedalia verba"; cronicus vero "silverstrem musam tenui meditatur avena." Sedet historicus "inter magniloquos et grandia verba serentes," et cronicus sub pauperis Amiclae pausat tugurio ne sit pugna pro paupere tecto. Proprium est historici veritati intendere, audientes vel legentes dulci sermone et eleganti demulcere, actus, mores vitamque ipsius quam describit veraciter edocere, nichilque aliud comprehendere nisi quod historiae de ratione videtur competere. Cronicus autem annos Incarnationis Domini annorumque menses computat et kalendas, actus etiam regum et principum quae in ipsis eveniunt breviter edocet, eventus etiam, portenta vel miracula commemorat.' *The Chronicle of the Reigns of Stephen, Henry II, and Richard I*, ed. William Stubbs, Rolls Series 73 (London, 1879), I, 87.

[14] The concept of *figura* and its foundation in historical fact has been discussed by Erich Auerbach in 'Figura,' *Scenes from the Drama of European Literature* (New York, 1959), pp. 11–76: '*figura* is something real and historical which announces something else that is also real and historical' (p. 29). It would be wrong to conclude that medieval chroniclers were without interest in God's Providential plan, even if their humility kept them from attempting to reveal it. They faithfully record comets and other portents for the interpretation of others. The *Anglo-Saxon Chronicle* stands at the beginning of the great English chronicle tradition and establishes many of its precedents. In the course of its careful dating and brief record of the acts of kings and princes, it occasionally notes the hand of God in this world by such phrases as 'as God had forseen' and 'such things happen because of the people's sins' (see C. A. Patrides, *The Grand Design of God* [London, 1972], p. 36).

[15] Collingwood, *The Idea of History* (Oxford, 1946), p. 53.

[16] Robertson, *Abelard and Heloise* (New York, 1972), pp. 100–01. Patrides shows that this view of Providential history was consolidated in the Bible, and he

notes that Augustine in the *City of God* refers to Isaiah to the effect that 'God "giveth kingdoms to good and to bad: not rashly, nor casually, but as the time is appointed, which is well known to him, though hidden from us" ' (*Grand Design*, p. 18).

[17] Charles W. Jones shows how Bede created a somewhat analogous combination of chronicle and hagiography in *Saints' Lives and Chronicles in Early England* (Ithaca, 1947).

[18] Vaughan, *Matthew Paris* (Cambridge, 1958), p. 125; Galbraith, ed., *The St. Albans Chronicle: 1406–1420* (Oxford, 1937), p. xxv.

[19] Eusebius, *The Ecclesiastical History*, trans. Kirsopp Lake, Loeb Library (Cambridge, Mass., 1926), I, 11.

[20] Because the original Latin is usually not necessary for our purposes and because of her careful work with Guido's often confused prose, in most cases I will quote the *Historia Destructionis Troiae* in the translation by Mary Elizabeth Meek (Bloomington, 1974). I will cite Meek by book and line number and also note the corresponding page number in Griffin's Latin text. Here the references are Pro. 1–16; p. 3. Further citations will be included in my text.

[21] *Bede's Eccesiastical History of the English People*, ed. and trans. Bertram Colgrave and R. A. B. Mynors (Oxford, 1969), pp. 6–7.

[22] *Eadmer's History of Recent Events in England*, trans. Geoffrey Bosanquet (London, 1964), p. 1. In the preface to his later *Life of Saint Anselm*, Eadmer again refers to his *History* as 'a brief record' of the events of his time, undertaken 'lest the knowledge of them should be entirely lost to future generations' (*Life*, ed. and trans. R. W. Southern [London, 1962], p. 1).

[23] Ordericus Vitalis, *The Ecclesiastical History of England and Normandy*, trans. Thomas Forester (London, 1853), I, 3. The first volume of the new edition of the *Ecclesiastical History* by Marjorie Chibnall has not yet appeared, though volumes two through six have been published (Oxford, 1969–78).

[24] Henry of Huntingdon, *Historia Anglorum*, ed. Thomas Arnold, Rolls Series 74 (London, 1879), p. 2: 'Historia igitur praeterita quasi praesentia visui repraesentat'; William of Malmesbury, *De Gestis Regum Anglorum*, ed. William Stubbs, Rolls Series 90 (London, 1887), I, 3: 'Quicquid vero de recentioribus aetatibus apposui, vel ipse vidi, vel a viris fide dignis audivi.'

[25] Ed. William Stubbs, Rolls Series 38 (London, 1864), I, 3–4. See also Matthew Paris who argues in his *Historia Anglorum* (or *Historia Minor*) that remembrance of the past is what separates men from beasts (ed. Frederic Madden, Rolls Series 44 [London, 1866], I, 3–4).

[26] *Continuatio Chronicarum*, ed. Edward M. Thompson, Rolls Series 93 (London, 1889), pp. 3–4. See also Ranulf Higden in his popular digest of world history, *Polychronicon*, ed. Churchill Babington, Rolls Series 41.1 (London, 1865), I.i.2 (p. 4).

[27] Isidore of Seville, *Etymologiarvm sive Originvm*, ed. W. M. Lindsay (Oxford, 1911), I.xlii.

[28] Hugh of St. Victor, *The Didascalicon*, trans. Jerome Taylor (New York, 1961), p. 86 (III.ii).

[29] Bede, *Ecclesiastical History*, pp. 2–3. The exemplary view of history found in clerical chronicles is more superficial and practical than Providential history since it concerns itself with men's morals rather than God's design. It is an inheritance from Roman historians like Sallust.

[30] Ordericus Vitalis, I, 1; Jocelin of Brakelond, *The Chronicle*, ed. and trans. H. E. Butler (London, 1949), p. 1; Roger of Wendover, *Chronica sive Flores Historiarum*, ed. Henry O. Coxe, English Historical Society 8 (London, 1841), I, 1; Matthew Paris, *Historia Anglorum*, I, 4.

[31] Henry of Huntingdon, *Historia Anglorum*, p. 2. Translation by Thomas Forester, *The Chronicle of Henry of Huntingdon* (London, 1853) Bohn's Antiquarian Library, p. xxvii.

[32] Higden, *Polychronicon*, I.i.2 (p. 4).

[33] William J. Brandt, *The Shape of Medieval History* (New Haven, 1966), see especially Chapter 3. Hereafter cited as Brandt.

[34] 'Pierre de Langtoft's *Chronicle*: An Essay in Medieval Historiography,' *Medievalia et Humanistica*, n.s. 3 (1972), 51–73.

[35] Brandt, p. 82.

[36] Brandt, pp. 85–86.

[37] Brandt, pp. 88 and 90.

[38] Paul Archambault, *Seven French Chroniclers* (Syracuse, 1974), p. 5, suggests that the new focus by historians on the particulars of their own time and place is a reflection of the 'nominalist crisis.'

[39] Archambault, *Seven French Chroniclers*, p. 119.

[40] *Les Chroniques de sire Jean Froissart*, ed. J. A. C. Buchon, 3 vols. (Paris, 1835). A convenient translation of Froissart's *Chronicle* is that by Geoffery Brereton (Baltimore, 1968). For the strategy before Crécy and its result see I, 233–238 (Brereton, pp. 83–89); for a similar account of the precise execution of a careful plan at the battle of Chevy Chase (this time to the disadvantage of the English) see II, 726 ff. (Brereton, pp. 341 ff.).

[41] Brandt, pp. 153–55.

[42] Archambault, *Seven French Chroniclers*, p. 69.

[43] Brandt, p. 99.

[44] This is Brereton's translation of Froissart (p. 343). Froissart's original is 'sans mesure, ainsi que un Hector, qui tout seul cuidoit et vouloit vaincre et déconfire la besogne.' (II, 728).

[45] Waller B. Wigginton, 'The Nature and Significance of the Late Medieval Troy Story: A Study of Guido delle Colonne's *Historia Destructionis Troiae*,' Diss. Rutgers 1965, p. 272. Hereafter cited as Wigginton.

[46] Wigginton, p. 209.

[47] Wigginton, pp. 122, 200, and 272.

[48] Wigginton, p. 204, does claim that Guido is at this point blaming Laomedon: 'he clearly [implies] that Laomedon should have acted otherwise.'

[49] See note 47 above.

[50] His long insertion on the development of paganism in Book 10, during which he condemns its deception and deviltry, is an anachronistic view from his own time and not integral to the narrative.

[51] Rarely do we find in the *Historia* that fortune is presented as a chastisement for sin, although this is central to Christian history—Providential or exemplary—and frequent in Herodotus. A reference to the punishment of Antenor (29.317–21; p. 226) is the exception that proves the rule and the only example I could find.

[52] See also Guido's proclamation of the irresistible hostility of fortune after the death of Pyrrhus (34.188–92; p. 267). Although Pyrrhus has just abducted Orestes's wife Hermione, he is not here being punished for lust by a just heaven anymore

than Hector was previously punished for magnaminity. Both are victims in a world without order or Providence, a world in which neither man's mind nor his virtue is any protection against the imminent blows of *fortuna* and *fata*.

[53] We will remember that because of his source Guido believed that Peleus of Thessaly (whose nephew Jason brought about the first destruction of Troy) was also the father of Achilles. Achilles, of course, killed Hector, and Achilles's son, Pyrrhus, killed Troy's last champion, Penthesilea, and Priam himself. For the confusion between Peleus and Pelias see 1.1–46; pp. 3–4.

II. *History into Verse: the prologues to the Middle English History of Troy*

[1] *The 'Gest Hystoriale' of the Destruction of Troy*, ed. George A. Panton and David Donaldson, EETS OS 39, 56 (London, 1869, 1874), lines 11–13. All further quotations will be from this edition and cited in my text. Chaucer also expresses the importance of the 'key of remembraunce' in recovering the past in the Prologue to the *Legend of Good Women* (see, especially, F 17–28).

[2] *The Laud Troy Book*, ed. J. Ernst Wülfing, EETS OS 121, 122 (London, 1902, 1903), lines 89–91. All further quotations will be from this edition and cited in my text.

[3] John Lydgate, *Lydgate's Troy Book*, ed. Henry Bergen, EETS ES 97, 103, 106, and 126 (London, 1906–35), Pro. 149–50. All further quotations will be from this edition and cited in my text.

[4] M. Dominica Legge, *Anglo-Norman Literature and Its Background* (Oxford, 1963), p. 28.

[5] Legge, *Anglo-Norman*, pp. 80, 278–79.

[6] Legge, *Anglo-Norman*, pp. 306–09.

[7] Ralph Higden, *Polychronicon*, ed. Churchill Babington, Rolls Series 41.1 (London, 1865), I.i.3 (p. 6).

[8] Manning, *The Story of England*, ed. F. J. Furnivall, Rolls Series 87, 2 vols. (London, 1887); *An Anonymous Short Metrical Chronicle*, ed. Ewald Zettl, EETS OS 196 (London, 1935).

[9] C. L. Kingsford, *English Historical Literature in the Fifteenth Century* (Oxford, 1913), p. 117.

[10] John Hardyng's *Chronicle* is often unreliable, but even it contains much useful and accurate information.

[11] Kingsford, *English Historical Literature*, p. 228.

[12] Manning, *Story of England*, lines 1–144.

III. The Destruction of Troy: *History as Poetry*

[1] I am discussing the *Destruction* first not because it was necessarily written before the *Laud Troy Book*, but because it is the closest Middle English translation of the *Historia*. The date of the *Destruction* is uncertain. The traditional date of 1350–1400 is repeated by Robert Lumiansky in *A Manual of the Writings in Middle English* (New Haven, 1967), 1.115, but William Ringler, 'An Early Chaucer Allusion Restored,' *Notes and Queries*, 174 (1938), 120, and the present author, 'A

Chaucerian Allusion and the Date of the Alliterative "Destruction of Troy," '
Notes and Queries, 219 (1974), 206–07, have argued that the *Destruction* borrows
from Chaucer's *Troilus* and thus must have been written after about 1385. C. A.
Lutrell, 'Three North-West Midland Manuscripts,' *Neophilologus*, 42 (1958), 38–
50, argues that the single surviving MS. of the *Destruction* (Hunterian V. 2.8) was
written in the mid-sixteenth century, which suggests that the poem itself may
have been composed much later than has ever been thought. We do know that the
Hunterian scribe was copying from a faulty exemplar as the disordered presentation of Ulysses's story shows, suggesting a minimum of three texts (the
autograph, faulty exemplar, and Hunterian). On this and other questions concerning the MS, see David Donaldson's discussion in the edition cited in my
previous chapter, pp. liii–v, and Gordon R. Wood, 'The Middle-English
Alliterative *Destruction of Troy*,' Diss. Princeton 1941, pp. 10–17.

² *Destruction of Troy*, p. viii.

³ Lumiansky, *Manual*, 1.116.

⁴ Atwood, 'English Versions of the *Historia Trojana*,' Diss. University of
Virginia 1932, pp. 138–40, 150; Wood, 'Middle-English Alliterative,' pp. 26–39,
52–68.

⁵ Gordon R. Wood, 'A Note on the Manuscript Source of the Alliterative
Destruction of Troy,' *Modern Language Notes*, 67 (1952), 145–50.

⁶ Griffin, *Historia Destructionis*, p. 167, n. 18.

⁷ Griffin, *Historia Destructionis*, p. 132, n. 30, and p. 153, n. 32.

⁸ George Kane, *Middle English Literature* (London, 1951), p. 58. See also
Atwood, 'English Versions,' p. 152.

⁹ Other passages in the *Destruction* that may at first appear to be mistranslations
turn out on further inspection to be caused by the MS. of the *Historia* used. The
poet adds a full day to his account of the Greek landing at Laomedon's Troy
(1091–93) undoubtedly because the MS. he used, like the related ones A, H, P¹, and
P² described by Griffin (p. 35, n. 13), omits to mention that certain events took
place at night during the light of the moon.

¹⁰ Such lists can be found in Herman Brandes, 'Die mittelenglische
Destruction of Troy und ihre quelle,' *Englische Studien*, 8 (1885), 398–410;
Atwood, 'English Versions,' pp. 138–40; Wood, 'Middle-English Alliterative,' pp.
21–39.

¹¹ J. P. Oakden, *Alliterative Poetry in Middle English* (Manchester, 1935), 2.34.

¹² Similarly, a reference to the deluge of Deucalion in the *Historia* (18.48–49; p.
156) becomes 'as oure lord wold/With water haue wastid all þe world efte' (7623–
24). A long passage on the adventures of Aeneas after the fall of Troy, which Guido
puts at the end of Book 12, is completely eliminated in the *Destruction* as a
needless digression.

¹³ Griffin, *Historia Destructionis*, p. 45, n. 13.

¹⁴ Nicolas Jacobs, 'Alliterative Storms: A Topos in Middle English,' *Speculum*,
47 (1972), 707, 710, 712, suggests some possible minor borrowings from Vergil in
the *Destruction*, but in view of the poet's larger errors I would consider such debts
very doubtful.

¹⁵ More puzzling is the poet's apparent use of a medieval source. In a passage
about the island of Delos which is generally reduced from Guido, the alliterative
poet adds a few details (4260–61) not in the *Historia* (10.80–95; p. 93). These details
do come from the ultimate source identified by Guido: Isidore of Seville's

Etymologies. Brandes, 'Die mittelenglische,' p. 402, notes the addition, but could not determine if it were the poet's own. An original assertion by the poet that emeralds are found in 'Judé, as Isoder sais' (923) tends to discredit his scholarship, and suggests his information is at second-hand, because Isidore does not say this (see *Etymologies* XVI.vii. 1–4, ed. W. M. Lindsay [Oxford, 1911]; Guido also gets the location wrong as Meek shows in her note to 3.296–307, though her reference to Isidore, XVI.3 should be to XVI.7).

[16] Atwood, 'English Versions,' pp. 149–50.

[17] The poet also increases the number of Trojan *Menons* (he has a *Merion*, *Menon*, and even *Seymon*), but there is manuscript support for each, and the poet works hard to make their stories internally consistent. He is also shrewd enough to realize that the two Greek *Merions* in the *Historia* (a blunder taken over from Benoît) are really a single character. Again he tries to make the history clear and consistent without fundamentally altering it.

[18] Griffin, *Historia Destructionis*, p. 153, n. 13.

[19] The alliterative poet also adds a passage on Envy that begins his Book VII (2725–28).

[20] Bloomfield, 'Chaucer's Sense of History,' *Journal of English and Germanic Philology*, 51 (1952), 305; reprinted in Bloomfield, *Essays and Explorations* (Cambridge, Mass., 1970), pp. 13–26.

[21] This list of crafts was considered convincing proof of the poem's Scots origin by its editors, but S. O. Andrew has shown that the crafts are not distinctively Scottish and can all be found in the medieval Guild rolls of Preston ('*Wars of Alexander* and *Destruction of Troy*,' *Review of English Studies*, 5 [1929], 269–70).

[22] Dorothy Everett, 'The Alliterative Revival,' in *Essays on Middle English Literature*, ed. Patricia Kean, rev. ed., (Oxford, 1959), p. 58; Jacobs, 'Alliterative Storms,' p. 713; John Finlayson, 'Formulaic Technique in *Morte Arthure*,' *Anglia*, 81 (1963), 372–93; Larry D. Benson, *Art and Tradition in Sir Gawain and the Green Knight* (New Brunswick, New Jersey, 1965), p. 146.

[23] It has often been shown that the *Destruction* is one of the most conventional and regular alliterative poems: James P. Oakden, *Alliterative Poetry in Middle English* (Manchester, 1930), 1.168, 170; Ronald A. Waldron, 'Oral-Formulaic Technique and Middle English Alliterative Poetry,' *Speculum*, 32 (1957), 796; Marie Borroff, *Sir Gawain and the Green Knight*, Yale Studies in English 152 (New Haven, 1962), pp. 58–59; Benson, *Art and Tradition*, p. 120.

[24] See Kane, *Middle English Literature*, p. 58; Wood, 'Middle-English Alliterative,' esp. 126; Benson, *Art and Tradition*, pp. 176–77.

[25] Oakden, *Alliterative Poetry*, 2.33.

[26] Benson, *Art and Tradition*, p. 168.

[27] Alain Renoir, 'Descriptive Technique in Sir Gawain and the Green Knight,' *Orbis Litterarum*, 13 (1958), 126–32.

[28] Renoir, 'Descriptive Technique,' p. 131.

[29] Borroff, *Sir Gawain*, pp. 93, 126; Benson, *Art and Tradition*, pp. 177–97.

[30] *Morte Arthure*, ed. E. Brock, EETS OS 8 (1871; rpt. London, 1961), lines 1283–98.

[31] Everett, 'Alliterative Revival,' p. 58.

[32] Benson, *Art and Tradition*, pp. 176–77.

[33] Oakden, *Alliterative Poetry*, 2.33; Atwood, 'English Versions,' pp. 146–47; Jacobs, 'Alliterative Storms.'

³⁴ Borroff, *Sir Gawain*, p. 92, discussing the bedroom scene in *Gawain*.
³⁵ Compare *Patience*, ed. J. J. Anderson (Manchester, 1969), line 143.
³⁶ Compare *The Wars of Alexander*, ed. W. W. Skeat, EETS ES 47 (London, 1886), line 558.
³⁷ Two other powerful descriptions of sea storms in the *Destruction* are 3688–714 and 4625–36.
³⁸ Oakden, *Alliterative Poetry*, 2.32; Atwood, 'English Versions,' pp. 141–43; Wood, 'Middle-English Alliterative,' pp. 82–88; but Finlayson, 'Formulaic Technique,' pp. 389–90 dissents and severely criticizes battle description in the *Destruction*.
³⁹ This is how the word is used in *Sir Gawain and the Green Knight* at 262, 1023, 1125, and 1513, although the first and third examples refer to the sinister game played by the Green Knight.
⁴⁰ Benson, *Art and Tradition*, pp. 185–97, discusses the whole subject of point of view; on p. 177 he shows how a definite point-of-view involves the reader in the winter scene from the *Destruction*; Borroff, *Sir Gawain*, p. 126, shows how the narration in *Gawain* often proceeds from a specific locus within the scene.
⁴¹ Borroff, *Sir Gawain*, pp. 126–27, demonstrates how this technique enhances the dramatic suspense.
⁴² Compare this with the distant and vague point of view in the *Laud*'s version (1641–48).
⁴³ To appreciate how real the speech seems in the *Destruction*, compare the same passage in the *Laud*, where Hector seems about to fight the Greeks single-handedly (5659–60), or in Lydgate's *Troy Book*, which adds abstract questions of chivalric honor (3.1686–89). Other examples where the alliterative poet changes indirect speech into direct include: 784–85; 6233–34; 6705–07; 7840–42; 8590–91; 8691–94; 9811–18; 9821–38; 10250–51; 10592–95; 10610–19; 11181–85; 11245–47; 11595–602; 11721–27; 11860–63; 12075–76; 12842–47; 13609–10.
⁴⁴ See Benson, *Art and Tradition*, p. 203, for a discussion of a similar shift from romance to realism in *Sir Gawain and the Green Knight*.

IV. The Laud Troy Book: *History as Romance*

¹ J. Ernst Wülfing, the *Laud*'s editor, asserts on the title page that the poem was written 'about 1400.' Dorothy Kempe, 'A Middle English Tale of Troy,' *Englische Studien*, 29 (1901), 5, and Atwood, 'English Versions,' pp. 86–89, argue for a somewhat earlier date without convincing evidence. A date of 1400 is accepted by Harry McKay Sundwall, 'The *Laud Troy Book*: Introduction and Commentary,' Diss. Harvard 1972, pp. 226–29, and Robert M. Lumiansky, 'The Story of Troilus and Briseida in the *Laud Troy-Book*,' *Modern Language Quarterly*, 18 (1957), 239–40.
² Root, review of Wülfing's edition, *Journal of English and Germanic Philology*, 5 (1904), 367. See also Kempe, 'Tale of Troy,' p. 26; Kane, *Middle English Literature*, pp. 26–28; Lumiansky, 'Story of Troilus in the *Laud*,' shows the author's care and intelligence, but he ultimately dismisses the poem.
³ Another example of the poet's desire to make the story clear to his readers occurs when Diomedes unhorses Troilus and sends the animal to Briseida. The

poet stops to remind us who Calchas is and briefly recounts the seer's trip to Delphos and his desertion to the Greeks (9065–77); the poet then gives a brief account of the exchange for Briseida which he had not narrated in its proper place (9078–92).

⁴ Atwood, 'English Versions,' pp. 109–111.

⁵ Another example from earlier in the story occurs when the Argonauts remember Laomedon's insult in refusing them permission to land at Troy. Guido describes the rising anger of Jason and Hercules briefly, indirectly, and generally (3.405–09; p. 32). The *Laud* brings the scene to life with a direct speech by Hercules that clearly conveys his anger and shame (1156–66).

⁶ The poet adds a similarly rhetorical introduction to the speech in which Antenor tries to persuade Peleus that Hesione should be returned to the Trojans (1993–98).

⁷ These similes have been catalogued by J. Ernst Wülfing, 'Das Bild und die bildische verneinung im Laud-Troy-Book,' *Anglia*, 27 (1904), 555–80 and 28 (1905), 29–80. I am greatly indebted to Wülfing's lists, but the interpretation offered here is my own.

⁸ For example, lion: 1434, 4973, 5368, 8777, 10473–74, 10844, 14197, and 14243; and leopard: 1432, 6096, 7562.

⁹ See also similes using sheep (4488), kite (5274), swallow (5304), swine (5707), flies (6240), eel (6255), bees (6294), wolves (6334), hound and hares (6420), hawk (6445), bulls (6704), rats and cats (6787–88), falcon and drake (7435), hound and deer (7438), bear (8013), and frogs (12756).

¹⁰ See also similes using silver (4535–36), water in a furrow (5284), honeysuckle (5382), a bird-trapper (7750–51), cherry-trees (8778), threshers (9336), leaves (9737), water in a well (10612), and flint (14057–58).

¹¹ Baugh, 'The Authorship of the Middle English Romances,' *Bulletin of the Modern Humanities Research Association*, 22 (1950), 13–28, especially 22 and 27.

¹² A similar mood is created by the use of more animal similes (birds again) when Achilles is told that his offer for Polyxena has been accepted at Troy (12227–32).

¹³ See my discussion of these techniques in the previous chapter and Larry D. Benson, 'The Use of a Physical Viewpoint in Berners' *Froissart*,' *Modern Language Quarterly*, 20 (1959), 333–38.

¹⁴ See, for example, 548, 18640, 18659; Paul Strohm, '*Storie, Spelle Geste, Romaunce, Tragedie*: Generic Distinctions in the Middle English Troy Narratives,' *Speculum*, 46 (1971), 354–56, argues that the *Laud*-poet deliberately identifies his work as a romance, but Strohm admits that the poet does use other terms also.

¹⁵ Erich Auerbach, 'The Knight Sets Forth,' *Mimesis*, trans. Willard Trask (1946; rpt. Garden City, N.Y., 1957), pp. 107–24. The *Laud*, like the other Middle English histories of Troy, follows Guido in avoiding the mysterious, the magical, and the marvelous, which figure so prominently in Benoît's romance.

Benoît de Sainte-Maure's *Roman de Troie*, Guido's source and a prototype of French romance, has often been suggested as a direct influence on the *Laud*, but the evidence is not convincing. The two poems share a common interest in battle and chivalric pageantry, but the *Laud* does not have Benoît's marvels or deep interest in love, and no exact borrowing has ever been absolutely proven. I am most persuaded by the argument that if the poet had known Benoît, his influence would have been extensive and unmistakable. Yet even if all the passages that have been suggested do actually come from Benoît, they serve only to demonstrate the English poet's respect for Guido's authority: each claimed borrowing from the *Roman* is merely supplementary, added to give dash and color to the narrative— none changes the truth of the history. Those arguing that Benoît's poem did influence the *Laud* include: M. Aristide Joly, ed., *Benoît de Sainte-More et le Roman de Troie* (Paris, 1871), 2.498; J. Ernst Wülfing, 'Das Laud-Troybook,' *Englische Studien*, 29 (1901), 378–81; Atwood, 'English Versions,' pp. 117–25; and Sundwall, 'The *Laud Troy Book*,' pp. 300–44 and notes. Kempe, 'Tale of Troy,' pp. 12–16, vigorously refuted Joly's conclusions and her argument is still convincing. The parallels between Benoît's *Roman* and the *Laud* are much too general and unexceptional to prove the influence. If the *Laud*-poet is really borrowing the specific details from Benoît that have been claimed, he must have a text before him. If this is so, why then does he choose to reproduce only such minor items? Sundwall concedes that the *Laud* would be little different if its author were unacquainted with Benoît (p. 344). If the poet must have a source for these romance details (which I doubt), it is surprising to me that no one has ever suggested the *Roman de Troie en prose*, ed. L. Constans and E. Faral (Paris, 1922).

[16] Kempe, 'Tale of Troy,' pp. 16–21; Atwood, 'English Versions,' pp. 107–09; Norman D. Hinton, 'A Study of the Medieval Poems Relating the Destruction of Troy,' Diss. University of Wisconsin, 1957, pp. 213–19.

[17] Kane, *Middle English Literature*, p. 27.

[18] Baugh, 'Authorship,' p. 22.

[19] For one example of this, see Robert M. Lumiansky, 'The Story of Troilus and Briseida According to Benoît and Guido,' *Speculum*, 29 (1954), 727–33.

[20] Lumiansky, 'Story of Troilus in the *Laud*,' demonstrates that the poet does not slight the love story of Troilus and Briseida, as had previously been thought. He only rearranges its beginning so that it will not interfere with a crucial episode concerning his main interest—Hector. The poet actually expands some parts of the love story, especially the military rivalry between Troilus and Diomedes.

[21] Similarly, the poet adds a passage when Hector returns from challenging Achilles to single combat that describes the chivalric love felt by the ladies of Troy for their champion (8571–76).

[22] The poet's hatred of Paris is extreme. At one point he has the Trojan women curse the man who began the war (8613–16), and after another battle he curses him in his own voice (12948–50).

[23] Mehl, *The Middle English Romances of the Thirteenth and Fourteenth Centuries* (London, 1968), p. 17.

[24] Lumiansky, *Manual*, 1.117.

[25] See also the original passage in the *Laud* in which Penthesilea describes Hector (16840–43).

[26] This section also contains two other original passages: one in praise of Hector, who is called as strong as Sampson and the equal of any knight (6721–34), and another in which Achilles makes a further attempt, this time with Thoas, to gang up on the weary Hector (6853–83).

[27] During the battle itself, Achilles, 'for al his myȝt & his prowes' (10695) is wounded several times and in a long speech, only barely suggested by the *Historia*, again insists on his intention to kill Hector by fraud (10759–78).

[28] Hinton, 'Study of the Medieval Poems,' pp. 208–11.

[29] In his defense as a historian, we must note that the poet's change is a relatively simple one (transferring some of the Myrmidons' actions to Achilles) and there is some justification for it. Guido accuses Achilles of treachery in the deaths of both Troilus and Memnon; but in the latter case all the Myrmidons do is hold off the Trojans and thus allow Achilles to defeat Memnon in a fair fight (26.325–39; pp. 205–06). The poet might have concluded that the same was true in the death of Troilus.

[30] Kempe, 'Tale of Troy,' p. 8; Strohm, 'Generic Distinctions,' p. 346.

[31] Atwood, 'English Versions,' pp. 93–98.

[32] An example of the poet's stylistic originality coupled with factual fidelity is the pledge of love Jason and Medea make to one another. Guido's lumbering rhetoric (2.407–20; p. 21) is replaced by a sprightly and more believable speech (793–814), but the basic statement remains the same.

[33] Lumiansky, 'Story of Troilus in the *Laud*.'

[34] There are some changes in the *Laud*, it must be admitted, that are inexplicable. During one battle (16.108; p. 150), the poet gratuitously adds two knights, Henes and Theseus (6222); and in a later one (25.70–77; p. 192) twice adds Nestor (12663 and 12679). Conversely, between lines 664–65, the poet omits two sentences from Guido that describe brief encounters between Troilus and Diomedes and between Achilles and Hector (17.57–58; p. 152). Corruptions in the poet's text that have not survived could explain these changes, and others like them, but probably they are the result of simple carelessness.

V. *John Lydgate's* Troy Book: *History as Learned Rhetoric*

[1] Bergen, *Troy Book*, p. 1.

[2] See, for example, K. M. Merritt, 'The Source of John Pikeryng's *Horestes*,' *Review of English Studies*, n.s. 23 (1972), 255–66; A. S. Cairncross, 'Thomas Kyd and the Myrmidons,' *Arlington Quarterly* 1 (1968), 40–45; Elizabeth Seaton, 'Marlowe's Light Reading', in *Elizabethan and Jacobean Studies Presented to Frank Percy Wilson* (Oxford, 1959), pp. 28–33.

[3] Alain Renoir, *The Poetry of John Lydgate* (Cambridge, Mass., 1967), pp. 7, 15. Hereafter cited as Renoir.

[4] Walter F. Schirmer, *John Lydgate: A Study in the Culture of the XVth Century*, trans. A. E. Keep (Berkeley, 1961). Hereafter cited as Schirmer. Derek Pearsall, *John Lydgate* (Charlottesville, 1970). Hereafter cited as Pearsall.

[5] See 2.4701–19 and 3.540–64; Pearsall, p. 63.

[6] Pearsall, p. 134.

[7] Pearsall, pp. 134–37 and 143 ff. Examples of seasonal descriptions not mentioned by Pearsall include: 1.623–44; 1.1197–214; 2.5067–91; and 2.6730–35.

[8] Pearsall, p. 129.

[9] Pearsall, pp. 7–11; Schirmer, pp. 43–44.

[10] Pearsall, p. 132.

[11] Schirmer, p. 46.

[12] The opening of Ulysses's speech in the *Historia* is extremely abrupt (25.169–72; p. 194). The *Laud*'s version begins a little more tactfully (13047–48), but in the *Troy Book* Ulysses is wonderfully self-effacing before the touchy Achilles (4.1701–10).

[13] Each of the Middle English histories of Troy translates these lines in its own characteristic style. Although the *Destruction*-poet appears to have misunderstood Guido's murky Latin, his version is compact and verbally precise (9781–84). The *Laud*'s version is more vigorous and again reveals a special delight in the gore of battle (13163–66).

[14] Pearsall, p. 151.

[15] After this section was first written, I was pleased to find that Pearsall reached many of the same conclusions about Lydgate's humor (pp. 134–36). He also notes that Lydgate's passages on women are the most annotated portions of the fifteenth-century MSS. of the *Troy Book*. See also Gretchen Mieszkowski, *The Reputation of Criseyde 1155–1500, Transactions of the Connecticut Academy of Arts and Sciences* 43 (1971), 116–26.

[16] Hinton, 'Study of the Medieval Poems,' p. 260; Bergen, *Troy Book*, 4.105 (notes to lines 1.2072–96 and 1.2097–2135), and 128–29 (note to lines 2.3515 ff.).

[17] Another bit of fun occurs earlier when Lydgate feigns concern for Guido's soul if he died unrepentent for his sins against women and claims that if Guido were still alive he would shrive him himself (1.2123–35).

[18] Atwood, 'English Versions,' p. 177, says that Lydgate is 'appreciative it seems of the humor of the situation'—a curious judgement since the poet had himself created the humor. And what do we make of Atwood's comment that Lydgate's ironic conclusion is 'a shrewd moral observation'? Atwood, 'Some Minor Sources of Lydgate's *Troy Book*,' *Studies in Philology*, 35 (1938), 31–32, says that the wit in the passage is clumsy (which it may be) and 'unnatural' for Lydgate (which we have seen is not true). John Gower plays similarly with the story of Venus and Vulcan in *Confessio Amantis*, ed. G. C. Macaulay, EETS ES 81, 82 (London, 1900–01), 5.635–728.

[19] For an early version of this section, with additional examples, see my article, 'The Ancient World in John Lydgate's *Troy Book*,' *American Benedictine Review*, 24 (1973), 299–312.

[20] Schirmer, pp. 47, 50.

[21] Atwood, 'Minor Sources,' pp. 27–33, and 'English Versions,' pp. 169–82.

[22] William Marquardt, 'A Source for the Passage on the Origin of Chess in Lydgate's *Troy Book*,' *Modern Language Notes*, 64 (1949), 87–88; R. A. Dwyer, 'Some Readers of John Trevisa,' *Notes and Queries*, 212 (1967), 291–92.

[23] Atwood, 'Minor Sources,' p. 29.

[24] For Chaucer's general influence on the *Troy Book*, see Pearsall, pp. 55 ff., and Atwood, 'Minor Sources,' pp. 35–42.

[25] Bloomfield, 'Chaucer's Sense of History,' *Journal of English and Germanic Philology*, 51 (1952), 301–13. Reprinted in Bloomfield, *Essays and Explorations* (Cambridge, Mass., 1970), pp. 13–26.

[26] Bloomfield, 'Sense of History,' p. 304.

[27] Elsewhere, in 'The *Knight's Tale* as History,' *Chaucer Review*, 3 (1968), 107–23, I have used Bloomfield's insight to argue that the *Knight's Tale* is a sort of classical chronicle in which Chaucer carefully modifies his source in order to convince contemporary readers that the events in Thebes took place long ago and far away in a world very different from their own. For Chaucer's playing with time see also E. Talbot Donaldson, 'Troilus and Criseide,' *Chaucer's Poetry* (New York, 1958), pp. 965–80.

[28] Although I believe Lydgate's interest in representing the ancient world was inspired by Chaucer, the *Troy Book* seems to be part of a general antiquarian movement in England at this time, especially in the regular orders. For one aspect of this interest, see Beryl Smalley, *English Friars and Antiquity in the Early Fourteenth Century* (Oxford, 1960). Another example of the 'classicizing' trend, this time in historical writing, is discussed by John Taylor in *The Universal Chronicle of Ranulf Higden* (Oxford, 1966), especially Chapter 3.

[29] Renoir, pp. 66–68; Pearsall, p. 131, also p. 142.

[30] Schirmer, p. 102, claims that 2.896–904 is a description of the poet's role in contemporary 'mummings,' though he offers no proof of this statement. See also Glynne Wickham, *Early English Stages 1300 to 1660* (London, 1959), 1.192–95, 321. In fact, Lydgate seems to be reflecting traditional medieval opinions about classical dramatic practice. For a discussion of these views, see M. H. Marshall, 'Theatre in the Middle Ages: Evidence from Dictionaries and Glosses,' *Symposium*, 4 (1950), 1–39.

[31] Bergen, *Troy Book*, 4.223 (note to lines 4.1054 ff.).

[32] Bloomfield, 'Sense of History,' p. 309.

[33] Other examples of such distancing phrases include: 1.1386 and 3.54.

[34] Although Lydgate is hostile to paganism, he labors to remind his audience of its reality. Guido's accounts of the supernatural powers of Medea and Cassandra stress the marvelous, but Lydgate expands both passages to create historical distance and to provide a detailed account of pagan practices (compare Guido— 2.183–84; p. 15, with Lydgate—1.1628–31; and Guido—5.71–73; p. 45, with Lydgate—2.363–68. Lydgate adds phrases throughout the *Troy Book* that insist on the pagan culture of Troy (e.g., 1.41; 2.2399; 4.5907). The poet also describes at length a sacrifice to Mars (4.4493–501), and later admits that he has previously given accounts of pagan rites (4.7024–26). On several occasions brief references to pagan worship in the *Historia* are given greater historical distance in the *Troy Book* by the addition of authenticizing detail (e.g., 2.3898–99 and 2.5990–95).

[35] Other examples of Lydgate's greater sense of anachronism not discussed here occur during the funerals of Deiphobus and Sarpedon (4.1601), those of Troilus and Memnon (4.3082–97), the proposed burial of Penthesilea (4.5381–97), the rites of Ajax (5.323) and Assandrus (5.1273), and a general burial of the Greek dead in which Patroclus and Prostesilaus are interred (3.2182; 3.2196–97; and 3.2205–08).

[36] Pearsall, p. 148.

[37] Lydgate shows little ability to compare and weigh authorities, a feature of Renaissance historiography, though he does at one point note the impossibility of some poetic fables (1.1711–15).

[38] *Journal of English and Germanic Philology*, 67 (1968), 145.

[39] Pearsall, pp. 127–28.

[40] Pearsall, p. 140.

[41] The following are characteristic examples of Lydgate's reductions: Guido describes Polydamas's tactical placing of his battalion during a battle (15.343–48; p. 137); but this almost entirely disappears in the *Troy Book* (3.1154). At 3.3330 Lydgate omits the names of four leaders that Guido says go out with Achilles (18.59; p. 156), and the poet says only that Achilles went to battle 'With his lordis & his knyȝtes bolde.'

[42] Paul Strohm, '*Storie, Spelle, Geste, Romaunce, Tragedie*: Generic Distinc-

tions in the Middle English Troy Narratives,' *Speculum*, 46 (1971), 351–52, discussing Lydgate's claim to write factual history in the *Troy Book*, argues that Lydgate makes a distinction between *transmew* (which is the radical transformation practiced by such as Homer and Ovid) and *translate* (which is his own faithful method).

[43] The importance contemporaries attached to the complete history of Troy is perhaps indicated by the production of the so-called 'Scottish Troy Fragments' to fill gaps in Scottish manuscripts of Lydgate's *Troy Book* (ed. C. Horstmann, *Barbour's des schottischen Nationaldichters Legendensammlung nebst den Fragmenten seines Trojanerkrieges* [Heilbronn, 1882], 2.218–304).

[44] Schirmer, p. 44; Studer, 'History as Moral Instruction: John Lydgate's Record of *Troie Toun*,' *Emporia State Research Studies* 19.1 (1970), 5; see also Robert W. Ayers, 'Medieval History, Moral Purpose, and the Structure of Lydgate's *Siege of Thebes*,' *PMLA*, 73 (1958), 464.

[45] Studer, 'History as Moral Instruction,' pp. 9–10.

[46] Pearsall, pp. 130–31.

[47] Pearsall, p. 139.

[48] Scattergood, *Politics and Poetry in the Fifteenth Century* (London, 1971), p. 288.

[49] Renoir, pp. 96, 100; See also Scattergood, *Politics and Poetry*, p. 45.

[50] For the practice of drawing such moral lessons from the story of Troy, see Durant W. Robertson, Jr., *Chaucer's London* (New York, 1968), pp. 2–4.

[51] Pearsall, p. 128.

[52] Schirmer, p. 49.

[53] Other examples of simple justice in the *Troy Book* include: 1.237–49; 2.4195–239; and 4.5477–501.

[54] See also the lines against paganism that parody the end of Chaucer's *Troilus* (4.3210–22).

[55] Willard Farnham, *The Medieval Heritage of Elizabethan Tragedy* (1936; rpt. Oxford, 1963), pp. 160–72.

[56] Farnham, *Medieval Heritage*, p. 165.

[57] John Norton-Smith, ed., *John Lydgate: Poems* (Oxford, 1966), p. 127.

[58] Phillippa Tristram, *Figures of Life and Death in Medieval English Literature* (New York, 1976), p. 141.

[59] Farnham, *Medieval Heritage*, p. 162. See also F. P. Pickering, *Literature and Art in the Middle Ages* (Coral Gables, 1970), p. 185.

[60] Lewis, *The Discarded Image* (Cambridge, 1964), p. 82.

[61] This section has been praised by Pearsall (p. 143) and is taken too seriously by Studer, 'History as Moral Instruction,' p. 9.

[62] To my knowledge, no one has analyzed Lydgate's use of the *Epistre* in his account of Hector's death. It is not mentioned in Atwood's 'Minor Sources,' pp. 25–42. In the notes to his recent edition of Stephen Scrope's translation of the *Epistre*, Curt F. Bühler refers the readers to Lydgate's version without discussion: *The Epistle of Othea*, EETS OS 264 (London, 1970) p. 190. Scrope's translation (ca. 1450) is extremely close to Christine's work and, since Lydgate's dependence on the *Epistre* does not extend to specific phrasing, it will be used hereafter for citations included in my text.

[63] For general accounts of the *Epistre* and its English translations, see especially P. G. C. Campbell, *L'Epître d'Othéa: Etude sur les sources de Christine*

de Pisan (Paris, 1924), and James D. Gordon, ed., *The Epistle of Othea to Hector* (Philadelphia, 1942), pp. 1–xxxi.

[64] See Mark Sacharoff, 'The Traditions of the Troy-Story Heroes and the Problem of Satire in Troilus and Cressida,' *Shakespeare Studies*, 6 (1970), 127.

[65] Dares is the ultimate source of the attempted plundering itself (see R. M. Frazer's translation in *The Trojan War* [Bloomington, 1966], p. 153), but Lydgate is here following the *Epistre*'s more extensive account as will be shown below.

[66] Hinton, 'Study of the Medieval Poems,' p. 269.

[67] Renoir, pp. 97–98. See also Pearsall, who claims that Lydgate's method of working from sources is 'always to add, never to alter' (p. 153).

[68] The last Middle English translation of Guido's history marks the decline of the tradition as serious literature. In about 1474, William Caxton published the first book in English, *The Recuyell of the Historyes of Troye* (ed. H. Oskar Sommer, 2 vols. [London, 1894]), his own close translation of a work by Raoul Lefèvre. This prose compilation was crucial to the Elizabethan conception of Troy and influenced even major writers like Shakespeare. After two books of only partially rationalized versions of other classical stories, Book Three of the *Recuyell* follows the *Historia* closely; but, unlike the Middle English poetic translators, Caxton makes no attempt to vivify the story through original artistry. All of Guido's stylistic decoration is eliminated (moral, educational, or simply decorative passages) and nothing comparable is added. In this, the *Recuyell* is like the fifteenth-century prose *Sege of Troye* (ed. Nathaniel Griffin, 'The Sege of Troye,' *PMLA*, 22 [1907], 157–200; and ed. Friedrich Brie, 'Zwei mittelenglische Prosaromane,' *Archiv*, 130 [1913], 40–47 and 272–85), a brief prose work whose emphasis on the factual highlights of the Trojan War is the ultimate, and slightly absurd, extension of Guido's concern with objective truth. The medieval history of Troy has ceased to exist in England as a complete and independent work.

VI. The History of Troy in Middle English Poetry

[1] *The English Works of John Gower*, ed. G. C. Macaulay, EETS ES 81, 82 (London, 1900–01).

[2] Alfred David, 'Gawain and Aeneas,' *English Studies*, 49 (1968), 402–09; *Sir Gawain and the Green Knight*, ed. J. R. R. Tolkien and E. V. Gordon, rev. ed. Norman Davis (Oxford, 1967), p. 70 (note to lines 3–5).

[3] *The Seege or Batayle of Troye*, ed. Mary E. Barnicle, EETS OS 172 (London, 1927). One version of the source of these romances is found in *Excidium Troiae*, ed. E. Bagby Atwood and Virgil K. Whitaker, The Mediaeval Academy of America Publication No. 44 (Cambridge, Mass., 1944).

[4] See, for example, C. S. Lewis, 'What Chaucer Really Did to *Il Filostrato*,' *Essays and Studies*, 17 (1932), 56–75; and Morton W. Bloomfield, 'Distance and Predestination in *Troilus and Criseyde*,' *PMLA*, 72 (1957), 14–26; rpt. in Bloomfield, *Essays and Explorations* (Cambridge, Mass. 1970), pp. 201–216.

[5] Geoffrey Chaucer, *The Book of Troilus and Criseyde*, ed. Robert K. Root (Princeton, 1926), 1.141–47. All further quotations from the *Troilus* will be from this edition and cited in my text.

[6] I am aware that it has been argued that Chaucer's immediate source may not

have been the *Filostrato* itself but a French translation of it, *Le Roman de Troyle*, by Beauvau (see Robert Pratt, 'Chaucer and *Le Roman de Troyle et de Criseida*', *Studies in Philology*, 53 [1950], pp. 509–39). But even if Chaucer's dependence on Beauvau should definitely be proved, it will in no way affect the substance of my argument here.

[7] Morton W. Bloomfield, 'Chaucer's Sense of History,' pp. 301–13.

[8] 'Chaucer's Influence on the Prose "Sege of Troy," ' *Notes and Queries*, 216 (1971), 127–30.

[9] Young, *The Origin and Development of the Story of Troilus and Criseyde* (1908; rpt., New York, 1968), pp. 105–39.

[10] At times Chaucer even goes beyond Guido and Benoît for 'historical' information. His statement that the war lasted ten years and brought a thousand Greek ships (1.57–60) comes from Vergil. Benoît and Guido give different and more precise numbers for the ships. See the note to this passage in Root's edition.

[11] John P. McCall, 'The Trojan Scene in Chaucer's *Troilus*,' ELH, 29 (1962), 263.

[12] McCall, 'Trojan Scene,' p. 273.

[13] W. W. Skeat in his edition of *Troilus* (*The Complete Works*, 2nd ed. [1900; rpt. Oxford, 1963]). 2. liii–lxii and notes, and George Hamilton in *The Indebtedness of Chaucer's Troilus and Criseyde to Guido delle Colonne's Historia Trojana* (New York, 1903), both argue that Guido was Chaucer's primary source for Trojan material not found in Boccaccio. Karl Young convincingly refutes this judgment in his *Origin and Development* and shows that where Benoît and Guido differ, Chaucer usually follows the French poem. However, as Young admits, Guido and Benoît are so often nearly identical that one cannot be absolutely sure which is the source for a particular passage. In a few places, at least, Chaucer's lines do seem closer to the *Historia*, and Young therefore considers it to be a probable source of the *Troilus* (p. 139).

[14] Chaucer, *The Works*, ed. F. N. Robinson, 2nd ed. (Boston, 1957), *House of Fame*, 1469; *Legend of Good Women*, 1396 and 1464.

[15] For a brief account of Chaucer's sources in the *Troilus*, see Root's edition, pp. xx–xlviii.

[16] E. T. Donaldson, ed., *Chaucer's Poetry* (New York, 1958), pp. 966–67; Bloomfield, 'Distance and Predestination,' 23; see also Dorothy Bethurum, 'Chaucer's Point of View as Narrator in the Love Poems,' in *Chaucer Criticism*, ed. R. J. Schoeck and J. Taylor (Notre Dame, Ind., 1961), 2.211–31.

[17] Donaldson, *Chaucer's Poetry*, pp. 977–78. Chaucer's account of the death of Hector is not in Boccaccio, but is based on Benoît and possibly Guido (see Root's note to 5.1548–61).

[18] *Chaucer's Use of Proverbs*, Harvard Studies in Comparative Literature, Vol. 11 (Cambridge, Mass., 1934), p. 49.

[19] Charles Muscatine, *Chaucer and the French Tradition* (Berkeley, 1957), p. 145.

[20] The stress on blindness in the poem has often been noticed. See especially Robert P. apRoberts, 'The Boethian God and the Audience of the *Troilus*,' *Journal of English and Germanic Philology*, 69 (1970), 425–36.

[21] Fortune in the *Troilus* is not random as in Guido, but is seen as ultimately controlled by Providence under God, as in Boethius and Dante. See, for example, 3.617–23, and 5.1541–47. Robertson's position was first set out in 'Chaucerian

Tragedy,' reprinted in *Chaucer Criticism*, 2.86–121; Ida Gordon echoes much of his view in her recent *The Double Sorrow of Troilus* (Oxford, 1970).

[22] In a very interesting discussion of Fortune, F. P. Pickering shows that Fortune and salvation operate in two different realms: *Literature and Art in the Middle Ages* (Coral Cables, 1970), p. 181.

[23] The exchange is one of the poem's few scenes for which Young suggests explicit borrowings from the *Historia* (pp. 115–16).

[24] apRoberts, 'The Boethian God,' p. 429.

[25] Robert Henryson, *Testament of Cresseid*, ed. Denton Fox (London, 1968), lines 107–09. All further citations to the poem are to this edition and will be included in the text.

[26] *Poems* (Oxford, 1963), p. xii.

[27] *Testament*, p. 22.

[28] *Robert Henryson* (Oxford, 1967), pp. 90–91.

[29] *Five Poems: 1470–1870* (London, 1948), p. 17.

[30] Duncan, 'Henryson's *Testament of Cresseid*,' *Essays in Criticism*, 11 (1961), 135; Harth, 'Henryson Reinterpreted,' *Essays in Criticism*, 11 (1961), 478.

[31] Stearns, *Robert Henryson* (1949; rpt., New York, 1966), pp. 97–105.

[32] Stearns, *Robert Henryson*, p. 100.

[33] Fox, *Testament*, p. 124, note to l.507. The MED records the technical use of the word to mean 'image formed on the retina' or 'an illusion' in a fifteenth-century translation of Guy de Chauliac's medical work *Grande Chirurgie*. But except in this one case, the other examples cited support Fox and the OED.

[34] Stearns, *Robert Henryson*, p. 100; Fox, *Testament*, p. 124, note to l.508.

[35] Tatyana Moran notes that line 513 of the *Testament* is an echo of Troilus's first sight of Cresseid in Chaucer's *Troilus* (1.229): 'The Meeting of the Lovers in the "Testament of Cresseid," ' *Notes and Queries*, 208 (1963), 11.

[36] The most ironic lack of insight in the *Testament* is Calchas's. When Cresseid first returns to him, the seer has to be told what Diomeid has done and he then vainly hopes that all will turn out for the best (99–105). After Cresseid has been ravaged by the gods, Calchas greets her with an astonishingly unknowing pun: 'Douchter, quhat cheir?' (367).

[37] I should emphasize again that there is no evidence that Henryson knew Guido directly. I assume that he, like any educated man of the time, had a general knowledge of the medieval history of Troy; but I imagine that his knowledge of the doom and despair that were associated with Troy comes principally from Chaucer.

[38] For the view that the *Testament* is 'pessimistic' see, for example, E. Duncan Aswell, 'The Role of Fortune in *The Testament of Cresseid*,' *Philological Quarterly*, 46 (1967), 471–87, and Tatyana Moran, '*The Testament of Cresseid* and *The Book of Troylus*,' *Litera*, 6 (1959), 18–24. For a brilliant recent reading of the poem that differs fundamentally from the one presented here, see Larry M. Sklute, 'Phoebus Descending: Rhetoric and Moral Vision in Henryson's *Testament of Cresseid*,' *ELH*, 44 (1977), 189–204.

[39] Cresseid's vanity and desire to keep up appearances are seen in her refusal to appear in her father's temple lest people know of her rejection by Diomeid (116–19) and the secret manner in which she goes to the leper hospital (380–90). In her accusation of the gods she shows her dependent nature by asking:

> Quha sall me gyde? Quha sall me now conuoy,
> Sen I fra Diomeid and nobill Troylus
> Am clene excludit, as abiect odious? (131–33)

For these qualities in Chaucer's Criseyde, see especially Ida Gordon, *The Double Sorrow of Troilus.*

[40] Fox, *Testament*, pp. 56–58.

[41] I agree with Fox's view that the gods represent natural forces (p. 34). They deal justly with Cresseid, but because they are inhuman, theirs is necessarily a harsh and mechanical justice. On this point see Aswell, 'The Role of Fortune.'

INDEX

This index does not include all minor characters in the *Historia*.

Eusebius, 8, 153
Everett, Dorothy, 58, 157
Excidium Troiae, 6, 133, 165

Fantosme, Jordan, 12, 37
Faral, E., 160
Farnham, Willard, 119–20, 122, 164
fate or *fata*, 25, 27–29, 120, 124, 139, 150, 155
Filostrato: see Boccaccio
Finlayson, John, 157, 158
Forester, Thomas, 153, 154
Fortune, 19, 27–29, 78, 109, 145, 149; in Lydgate, 120–23, in Chaucer, 141–42, 166–67
Fox, Denton, 144, 147, 148, 167, 168
Frazer, R. M., 4, 151, 165
Froissart, Jean, 5, 12, 14, 15, 17, 19, 21, 38, 154, 159
Fulgentius, 107
Furnivall, F. J., 155

Gaimer, 37
Galbraith, V. H., 7, 8, 152, 153
Gawain, 56, 57, 62, 165
Gawain and the Green Knight, Sir, 49, 56, 57, 58, 59, 62, 77, 101, 133, 157, 158, 165
Geoffrey of Monmouth, 5
Geoffrey of Vinsauf, 101
Gervase of Canterbury, 6, 8, 152
Gesta Friderici I Imperatoris: see Otto of Freising
Golden Fleece, 15, 20, 24, 27, 45
Gordon, E. V., 165
Gordon, Ida, 141, 167, 168
Gordon, James D., 165, 168
Gower, John, 117, 118, 133, 162, 165; *Confessio Amantis*, 117, 133, 162, *Vox Clamantis*, 118
Gransden, Antonia, 152
Gray, Thomas, 12
Green Knight, 56, 62, 158
Griffin, Nathaniel, 43, 45, 86, 87, 92, 151, 152, 153, 156, 157, 165
Guido delle Colonne, 3, 4–6, 9, 10, 11, 12, passim, 133, 134, 144, 145, 146, 148, 149, 150, 151, 153, 154, 155, 156, 157, 159, 160, 161, 162, 163, 165, 166, 167; classical chronicle 14–15, eyewitness style, 15–19, heroes and battle, 19–23, pessimism, 23–31, proverbs, 26–27, prologue, 35–41, used by *Destruction*, 42–66, by *Laud*, 67–96, by Lydgate, 98–129, by Chaucer, 135–43
Guy de Chauliac, 167

Hamilton, George, 166
Hardyng, John, 155
Harth, Sydney, 144, 167

Havelok the Dane, 68, 82
Hector, 9, 14, 19, 20, 21, 22–23, 26, 27, 28, 29, 31, 39, 51, 52, 53, 55, 61, 64, 66, 67, 68, 69, 70, 71, 73, 74, 77, 79–80, 81, 82–88, 89, 90, 91, 92, 93, 94, 105, 117, 118, 124–29, 139, 145, 155, 158, 160, 161, 164, 166
Hecuba, 22, 29, 93
Helen, 14, 18, 19, 22, 29, 30, 31, 50, 53, 54, 80, 82, 101, 103, 108, 110, 117, 137
Henes, 161
Henry V, King of England, 40, 97, 118, 123, 126, 136
Henry of Huntingdon, 10, 11, 13, 153, 154
Henryson, Robert, 4, 6, 31, 54, 143–50, 167–68
Hercules, 17, 50, 159
Hermione, 30–31, 154
Herodotus, 154
Hesione, 20, 26, 28, 65, 93, 159
Heywood, Thomas, 104
Higden, Ranulf, 11, 12, 38, 39, 153, 154, 155, 163
Hill, Archibald, 151
Hinton, Norman D., 126, 127, 160, 162, 165
Histoire de Guillaume le Maréchal, 38
Historia Destructionis Troiae: see Guido delle Colonne
Historia Ecclesiastica Gentis Anglorum: see Bede
Homer, 3, 8, 10, 29, 37, 40, 90, 135, 164
Horstmann, C., 164
Hotspur, 22
Hugh of St. Victor, 11, 153
Hupon, 52

Ilion, 92
Innocent III, Pope, 29, 128
Iphigenia, 107
Isaiah, 153
Isidore of Seville, 11, 49, 107, 153, 156–57
Ithaca, 14
Itinerarium Peregrinorum et Gesta Regis Ricardi, 10, 11

Jacobs, Nichols, 156, 157
Jacobus de Cessolis, 107
Jason, 20, 24, 31, 45–46, 47, 49, 55, 80, 104, 111, 118, 121, 155, 159, 161
Jerome, St., 8
Jocelin of Brakelond, 11, 154
Joly, M. Aristide, 160
Jones, Charles W., 153
Joseph of Exeter, 17, 138
Joyce, James, 3
Jupiter, 50, 109
Justin, 11
Juvenal, 142